CHINA

*Empire of the
700 Million*

CHINA

*Empire of the
700 Million*

BY HARRY HAMM

Translated by Victor Andersen

DOUBLEDAY & COMPANY, INC.

Garden City, New York 1966

Contents

PREFACE

There is hardly a country on earth which has intrigued the peoples of the West down the centuries as China has. The history of the Chinese people, their exotic customs, their alien mentality and tradition, all these are full of paradoxes and strange contradictions. The history of the country extends over four thousand years, during which the Chinese nation, despite innumerable periods of confusion and despite conquests by foreign armies, has always managed to retain its identity. Throughout these four millenia the consciousness of a recurring rhythm in the ebb and flow of history has induced in the Chinese a stoic calm in the face of even the most momentous turns of fortune.

These four thousand years were dominated by the concept of imperial authority. The Emperor was attended by ceremony and adulation such as are properly reserved for the gods, but the Emperor could lose his Heavenly Mandate and was deposed if he lost the trust of the people, however innocently. These were four thousand years marked by a sense of cultural superiority but lacking the formation of any feeling of nationhood in the true meaning of the word: in which periods of impressive tolerance toward alien learning and foreign ideas, when foreign scholars and missionaries were to be found among the Emperor's closest advisers, alternated with periods of brutal and unbridled lust for conquest that sent the Chinese roving far across the neighboring seas.

Chinese culture has fascinated men for hundreds of years. For over two thousand years Chinese thought and life were shaped by the teachings of the great philosopher Confucius. Simultaneously, as a kind of opposite pole to Confucius' lessons of kindliness, tolerance and harmony, and accorded equal standing, there flourished the teachings of Lao-tse, the unfettered individualist and proponent of naturalism.

The elite of the ruling class continued all their lives to advance through the classes of the mandarin hierarchy by means of one examination after another. They devoted themselves almost exclusively to perfecting their knowledge of ethics, literature, philosophy and history. Respect for wisdom was universal: a polished literary style and refined calligraphy were regarded as the significant criteria of a meaningful life. And yet China was the country in which robbers and bandits were as much a part of everyday life as was the widespread illiteracy.

The Middle Kingdom was pre-eminent in the field of technical progress long before the birth of Western civilization. Chinese invented the compass, gunpowder and the art of printing. Chinese constructed the first rockets and produced porcelain and delicate silk. At a time when the peoples of the West were still in the semidarkness of history, the Chinese were creating architectural wonders such as the Great Wall and the Grand Imperial Canal. In spite of all this, however, the last few centuries saw China fall hopelessly behind in technical accomplishment.

Chinese art was a striking symptom of a propensity to value beauty above utility. Chinese literature is without parallel for poetic depth and sensitivity of language. Chinese painting, while it is distinguished by perfection of form, never lost the sense of a world pervaded by mysterious natural forces. Chinese bronzes are regarded as the finest examples of creative art ever shaped by the hand of man. Their pottery, porcelain and brocade have become symbols of an attitude to life permeated with a feeling for beauty. Yet there is hardly a race which showed so little regard for its own art treasures, hardly a country in which artistic refinement and unbridled barbarity lived side by side so much as a matter of course.

The Chinese are said to display humility and patience. As an old saying put it, a man must be able to bend with the wind, like the bamboo. But in the history of China there has been one bloody revolt after another and acts of revenge of unimaginable cruelty. Family and kindred formed the basic unit of the community. In this circle, and only there, ruled security, human warmth, obedience and absolute unselfishness. What happened outside of the circle of kith and kin was of no concern. Social conscience or even good-neighborliness were alien concepts. The desire for freedom was confined to the individual: there was little in the political field to correspond to it. Nevertheless, strange as it may seem, pronounced individualism did not conflict with the nation's inner spiritual and cultural security.

China's customs, manners and usages, too, seemed contradictory and incomprehensible. The color of mourning was white; for weddings it was red. In her gorgeous silk robes closed up to the neck, the elegant Chinese woman might have appeared to be a model of virtue if it had not been for the subtle way in which she coincidentally contrived to allow a glimpse of an uncovered leg. Again, Chinese cookery represents a high degree of refinement, and yet in no other country were there so many and such disastrous famines as in China.

"Losing face," the exposure of some fault or deficiency, was thought to be the worst thing that could happen to a man. It was the continual effort to avoid losing face that gave rise to stories of Chinese secretiveness, cunning opportunism and calculating self-interest. But behind the mask of permanent imperturbability and self-control there lay a sensitiveness which could only too easily turn to irritability.

Finally, the strange language and complicated written characters made their own contribution to the ineradicable myth—the myth of "China the unfathomable."

More recently there have appeared new phenomena which have stimulated Western imagination to fresh heights and have added to the existing myth a new dimension, which can be expressed as the myth of "China the terrible." The giant in the Far East seems to be awakening from the long slumber of centuries. With primordial energy China is beating out the road which will lead her out of misery, poverty, chaos, disunity and political impotence. China is striving after a standing in the world, a prestige which will correspond to the size of the country and the importance of her people. With her three million square miles she is the second largest country in the world after the Soviet empire, bigger than the United States of America and bigger than the whole of Europe. Her frontiers are nearly sixteen thousand miles long. The traveler who journeys across the whole of China will cover three thousand miles from north to south and the same distance again from east to west.

The country's staggering population growth provides even more food for thought. The population today is estimated to be 700 million, which, in terms of numbers, makes the Chinese the greatest people on earth. This figure is believed to be increasing at the rate of 2 to 3 per cent, by some fifteen to twenty million, every year. The thought that within a few decades there will be one billion Chinese in the world is a nightmare prospect.

The conclusions suggested by these bare facts would still not justify great apprehension if it were not for the other, the decisive factor, that of the existence of an ultrarevolutionary and uncompromising political regime. Communism in China has shown itself to be a molding and directing force which is hustling the Middle Kingdom along the road to a new and more promising future. Its iron hand has brought discipline and order to the country. The sacrifices demanded of the people by the government's draconic measures may strike the Western observer as too high a price to pay, but the Communists—and not only they—believe them to be essential for the creating of the basic conditions out of which a viable form of state and society, capable of further expansion and development, can grow. Today, after many setbacks and mistakes, China is more and more clearly presenting the outward appearance of a united and undivided power which is not only convinced that its painful road will lead to the solution of its immense problems but is equally certain that it is destined to play a part on the world's political stage corresponding to its own belief in itself.

Within the space of a few years China has emerged from its provincial shadow-existence. On the continent of Asia she has already attained the stature of a decisive regional power and there are many indications that she is on the way to becoming a world power. The leading world powers can no longer leave out of account the way in which the Chinese Communists see and evaluate problems outside of China, whether they be in Europe, Africa or Latin America. Peking is everywhere trying, with varying degrees of success, to make China's influence felt, a fact which has been reinforced by her entry into the circle of atomic powers. This new development has raised China's prestige and power-political standing, but it has also increased the apprehension felt by many people outside China.

There can be no doubt that one of the factors contributing to this sudden, unmistakable development has been the antagonism between China and her former ally and ideological partner, the Soviet Union. The break with Moscow demonstrated the resolution and self-confidence of the Chinese Communists. But even more, it demonstrated that they had political ideas and aims very different from those of the Soviets. The consequences of this have since become plain. The Chinese Communists now claim to be the only remaining prophets of the true Communist gospel. The Peking center is successfully enlisting support among other Communist parties. The most important Asiatic parties have already fallen in line with Peking, and there are pro-Chinese factions, overt or disguised, in all sections of the world Communist movement.

But it is not the disintegration of a once apparently monolithic Communist movement that is the central factor in a new development, which is leading to a regrouping of forces and relationships within the existing power-political firmament. China has decided to engage in a political and propaganda war on two fronts. Pride of place is still taken by the fight with the leading Western power, the United States. Over and above the internal ideological sphere, the challenge to the second world power, the Soviet Union, is coming more and more into the foreground. These two decisive elements of Chinese foreign policy provide wide scope for all kinds of tactical or strategic political maneuvering by the two Communist centers, both in the relationships between Moscow and the countries hitherto regarded as the Soviet Union's archenemies and in those between Peking and powers which the Chinese have hitherto despised as satellites or satrapies of their opponents. The "alliance between the enemies," as the current relations between the United States and the Soviet Union are sometimes called; the calculating nationalist policies of Roumania; the shift in Pakistan's attitude toward America and China; and the widely differing attitudes of the Chinese and the Soviets toward the Vietnam crisis—these are some of the symptoms of a transformation in the play of international forces which is silently taking place.

Who knows, future historians may well reach the conclusion that the entry of China upon the stage of world politics was the most decisive and momentous event of the second half of the twentieth century. Every Western politician already follows events within China and China's forward thrust in the foreign policy sphere with breathless interest. The political reporter can hardly conceive of a more important task than that of trying to fathom Chinese intentions and the reasoning behind them.

A stay in China itself might do something toward this. Brilliant analyses by individual experts and specialist agencies, based on official Chinese publications, provide a solid starting point for evaluation and judgment, of course, but they can never be more than a skeleton, needing the flesh and blood of personal observation. Getting to know the real China seemed to me to be a necessary supplement to all the detailed academic research which has been done on China, particularly in recent years. To make this reality known to a wider audience seemed especially important at a time when the Far Eastern giant was increasingly striving to make its voice heard.

I had been trying for years to get permission to enter China. At the embassies of the Chinese People's Republic I had been received with polite amiability, my requests had been patiently heard and I had always been assured that the matter would be referred to Peking. But the authorities in the Chinese capital had remained obdurate, as they had to other colleagues of mine who had tried to get into China. The Bamboo Curtain remained impenetrable for Western observers, apart from a few Western technical delegations, the odd fellow-traveling newspaperman or the occasional reporter from countries which recognized Communist China. As far as I could establish, it had been years since political journalists of any of West Germany's leading newspapers had been allowed to travel about in China.

The reasons for this attitude on the part of the Chinese seemed obvious enough. Things had been going downhill in China ever since 1958. As a result of the setting up of the People's Communes, the tremendous expenditure of effort involved in the radical economic program known under the poetic name of the "Great Leap Forward" and a series of natural disasters, the Chinese had suffered serious setbacks. Piecing together official Chinese government statements and the testimony of thousands of refugees who reached Hong Kong, particularly in 1961 and 1962, one got a picture of distress and suffering throughout the entire country. The Communist regime was poised on the brink of catastrophe. It was only too clear why a totalitarian machine, caught in the meshes of its own propaganda boasts, was unwilling to allow reporters into the country at this time and in the subsequent difficult years of gradual economic and social convalescence, especially since Peking was well aware of these reporters' fundamental opposition to Communism. "Lackeys of the class enemy," as Western journalists are usually considered by the Communists to be, are not welcome to snoop about in the

most private internal affairs or, even worse, to ferret out genuine
facts about the situation in a period of recession, facts which
could, in the eyes of the world, damage the prestige of the sup-
posedly most progressive ideas man has ever had. Much that
had hitherto only been guessed at would have been confirmed.
Much that the regime would have preferred to keep concealed
would have been revealed and described in the most vivid
colors, and no amount of control could have prevented it.

When my applications for a permit to enter China were rejected, this was never the kind of explanation I was given, however logical and understandable it might have been, seen from
the point of view of a totalitarian system. Instead, there were
hints of other reasons why the competent authorities in Peking
had rejected them. China, it was suggested, had had unfortunate
experiences with reporters from West Germany. They were not
"objective," they tended to "distort the facts" and some of them
had made nothing but malicious comments on the difficulties
which admittedly existed in China. The Chinese, it was added,
thought they could understand the reasons for this attitude on
the part of West German newspaper correspondents. After all,
West Germany was the most pliant of all the satellites of America, China's Enemy Number One. Unless they wanted to risk
losing their jobs, how could West German journalists be expected
to report on China other than in terms acceptable to the Americans?

Whatever the real reason may have been, the fact was that
there had been a strict ban on the granting of entry permits to
West German journalists. It was not until 1964 that a change
came about. I was suddenly given permission to make two
journeys to China, one as a member of an official delegation, on
the occasion of the inaugural flight of the Pakistan International
Air Lines service to China, and the second as an individual, this
time with permission to visit extensive areas of inland China, including some areas that had been made accessible to few, if any,
Western observers until that time.

What was the explanation of this change of heart? On the face

of it it might seem that conditions in China had so far improved
since the terrible, catastrophic years that Western correspondents
could now be allowed into the country. But this explanation does
not seem to me to be enough. The real reason must be sought
elsewhere. It was surely no coincidence that this permission to go
to China was given just at the time when the dispute between
Peking and Moscow had reached its height. The Chinese leaders must have been concerned to ward off the frontal attack by
the Soviet Union and her supporters and not to let themselves
be driven into a position of hopeless political and economic
isolation. A harmless flirtation with the West German Republic
might be one way, out of a number of possible tactical moves, to
achieve this.

This automatically brought in the German question, a particularly sensitive matter for all Communist states. Moscow was not
only to be provoked and irritated. The Soviets were also to be
warned, to be threatened with weapons up the Chinese sleeve,
so to speak, and reminded that if the worst came to the worst,
Peking would have no difficulty in thwarting Soviet plans in
Central Europe in one of the most touchy questions in world
politics. Accordingly, Bonn's first cautious feelers on the subject
of establishing trade relations brought a favorable reaction from
the Communist headquarters in Peking. The immediate cries of
outraged protest from the East German government seemed to
confirm the correctness of Peking's tactical thinking. The ex-
travagant assertion by Hermann Matern of the Central Committee of the East German Communist Party, in April 1964, that
China was now willing, like Beria before her, "to sell out East
Germany to the West German militarists and revanchists" was
greeted in Peking with a suppressed smile.

At the same time, these cautious attempts to make contact
with Bonn did fit in with China's genuine interest in setting up
connections with Western industrial states now that the flow of
help and support provided by the European Communist bloc
had dried up.

Such considerations led logically to the next step, the ex-

perimental lifting of the ban on visits by West German journalists
to China. It was no accident that I, a member of the editorial
staff of the *Frankfurter Allgemeine Zeitung*, regarded by the
Chinese as the most influential newspaper in West Germany,
should be the first reporter to receive permission to travel to and
within China.

Everything seems therefore to point to the conclusion that it
was tactical political considerations which led to the fulfillment
of my long-standing wish. It was also tactical political considerations which led to my being allowed to see and hear so much
that had not hitherto been made accessible to others because it
was not in China's interest to allow it at the time. As a result, my
two trips to China became more than a mere tourist visit. They
enabled me to gather impressions which may well help to lift a
corner of the veil which covers the life of a people and the enigma
of the political views and aims of their leaders.

"Anyone who thinks China can be isolated is going to be
deeply disappointed." As the Chinese Foreign Minister shouts
these words at his audience, the members of the diplomatic corps,
with the exception of those from pro-Chinese countries, react in
routine fashion. Bored and sleepy, the ambassadors and envoys
from all over the world, sunk deep in long rows of soft armchairs,
applaud dutifully, as if they are duly taking note of one of those
often-repeated slogans which nobody can really believe. The
other foreign guests behave more politely. But the Chinese
functionaries break out into thunderous applause. Their expressions change to one of grim determination, their eyes light up.
Chen Yi is striking a note which echoes their most heartfelt hopes
and desires.

The occasion itself seems to support the Chinese Foreign
Minister's claim. In the Peking Hotel, the most elegant and distinguished in the Chinese capital, a resplendent company is
gathered for the banquet to celebrate the opening of the airline
service between Karachi and Shanghai. Everybody of any consequence is there and even the Premier, Chou En-lai, has not

wanted to miss this occasion. The toasts are endless. The faces of the Chinese functionaries show their pride and confidence. There can be no doubt, Peking sees the new airline service not as a welcome expansion of communication between countries, as would be the case anywhere else in the world, but as a political victory. The speeches and toasts contain repeated praise of the visitors from Pakistan for having decided to take this step, "in spite of numerous difficulties, despite attempts at blackmail and in the interests of peace and friendship between peoples."

One can feel the satisfaction of the Chinese at having succeeded in breaking through the transportation cordon surrounding the Chinese mainland and that, moreover, in collaboration with a pro-Western country, a country linked to the free world by military alliances. The genuine pleasure the Chinese feel is mixed with high glee at having been able, with this move, to thumb their noses at both of their mighty opponents, the "American imperialists" and the "Soviet revisionists."

My first visit to China was pervaded by the atmosphere of victory and cheerful confidence which was so marked a feature of the gathering in the Peking Hotel. The members of the group that I was in were treated as honored guests and titled "particular friends of the Chinese people." From the moment of our arrival until the last minute of our departure there was no escape from the pomp and ceremony which is unfailingly accorded to "friendship delegations" in all Communist countries.

It began when we landed in Shanghai. Thousands of "workers from all sections of the people" had gathered to greet the delegation. As we left the airplane our ears were assailed by the noise of shrill gongs and deep-throated drums. Hundreds of silk flags of all shades provided a background of magnificent color. Girls threw bunches of paper flowers and garlands in rhythmic unison. Choruses of young people chanted greetings. Only the expressions on the faces of the crowd betrayed the fact that these greetings were more the result of duty than the product of spontaneous enthusiasm. Officials in clean, identical suits of high-quality material were lined up, young intelligent faces, charged

with energy, faces that seemed to bear the stamp of thousands
of years of Chinese history. Endless handshakes were followed
by interminable speeches, in which representatives of provincial
and municipal councils, of the national transport authority and
of the Chinese state airline gave full expression to their official
pleasure and satisfaction.

The whole of our stay of just under a week was on similar lines.
One reception followed another, one banquet was succeeded by
another banquet and the speeches and toasts were word for
word identical. In the meantime there were inspection tours,
excursions and entertainments. Nothing but the best was good
enough, it seemed. It started in Shanghai. From the airport we
were taken to our hotel and then immediately to a banquet given
by the mayor of this, the biggest city in China. After a
sumptuous meal and numerous speeches we were treated, despite the lateness of tho hour, to a monster program of artistic
entertainment, in which choirs alternated with music and variety
acts. The climax was a performance of Beethoven's *Fidelio*
Overture, but even though this was doubtless meant to be a
special treat, hardly any of the foreign visitors was in a condition to appreciate it. The thirty-hour flight from Western
Europe to Shanghai, the tumultuous reception at the airport and
the countless new impressions, one treading on the heels of the
other, would have knocked out even the hardiest globe-trotter.

The next morning at cockcrow we were flown on to Peking.
The welcoming ceremonies which met us there were identical
with those we had experienced on our arrival in Shanghai. For
several days thereafter we were swept along in a minutely
prepared program which left the visitor little time or opportunity
even to sit back and think, much less wander off on his own away
from the route laid down for the delegation. The guests were
shown everything Peking had to offer, including the Great Wall
of China and the Ming tombs. In return, they served as extras for
the May First celebrations which were going on just at this time.
It was carefully arranged that we should be taken to the locations
of the most important parades, where we could be loudly ap-

plauded by the wondering masses as examples of a new movement toward peace and friendship.

From Peking we went on to Hangchow, the romantic ancient
residence of the Sung dynasty and the present-day capital of
Chekiang Province. In one single day we saw a large number of
temples, pagodas and monasteries, took a boat trip on the
celebrated West Lake and inspected a silk-weaving mill. This
left us two days for Shanghai. Our stay in this city of ten million
people could of course only give us a very superficial glimpse of
it.

What remained after this hectic merry-go-round was really
nothing more than a multitude of impressions and sensations
which satisfied hardly any of us. The Chinese had been too
eager to show the visitors what they wanted them to see. One
felt they had given their guests too much kid-glove treatment.
They had not asked a single provocative question, nor did they
seem to expect from their guests either words of praise or
simulated enthusiasm.

Even on the few occasions when we did meet with Chinese
other than our official escorts, the same sort of thing happened.
Whenever our delegation appeared, the people were curious but
at the same time overwhelmingly friendly. They beamed at us
and there was usually loud applause. Wherever our motorcade
came in sight, the people would smile and wave at the column
of cars as it passed, in the streets of the towns, in the villages or
out in the fields of the countryside. Visits to plants and communes were skillfully arranged and planned down to the last
detail. Meetings with individual workers and farmers seemed to
be equally well planned and fell neatly in with the rest of the
propaganda pattern. We were never free of the feeling that we
were witnessing a spectacle, long prepared and staged on a
gigantic scale. Quite apart from that, every Chinese seemed to
know how he had to conduct himself in the presence of a group
of the government's honored guests.

We had an amusing example of this in Peking, when a small
group of us took advantage of one of the rare breathing spaces

in the program to take a short walk, unescorted, in the side streets off the Changan Boulevard, the capital's finest and broadest street. In the course of our walk we came across some men sitting in the spring sunshine before an old wall, playing a harmless game of chess. This idyllic scene seemed to be positively asking to be photographed, but almost as soon as we pulled out our cameras, an official came bustling up and gave us to understand, with violent gestures, that it was forbidden to take pictures here, for some mysterious reason. One word led to another and people came up from all directions, looking anything but friendly and waiting to see how it would all end. Then one of my companions had the bright idea of bringing out and showing to the aggressive official a badge which identified us as members of a "friendship delegation." In a second the situation changed completely. The official at once became friendly and the crowd standing around put on courteous smiles. Now we were actually encouraged to take photographs and were finally sent on our way with many good wishes.

In spite of its highly official nature, I did gain some profit from this first visit to China. It not only gave me a general idea of conditions and living standards, it also offered me the opportunity, by reason of continual contact with functionaries and officials at receptions and banquets, for some political conversation. Moreover, our status as guests of honor meant that we were invited to functions attended by leading members of the Party, which gave us an interesting opportunity to study them at close quarters.

Yet I still had serious doubts. The journey had been too short, too official, too collective, too planned and organized, too tailored to the purpose of displaying what our hosts had wanted us to see. It gave too one-sided a picture of certain aspects of Chinese life which could, after all, be only a part of the whole picture. This itself taught me something, admittedly. I can now envisage more clearly the kind of impressions governmental or specialist delegations from Western or neutral countries would take back with them from China after an officially arranged series of flying visits such as the one we had. Many of those who undertake similarly planned tours in China as members of Western tourist groups may well return with the same sort of impressions.

But the few "authorized" towns and cities are not typical and their manner of life is not representative of the whole country. Just as Paris is not France and New York is not America, so are Peking and Shanghai not China. Only a journey into the vast and many-sided hinterland, in which more than 90 per cent of the population of China live, would justify the attempt to draw a reasonably accurate picture of the China of today.

Six months later I was given the opportunity to make such a journey. Traveling on my own, I was given permission to follow a route which largely corresponded to my own proposals and which was to take me, in the space of several weeks, six thousand miles through the interior of China.

Part One

LOOKING INTO THE
KALEIDOSCOPE

The less one has seen, the
more there is to wonder at.

—*Old Chinese proverb*

Chapter 1

TRAVELING ALONE IN CHINA

The features of the customs officer at Kunming Airport, the starting point of my second journey to China, radiated friendliness as he greeted me in fluent English. "Welcome! You will be a guest at the celebrations to mark our national day. Please fill out this currency declaration blank. All other formalities have been taken care of." He saluted politely and went off with self-assured step.

I was dumfounded. On the journey across India and Burma I had had to endure the deep mistrust of the frontier officials in neutral Asian countries, and I had been wondering what mountains of paper, endless questionings and minute searches I would be faced with on setting foot on the soil of anti-imperialist, Communist China, so suspicious of anything foreign. But nothing of the kind happened.

I was to have a similar surprise the day I left China. At Nanning Airport, the handful of Soviet and Eastern European specialists who were to travel in the same plane as far as Hanoi were subjected to a detailed examination of their baggage. When it came to my turn, however, the official expression on the face of the customs official relaxed into a courteous smile. He riffled negligently through the pages of my passport and then gave a careless wave of his hand to indicate that the formalities were over. He showed no curiosity about my camera case, maps or the dozens of rolls of undeveloped film. "Have a good flight and come back soon" was his laconic farewell, as if a journey to China were one of the most natural things in the world and political differences existed only on paper.

Between that first impression on my second arrival in China and my last pleasant experience as I departed, there had been six weeks crammed with experiences, impressions and observations, as varied and as kaleidoscopic as the landscape, the people and the conditions in the course of a six-thousand-mile journey through the Chinese mainland.

Traveling across the forbidding plains of the Northeast, I had a depressing feeling of dreary monotony. Even the enormous industrial centers of Manchuria seemed unable to overcome the influence of the yellow-gray wastes. An unceasing merciless wind beat down the smoke and grime which hung over the industrial landscape and forced them into the streets and alleys, covering the unending slums, the factory chimneys and the factories themselves with a fine smoky mist, so that all activity was transformed into a shadow play. Only the sun could occasionally banish the spectral veil for an hour or two and lighten up the hard features of the people.

Nature is inexorable in Inner Mongolia. The storm wind from Central Asia has swept the first snow from the hills and valleys, as if to ensure that nothing shall soften the unending barren landscape or make it less intimidating to mere humans, of whom only a few lonely souls seem prepared, out of tradition or habit, to endure its rigors.

Returning to Peking from the inhospitable plains, the traveler feels a sense akin to homecoming as he re-enters the walls of the capital. Peking has lost none of the famed intimacy of its tortuous maze of streets, the intoxicating loveliness of its palaces and gateways and the esthetic beauty of its extensive, artistically laid-out parks and gardens. Even in the overcast and muggy days of autumn, when mist and drizzle dampen the spirits and depress the mind, they still cast their spell over resident and visitor alike.

Towns like Sian and Loyang, on the other hand, have a very different effect. At one time, thousands of years ago, these were the seats of mighty imperial dynasties, citadels of a flourishing culture. Today they are atrophied, shrunk, impoverished. Time seems to have stood still here. Within the ancient city walls there is a scene of bustling, almost medieval activity, but the industriousness is not that of the technical age. Only in the outlying suburbs is there a new stirring, a sparse growth of modern industries. But these are a long way from setting the pace of the towns.

Was it their proximity to the Hwang Ho, the dreaded Yellow River, that drove the life out of these places? Like a raging monster the river thrusts its way south through massive mountain gorges until, released from the confinement of the rocky canyons, it hurls its boiling mass onto the plains as if to take them by storm. Broadening out, it pushes its way forward in gigantic muddy-yellow tongues, untamed, the arbiter for good or ill of the destinies of millions.

Compared with the Yellow River, the broad placid waters of the Yangtze Kiang seem to exude life-giving benevolence. The faces of those who live on it are much less deeply marked by toil and sorrow than the faces of those who live in the Yellow River valleys. This is particularly so in Wuhan, the thriving metropolis, whose outward appearance stems from the pre-Communist era.

If the traveler presses on south for another hundred miles or so, he sees yet another change in scenery and character. Life does not seem to have changed much in Hunan Province, either. The capital, Changsha, is typically Chinese and even the few modern buildings do not spoil the picture of the town as an entity. It is as if the spirit of progress, however extravagantly it may express itself in words, suddenly checks itself when it comes to putting the theory into practice. Is this because of the people themselves, who, particularly here in Central China, seem more attached to the old traditions than those elsewhere? Or is it that the tender, charming landscape, the pine-covered slopes and hilly contours exercise a softening influence on them?

Finally, South China takes the traveler into a completely different world. Heat and tropical humidity prevail in the provinces of Kwangtung and Kwangsi. The landscape has the serene and dreamlike quality which has always delighted the European in classical Chinese watercolors. The commercial center, Canton, bubbles with life and vitality. For someone coming from Central China, it is as if he had crossed into another region, another age. The people here seem more advanced and intelligent than in many other parts of the country.

As the traveler journeys across the Middle Kingdom he passes through landscapes of many different types and meets people of every kind. The only thing that never varies is the way he is conducted to what he wants to see and the way it is presented to him. He is always in someone's care. There is always some official government department responsible for him. In the case of Western journalists this is the Information Department of the Foreign Ministry in Peking. This is where he expresses his wishes, where every proposal is haggled over and where it is decided where he may go, and when.

Once permission has been given and he has in his pocket the travel permit showing the exact details of destination and dates, the traveler has nothing more to worry about. The plan functions with clockwork precision. The stranger cannot get lost, no difficulties can arise. Air and railroad tickets are booked for him, hotel accommodations and sleeping-car berths provided: he does not have to bother about a thing. If he is escorted by an interpreter—something which sometimes proves very useful, since the ability of the local interpreters varies considerably—he travels like a king. The interpreter arranges everything. But even when he is traveling by himself he need still have no worries. He is escorted to the airport or railroad station and when he arrives at his destination he will be met by another broadly smiling interpreter and a representative of the municipal or provincial administration.

When he is traveling, even without an official escort, the stranger in China is continually surrounded by solicitous care. If he is in a hurry, he will travel by air whenever possible. This will allow him to visit more places with less loss of time, an important consideration in view of the enormous distances to be covered. Only a decade or so ago, a journey into the far interior could take weeks or even months. Even today one can occasionally lose a great deal of time. Kunming, for example, although it is the capital of the province of Yunnan, still has no railroad connections with the Chinese interior. An official who had only recently been transferred from Peking to Kunming told me it had taken him nine days to reach his new post, sometimes traveling by railroad but more often by bus over rutted country roads. The same journey by air, including stops in Sian and Chungking, takes rather less than nine hours.

However, air traffic is confined to a few important routes. There are still not enough airplanes and fuel is scarce. The airplane most commonly used is the reliable Ilyushin 14. The Chinese pilots fly remarkably safely and never take any chances. There are no night flights and if weather conditions become even slightly dubious, all flying is stopped.

The only other passengers one meets when traveling by air are officials and foreigners, and it is a matter of course that the foreigner will enjoy certain privileges. He is made aware of his special status immediately after takeoff, when he is the first one to be offered refreshments. On one occasion, when I found that my seat could not be adjusted to a more comfortable position, the stewardess called on another passenger, clearly a senior official, to change places with me. Without complaint—indeed with a friendly gesture of invitation—he vacated his seat for me. The foreign passenger also receives regular special bulletins, usually in Russian, telling him the aircraft's position, and informing him what town, river or mountain range is now below him.

Even on long flights, meals are not provided on board airplanes, but are served at intermediate stops. The stranger does not need to do anything about this: when the airplane lands he finds a waitress already waiting for him in the airport building. She leads him to a reserved table piled with food of all kinds.

He will seldom be able to consume even half of what is provided, no matter how temptingly it is prepared. However, this kind of thoughtful service can sometimes be the cause of disappointment. One time, early in the morning, when the sun was just showing itself above the horizon, the stewardess brought me a tray on which, as she proudly indicated, was a glass of beer. When I tried to explain that I was not accustomed to drinking beer in the early hours, the world seemed to collapse about her. A German who refused a glass of beer—that was something she just could not imagine.

When traveling by rail, the traveler will encounter the same kind of treatment, quite apart from the fact that rail travel has other advantages to offer. In the densely populated areas of China there is a closely knit railroad network. One can always make a good connection and one can also travel by night and thus save time. Then, too, since the long journeys mean that one spends a long time in the train, one has a very good opportunity of getting closer to the life of the people. Train travel is slow. Not only do the trains never reach high speeds but they also stop at every place of any size, in order that passengers, some of whom travel for days, can stretch their legs or get something to eat from one of the stalls or eating houses that abound everywhere.

The trains are kept scrupulously clean. An army of employees is constantly engaged in sweeping, polishing and dusting. The outsides of the cars are washed down at every stop. Service and cleanliness are particularly good in the higher-class cars in which officials and foreigners normally travel. As soon as the journey begins, cigarettes and matches are placed before the foreign passenger, not just one pack but four. A pair of soft slippers is provided so that the traveler will feel completely comfortable. In every compartment there is a radio which, notwithstanding the widespread belief to the contrary, can be switched off at any time. Hot tea is served as a matter of course and a waiter comes round at regular intervals to see if the traveler needs anything. In the dining car the foreigner will find his place specially reserved and his table, unlike the others, will boast a white tablecloth. Should the foreign guest elect to eat Chinese food, the kitchen staff will put their best efforts into its preparation, and should he also know how to manage chopsticks, the staff will be enchanted.

An incident during my travels in the Northeast will illustrate the extent to which the foreigner's welfare is taken care of. After visiting the Anshan steelworks, I wanted to travel on to Shenyang, less than sixty miles away, that same evening. However, the timetable revealed that the only train running at this time was an uncomfortable one with wooden seats. A message was sent at once to Dairen, the home station of the train, and a sleeping car was specially attached to the train for one passenger. This enormous, comfortable car belonged exclusively to me for the short trip from Anshan to Shenyang. The same politeness was displayed, incidentally, when my solitary splendor became too much for me and I decided to take my place among my fellow humans in the dining car.

What is true of conditions in public transport holds good for the hotels as well. It is not very long ago since the foreign traveler could tell many a dismal story about the inns and hostelries of China. The well-known Sinologue Perzyński, neither prejudiced nor particularly sensitive, described his experiences in Chinese inns about fifty years ago in these words:

In the courtyard of the inn, pigs, hens and dogs play peacefully together, mules are tied up outside the rooms and there are garbage heaps, feet high, in each corner. The "guest room" is an empty stable, the sky can be seen through the board ceiling, the paper door and windows are torn and unspeakably filthy. My kerosene stove is too small to heat this leaky shed. The other rooms have mud walls and mud stoves. In these rooms sleep indigent traders or draymen, who feed the stoves with poor Chinese charcoal and wake up rosy-cheeked and cheerful after a truly animal sleep, where we would have been suffocated by the carbon monoxide.

His Chinese fellow travelers frankly admitted, ". . . even for a Chinese a night in an inn is a grueling experience. Europeans are not wanted; they cause too much bother. Recently an inn-keeper, who did not even serve tea, was heard to grumble about modern effeteness. Once upon a time, he said, people had been content to sleep all together in one big room. Now only three or four people were willing to share a room. If you travel in summer, nothing will surprise you more than the astuteness of the Chinese bedbugs. They crawl up the walls to the middle of the ceiling and then drop boldly onto your bed."

The present-day traveler in China will miss the colorful adventures which so shocked and fascinated travelers in former times. Instead, he will find a uniform standard of hotels and perfect service. The hotels for foreigners are all enormous boxes in the stern splendor of socialist realism, relieved only here and there with Chinese ornamentation. Most of them were built at a time when Soviet and Eastern European technical experts were living in the towns and cities of the Chinese interior. Since these advisers and helpers left the country, the hotels are silent, a ghostly silence like that of the beehive when the busy swarm has left. In some of the hotels in Central China I sometimes seemed to be the only guest. I would be seized by a feeling of infinite forlornness, sitting in the gigantic dining rooms against a silent backdrop of pompous chandeliers and marble columns, or when my steps echoed monotonously through endless, deserted corridors.

The service provided by the hotel staffs largely makes up for this, however. A throng of smiling "boys" and chambermaids anticipated one's every wish. The service is always there when wanted and then, when it is clearly not desired, disappears as if by magic. In contrast to some other Communist countries, the plumbing and technical installations in the rooms really work. Cleanliness and honesty are paramount. Most of the rooms cannot be locked, but the guest need not fear that things will go astray. For example, I left a pair of shoes lying in a hotel in North China because the welts had begun to go. Weeks later, in the South, they were returned to me, carefully wrapped, and handed to me with beaming smiles. Tips are forbidden, and the bill is always correct to the last cent.

Should the traveler occasionally wander off the smooth path laid down for him by the tourist travel machinery, he will still meet tact and politeness everywhere. In Central China I traveled in the company of a Norwegian Sinologue. The interpreter was thus unnecessary and we took long, unescorted walks together through the town centers, especially in the evening. We found that the attitude of the ordinary Chinese toward the foreign guests was just the same as it would have been if we had been escorted. When we strolled through shops and department stores we were still accorded preferential treatment. If we got on buses and streetcars, people would immediately jump up and smilingly offer us their seats. We found the same thing in the innumerable tearooms we went into to get into conversation with the ordinary man in the street. A table would be cleared and, as soon as we had sat down, the people would sit down with us. The owner of the teashop would feel himself honored to serve us and dozens of other people would gather around, inquisitive but polite, to listen to the unusual conversation.

The desire to make the best possible impression on the foreigner during inspection tours of People's Communes, factories or cultural institutions sometimes took on grotesque form. Heaven and earth would be moved to ensure that everything went well and that the guest's wishes were fulfilled. One afternoon in South China, for example, when I expressed the wish to take some photographs of a work brigade harvesting rice, having seen this brigade at work during a tour of the commune that morning, it was at first explained that this brigade had already finished work for the day. However, they said, as a favor to me they were willing to send another unit into the fields. In spite of my protests that I did not wish any special demonstration, an hour later I was taken out to the fields to see in action the brigade which had been especially called into service for me.

During my inspection of a primary school in Peking I found at the entrance a blackboard bearing a long and beautifully written greeting to "the guest from West Germany." The children revealed that they had been told about my visit in advance and had put on their nicest clothes. Portraits of Bach and Beethoven had been hung up in the music room specially for the occasion.

Nor was any effort spared during a visit I paid to the Academy of the Peking Opera. After I had toured the classrooms I was told that a number of dress rehearsals happened to be taking place on that day. For two hours, a one-man audience in the large auditorium, I was treated to one extract after another from classical and modern Peking operas, with the whole cast in full costume, involving hundreds of actors and musicians, who had had to rehearse for many hours.

This overeagerness to please can sometimes lead to farcical situations. One evening I was visiting a workingmen's club in a town in Central China and the workers from a local factory had been mobilized to demonstrate organized spare-time activities for the visitor. Some were practicing musical instruments, others were playing chess, cards or table tennis, gravely reading books in the library or reading rooms and some were watching a movie: all without paying the slightest attention to the unusual visitor. If I had not already been struck by the tremendous interest my appearance had aroused and if I had not been stared at as if I were some exotic animal everywhere I went in that same town during the day, I might almost have believed that I was seeing the normal evening activities of a group of Chinese workingmen.

The sheer perfection of the organization and the efforts made to show things in the best possible light may be impressive. But despite all the politeness and helpfulness of the individual Chinese, who is anxious to do what is right for the visitor and is always tactful and patient, never aggressive or offensive, there is one important element in the relations between people which is missing. There is never any human contact between person and person, no opportunity for the development of natural and unforced feelings of friendliness. I did occasionally have the feeling that this might be about to happen, but then it always seemed as if an invisible wall, some insuperable obstacle, stood between us. A personal invitation from a Chinese is apparently as little possible as a confidential man-to-man conversation, even on nonpolitical subjects.

Part of the reason for this lies in the national character of the Chinese, of course, but the main cause is the psychological effect of strict political control. There can be no other explanation for some of the things I saw almost every day during my travels. In the course of a number of conversations I had with ordinary Chinese when officials were also present, I could feel the nervousness of the people I was talking with and their fear lest they should say something not in accordance with the prescribed official line. Another symptom was the disinclination of most senior Chinese officials, without any special cause or instructions, to have any contact with foreigners. For example, on all my trips by air, the seat next to mine in the plane was always left empty, even when, as happened on one occasion, the plane was full and one official preferred to sit on a makeshift seat rather than take the one next to the foreign passenger.

I had the clearest evidence of this general tendency to be cautious in relations with foreigners when I used to get into informal conversation with people in restaurants and teashops, if I went into them without my official escort, as I sometimes did. It would never be more than half an hour before an official would suddenly appear and sit down at my table, uninvited, as though this were the most natural thing in the world. The conversation, which up to then had had the peaceful, unsensational character of a quiet chat between friends, would grind to a painful halt. What was most significant was the reaction of the people I had been talking to. Whereas up to this point they had all been relaxed and talkative, now some of them would lapse into silence and leave the official to do the talking, others would try to slip away unnoticed, while a few of the others would suddenly break out into paeans of praise of present-day conditions.

After these and similar experiences, one is not surprised that the official tour programs are also made to serve the purposes of political opportunism. Any desires on the part of the visitor which do not conform with this are simply ignored. It could be argued that every country has a legitimate right to put on display as far as possible only those things which will show conditions in the best light. But what is particularly striking in China is the staged demonstrations and the perfectly organized performances, which cannot help but evoke skepticism. Things are not so bad as they were a few years ago. Official agencies are more forthcoming. I was told in Peking that during Chou En-lai's African tour in early 1964, well-disposed Africans had complained to him about the rigid planning of tours in China, pointing out that this produced precisely the opposite propaganda effect to the one intended. It was due to these complaints, for example, that it was now possible to take photographs in China without hindrance. Even when the photograph is of some aspect of abject poverty, little attempt is made to prevent the picture being taken, and when this does occasionally happen, it is apparently because the official concerned is not *au fait* with the latest instructions. In fact, the current line seems to be, "Go ahead and take whatever pictures you want. We want the world to know we are poor and to see what enormous tasks we are faced with."

Only once did I find myself in an awkward situation. This was in Changsha, the capital of Hunan Province, in the South. I had gone off by myself into the center of the old town with the intention of finding some picturesque scenes to photograph. All went well for some time. The usual troop of lookers-on followed or surrounded the long-nosed stranger, nobody showing any signs of unfriendliness. All at once there appeared a scowling official, probably the Party informer for this street. He began to bawl at me, pointing to my camera and looking as if he were about to attack me. I could think of nothing to do but to bawl back at him, just as loudly and in German. The official stopped short, taken aback. In his eyes I could read apprehension and doubt.

Clearly he was wondering if he had made a mistake for which he might be called to account. I quickly took advantage of his confusion to leave the scene, head held high but not feeling very comfortable. My faithful escort of spectators, grinning with amusement, followed behind me.

When permission to travel to a particular place is denied, the refusal cannot always be put down to the fact that the authorities in that place have something to conceal. It is more likely that the absolute insistence that the foreigner must go short of nothing means that good hotels and capable interpreters are a prerequisite. If these conditions are not met, then there is simply nothing to be done. Regarding interpreters, I seemed to be fortunate. During the working out of my route, I had said in Peking that it was not essential to provide a German-speaking interpreter, as I could equally well manage with interpreters in English, French or Russian. This was accepted, and I am sure it made things easier for me. There was only one point on which the authorities never gave way. I never at any time had a Russian-speaking interpreter, although there are large numbers of them available owing to the requirement for Russian-speakers during the years of close friendly relations between Moscow and Peking. There was only one explanation for this. The conflict with Moscow being at its height, the Chinese authorities wanted to forestall the possibility of painful and possibly even offensive misunderstanding and confusion on the part of my Chinese hosts during inspection tours or interviews.

Other reasons for the refusal to allow visits to certain towns or areas sound reasonable even to Western ears. My request for permission to visit Lanchow in the West and Paotow in Inner Mongolia, for example, was refused despite the fact that only a few weeks before, French and Swiss journalists had been allowed to go there. The explanation was probably to be found in the atomic explosion which took place shortly afterward. Western experts believe there are nuclear reactors in Lanchow and Paotow and there were rumors in Peking shortly before the exploding of the first atomic bomb that all roads to and from these towns in the Central Asian proving area are barred to foreigners.

On the other hand, the Chinese are not so sensitive about military secrets as many people think. I was given permission to go to both Kunming and Nanning, even though the airports in both places are also, or even mainly, air-force bases. At Nanning Airport, indeed, there was considerable military activity. The area round about was dotted with anti-aircraft guns and uniforms were to be seen everywhere in the streets of the town. This increased military activity in Nanning was due to the immediate proximity of the North Vietnamese border. At a time when the Vietnam crisis had reached a critical stage, this would have been reason enough to keep certain things hidden from foreign eyes, but the Chinese authorities apparently saw no reason to keep me out of the area.

The reasons for the ban on visits to certain provinces and districts, particularly the peripheral regions of Sinkiang and Tibet, were obviously political. In Sinkiang, according to Soviet statements, there is friction between the Chinese administration and the minorities living in the area, especially the Kazakhs and Uighurs. While I was in Nepal on the way back to Europe, I was told by Tibetans who had just fled from their homeland that things were not looking very bright for the Chinese administrators in Tibet, either. Other areas are closed to visitors because of "poor economic conditions," as was indirectly indicated to me by prominent Chinese in Peking. The true interpretation of this seems to have two sides. In the first place there is always some place in China that is in the throes of a natural disaster such as floods or drought, even if these do not attain the proportions of those of the period 1959–61. Individual regions still do not have sufficient emergency reserves to be able to relieve the sufferings of the people immediately, nor is it always possible to get supplies from better-situated provinces elsewhere. In the second place, just at the time I was in China, or so I heard from a reliable source in Peking, central Party agencies were reported to have dispatched commissions of investigation to various remote districts to inquire into cases of corruption and embezzlement. The Chinese were not willing to allow such matters, which would throw an unfortunate light on certain regional goings-on, to be served to the foreign visitor on a plate.

It follows from all this that there are limits to the amount of information that can be gathered during a journey through China. One does not get to know what is happening behind the scenes and the reporter must realize it. Anyone who claims to understand conditions and the political scene in the colossal empire because he has been there and has seen the reality with his own eyes is either presumptuous or naïve. At the same time, however, it would be just as wrong to claim that every visitor to China must necessarily fall a victim to the cunning propaganda of the system. A reasonably long stay and extensive travels in the country provide a large number of opportunities for picking up signs, hints and intimations from conversations and personal observation, and these can be put together to make a mosaic which will allow conclusions to be drawn as to the political situation and the problems of the country.

Anyone who makes it clear that he has not come to China with the intention of portraying everything in black and white, but simply wants to inform himself, to try to get some understanding of certain conditions, certain methods—even if he is not able to fully approve of them—will be met with a frankness, even in respect of sensitive political matters, that he will seldom find in any other Communist country. It is certain, therefore, that in spite of all the obstacles and difficulties, a visit to China goes a long way toward giving a better understanding of what is really happening in the Middle Kingdom.

Chapter 2

PEKING

"The town is built in the form of a square, entirely en-
closed by earthen ramparts, ten paces thick and crowned with
battlements. The whole design of the town displays the greatest
regularity and the streets are for this reason so straight that he
who enters by one of the town gates and gazes straight ahead
sees the opposite gate at the other end of the town. In the
center of Peking lies a palace, the largest ever seen, surrounded
by stretches of park land and stately trees bearing diverse fruits.
In the north, a bowshot removed from the palace, stands an
earthwork fully a hundred paces in height." This was how Marco
Polo described Imperial Peking at the beginning of the four-
teenth century; and the description still holds good today.

Peking has retained a great deal of the character of an imperial city. The view from Prospect Hill, which was erected
when the artificial lakes were being constructed, takes the eye
over the elegantly curved, golden-gleaming, glazed roofs of temples and palaces, bedded in a sea of green. In the distance,
through the misty haze, tower the massive city gates, looking
like the grim guardians of an idyll of tranquillity. To the south
one sees the gleaming turquoise of the Temple of Heaven, like
a glowing jewel eager to soar into the air from among the hud-
dled houses. In the far distance, like a filigree decoration on the
horizon, stand the Western Hills so dear to every native of Peking, closing the great circle that surrounds the colossal dimen-
sions of the Chinese capital.

The area of the Imperial City, once the realm of monarchs, eunuchs, mandarins and concubines, with its maze of harmoniously laid-out halls, temples, pagodas and pavilions; and the Forbidden City, which still carries a savor of long-dead formal etiquette, intrigue and counterintrigue, courtly manners and courtly vices—both fill the center of Peking with an atmosphere that not even the challenging placards, the banners and the uniforms of the visitors can dispel.

Surrounded by a red wall and a moat, this domain is still a fairy tale in wood and stone. In days gone by, ordinary mortals were forbidden to enter it. In the days of the Republic only foreign tourists and a few Chinese used to come here to contemplate the silent evidence of a sublime past. Nowadays thousands stream along the broad avenues of the city of temples. Palaces and gates stand side by side, each with its heavy gleaming roof of glazed tiles and separated from the others by squares laid out in beautiful symmetry, marble staircases and intersecting walls of dull red. The gates all bear poetic names, each one heightening the expectation of the visitor as he penetrates deeper into the interior of the palace area. Finally he reaches the culminating glory, the architectural heart of Peking, the Gate of Heavenly Purity, the door behind which lay the imperial residence. The modern Chinese is fond of these wonderful palaces within his capital, not in nostalgia but as places of interest that fill him with national pride.

Even the intrusion into the center of the city of new buildings in the bloodless style of socialist realism has little effect on its dignity and elegance. The massive modern structures on the great Tien An Men Square and the Changan Boulevard, which, lined with street lamps in Stalinist style, forms the east-west axis of Peking for a distance of almost sixteen miles, are made to look unassuming. Tree-lined avenues and parks conceal a good deal of ugliness. It is as if the modern were trying to disguise itself, overawed by the spirit of perfect harmony in the ancient architecture. There are only a few skyscrapers. The invasion by the prosaic and the unesthetic, which has destroyed the character of many an old town, has not yet begun in Peking.

Within the historic city walls, much has remained as it was. True enough, the noisy carnival atmosphere and bustling trade have disappeared, along with the dust and the garbage. China's capital is now scrupulously clean. The demands of hygiene have made their mark. As a result, much of the old romantic atmosphere, the warmth and the life have also gone. And yet there is still a good deal of the spirit which led the chroniclers of bygone days to sing the praises of Peking as the greatest and most home-like garden city in the world.

Buildings in the modern style have mainly been pushed out into the suburbs. People have been talking for years about tearing down the old sections of the city and putting up practical apartment houses, based on the latest designs. But as yet nothing has been done. Nobody can say whether this is due to lack of money or to inertia, the unwillingness among even the most fanatical of the Party functionaries to do away with the things that are such an essential element in the native Chinese way of life.

Outside, however, on the other side of the city gates, furious efforts are being made to realize new constructional schemes. To the west, government buildings and innumerable schools have sprung up, together with their own living quarters. To the east there are extensive industrial complexes with miles of working-class homes in the style of barrack blocks. The predominant color in these areas is an insipid brick red: cement is still scarce in China. The monotonous rows of housing estates, each one built on exactly the same pattern as all the rest, make an infinitely dreary picture. Everything needful has been provided—parks, green spaces, schools, kindergartens, moving-picture theaters, workers' clubs and all the other things that go with the Communist idea of paradise. But the sameness is still there. The monotony cannot be disguised. It breathes its spirit into the people and weighs them down.

Even the insides of the apartment blocks are stereotyped. The apartments themselves are tiny and impractical. Often enough even the proportions are out of balance. The motto has clearly been, "Don't spend a cent more than you have to." Agreeable touches such as balconies, for example, are completely lacking. The inhabitants do not seem very concerned to care for their homes, although Party deputies see to it that they are kept spotlessly clean. It is only a little while since the apartment blocks were completed, but already everything looks dilapidated and miserable.

The foreign visitor will not be surprised at all this. In order to hurry the plans for industrialization, everything must be built quickly, cheaply and to a standard pattern. And in any event, for the majority, who have previously been living in grinding poverty, even the smallest apartment, no matter how miserable it may be by Western European standards, is something worth striving for. The same thing has happened elsewhere in the world, including Europe and America, at one time or another in the past. But what is so saddening here is another feature, about which the visitor can only agree with the old hands. Every Old China hand one meets in Peking, and who knew the Imperial City as it was twenty or thirty years ago, has the same complaint about it. The capital has lost most of its color, its life and its sparking vitality. It has become monotonous and drab, as if it had been robbed of its very essence.

One sees this in the very streets. Gone forever are the scenes of noise and hubbub, the boisterous throng of laughing, shouting people, the confusion of exotically draped figures, the astounding variety of shops, sidewalk stalls and pavement peddlers, the legions of hurrying, perspiring pedicab drivers pushing their way through the crowd, the all-pervading, overpowering smell compounded of garlic, onions and sesame oil, the strolling players putting on their show before a verminous audience, the hundreds of storytellers and soothsayers casting their spells on the illiterate peasants in squalid holes and corners. The traffic is thinner, the people more serious, the stores, except for one or two, more stereotyped. There is a depressing sameness about the people's clothes. Admittedly, no one nowadays has to go about in rags, but neither is there any of the chic and elegance that once dotted the streets with splashes of vivacious color.

The old Peking that is looked back on by the Europeans who used to live in this exotic and romantic city in prosperity and comfort is no more. But anyone who wishes to recapture a faint breath of the past can do so. He can still wander through the stillness of the Forbidden City, lost in dreams, undisturbed by any sound from the modern world outside. Or in the thousands of walled alleys, in the late afternoon, when the city is wrapped in a veil of melancholy, he will meet characters who seem to have stepped out of pictures of a bygone age. Here he can see the noisy intimacy of Chinese families in their back yards or join groups of men playing cards or chess, whose serenity and unhurried wisdom are in such contrast to the clamorous pro- ductivity-mania continually being demonstrated to the visitor by the official machine outside.

He can go to the bazaar which winds its way through narrow lanes covered with straw matting, and listen to the discordant babel of the hustling market. There, in the Market of Oriental Peace, parallel to the Wang Fu-ching, the main business thoroughfare of Peking, he can still feast his eyes on a colorful profusion of wares, where fountain pens, crockery, stationery, lamps, cakes and biscuits, cigarettes, pottery, souvenirs, cheap jade statuettes, shoes, clothes, toothbrushes, mountains of candies and much else besides are offered for sale among the crowds of happily chattering passers-by and playing children.

He can browse through the shelves of the secondhand book- shops and throw the owners into dreadful confusion by protest- ing the presence, among the stock of National Socialist books from the library of the former German colony, books which bear bombastic titles to do with race hatred and are nevertheless to be found in the heart of the strictly organized and controlled Communist metropolis. Or he can go into the numerous antique shops and yield to the intoxication of the passionate collector, even though he will not be allowed to take out of the country any article more than a hundred years old.

On a wonderful, azure-blue autumn day he can go to the Tien An Men Square, where the children fly their kites before the colossal statue of Mao Tse-tung at the Gate of Heavenly Peace. The kites darting about the sky are no dull rhomboids or standard paper kites, but ingenious structures of silk in tho most amusing shapes, from multicolored butterflies to stylized tadpoles and symbolic dragons brightly painted to show up at a distance and constructed so as to produce comical evolutions.

The foreign visitor will have to forego much that he may be used to in the way of Western-type entertainment. There are no bars, cabarets, popular movies, cozy cafes or establishments of that kind. The evening's whiskey and soda and society gossip such as the European colony used to indulge in the attempt to create a feeling of the fashionable world of luxury hotels and clubs in Peking—that, too, is no longer obtainable.

To make up for it the visitor can visit the traditional Peking Opera, whose fantastic artistry still thrills audiences just as much as ever it did. He can go with friends to one of the many excellent restaurants and spend hours in a tastefully decorated private room enjoying the superb service and the dozens of different courses of classical Chinese food, which is still to be numbered among the world's supreme culinary achievements.

Life in Peking was certainly more pleasant, more colorful and more interesting in the old days, and the visitor may look back on the old times with nostalgia and regret. He can only console himself with the thought that China is in the toils of a gigantic transformation process that is being forced on with sinister totalitarianism. The consequences are inescapable. In China, as everywhere else, even without Communism, there is a price which has to be paid for modernity, progress and prosperity.

Chapter 3

SHANGHAI

Peking has retained the enchantment of an imperial garden city. Shanghai, too, is in one respect the same as it always was. It is the quintessence of ugliness.

The distinguishing feature of the city is still the Bund, the waterfront along the Hwang Pu River. Shanghai is the only city in China with a façade of skyscrapers, giving it the character of a real metropolis. Decades ago the office buildings, commercial businesses, hotels and banks were controlled by European and Japanese managers, who held the reins of the economy in their hands; and the quays along the waterfront throbbed and echoed with commercial din and bustle. Today the soporific rhythm of the bureaucrats has moved into the skyscrapers and only a few coastal steamers and an occasional liner tie up alongside the quays. The junk and sampan traffic is only a fraction of what it was. The promenade is no longer a place where thousands struggle to eke out a living. Nowadays there are well-cared-for gardens and ornamental grounds where children play, old and young practice their shadow-boxing in the early morning and old people sit on the benches in the sun, doze, read or play mah-jongg. The celebrated sign at the entrance to the park, "No Entry for Dogs or Chinese," has gone. Only at night do the advertising signs along the Bund remind one of the vanished greatness of Shanghai as one of the most important transshipment ports in international trade.

The business streets still bear the old resounding names, names like Nanking Road and Bubbling Well Road. But where the elegant stores used to sell luxury commodities, especially the world-famous high-quality silks of this region, nowadays it is the state sales organizations and cooperatives which offer consumer goods, usually of inferior quality. Squeezed in between them are department stores containing surprisingly large stocks of every-day commodities. Other well-known places have changed their names and much else besides. The Shanghai race course, once the meeting place of the cosmopolitan smart set, has been ex-panded into a park with not only many pleasant walks but a stadium and a parade ground to boot. The former French Club is now a People's Palace and the American Club is the police headquarters.

There has also been a change in the atmosphere of Shanghai, which, with its depravity, its tinsel glitter, its bedlam of noise and the stark contrast between its rich and its poor, had become the most colorful but also the most notorious city in the East. The business quarter, with the international settlements, which used to stand out against the surrounding slums like an oasis of foreign power and suspect wealth, is now something like a burned-out, useless stage set. The tyranny of the gangsters and the mob leaders, the one time dictators of the harbor area, has been smashed. The kidnapings, the blackmail and the un-ashamed exploitation which used to terrorize the inhabitants have all been done away with. All the accompaniments of the ruthless pursuit of wealth and influence which knew no scruples as to methods or the fate of the victims, the bodyguards of the sinister rulers of the underworld, their bulletproof automobiles, the servile "boys," the beggars in their tattered rags, the suicides and the emaciated children's corpses which used to be found in the sewers—all these are things of the past.

Gone, too, is the orgiastic night life that once gave Shanghai the reputation of being the most immoral city in the world. The opium dens and the gambling saloons, the countless dance halls, the brothels and the dilapidated bars of the harbor area have vanished along with the singsong girls with their lacquered hair and skintight dresses slit up the side to the hips. The thousands and thousands of prostitutes and waterfront bums who infested both the main streets and the alleys have been re-educated— "no easy task," as an official said to me. There are still said to be some prostitutes about, but considering the network of organized controls that covers the entire country, it is difficult to know how they manage to operate.

In the space of a few years Shanghai has become prudish and puritanical. Even the International Seamen's Club, used by the crews of the few foreign ships that tie up in Shanghai and formerly known as the Shanghai Club, famous for having the longest bar in the world, is more like a pleasant boarding school for girls than a place of entertainment. "We know what sailors need after weeks at sea," said the manager of the club, a model of respectability. "We organize excursions for them and walks in the parks, so that they can at long last enjoy the sight of foliage and greenery."

Shanghai has taken on the typical Chinese character of all the other towns and cities in the Middle Kingdom. The teeming throng in the narrow streets of the most populous quarters is the same as in Peking, Sian or Wuhan. Bicycles, pedicabs and buses are the usual means of transportation here as elsewhere. Their standardized clothing renders the masses hardly distinguishable from those in other places. The leveling-out process has succeeded so well that it is turning to sheer monotony. Sex appeal has been eliminated. In fact, from a distance the foreigner sometimes finds it difficult to tell the man from the woman, so completely have the outward signs of the difference between them been eradicated.

Shanghai is no longer the place people outside of China picture in their minds when they hear the name. Its character has changed and not only in the ways I have described. The city's very livelihood has shifted. What was once a commercial metropolis is now mainly a thriving industrial city. This may be in fact the real measure of the transformation in Shanghai.

This is not to say that there were no industries in Shanghai before the Communists took over. There were, mainly in textile plants, machinery manufacture and a small steelworks. But the industrial capacity of Shanghai has now been greatly expanded. West of the city there are some dozen satellite towns extending out into the plains, and reputedly increasing the residential area of Shanghai by more than a third. Here live the workers from the many newly constructed factories. The housing estates are built on the most modern lines, with shopping centers, multistory apartment houses, hotels, schools, children's playgrounds, movie houses and theaters. These would certainly not stand comparison with housing estates in Europe, especially when one is taken inside the apartments. The brickwork is unplastered, the staircases are of raw cement and the rooms are overcrowded. The furnishings reveal the poverty of the occupants, the furniture is wretched, there are seldom curtains on the windows and the decorations are trashy.

All this may perhaps not make an overwhelming impression on the Western visitor, but it would be wrong to make unwarranted comparisons. A visit to the slums makes this clear. Shanghai still has its slums, too, and a considerable number of people still have to live in them. In "Pumpkin Town," for example, which has always been a loathsome slum, people still live in shanties made of broken-up packing cases and weatherproofed with mats, newspaper, bamboo or beaten-out oilcans. The streets that wind through the chaotic confusion of these shacks are muddy when it rains and dusty when it is dry, and only a photographer looking for out-of-the-way local-color shots would find anything good about them.

Things are getting better, however. Water supplies, sanitation centers and even an infants' home have been provided and there are determined drives to introduce cleanliness. The repeated cry is, "We are not yet in a position to give every inhabitant of Shanghai a modern apartment." Bearing in mind the prevailing poverty and the shortage of capital, is it reasonable to expect that within the space of a few years the massive concentration of slums in a city of ten million people can be replaced by hygienic dwellings fit for humans to live in?

After seeing a number of plants and factories in all parts of China, I do not think there can be any doubt that Shanghai is now the industrial center of China. Its industrial products range from antibiotics and disposable diapers to steel rolling mills and hydraulic presses, from television sets and cameras to automobile tires and generators, from surgical instruments and X-ray apparatus to drills and diesel tractors.

As in almost every Chinese town the products of the region are on display in a permanent exhibition. In Shanghai this is located in an enormous building which still, curiously enough, bears the name "Palace of Sino-Soviet Friendship." Many of the articles on display are never seen in the department stores outside, such things as electric shavers, refrigerators, pianos, radios, many different kinds of canned food, delicate silks, carpets and fine porcelain. These are the items which are only available for export or for purchase by collectives. I noticed in this and similar exhibitions the great interest the displays arouse in the citizens who come to see them. They go around in groups listening to the explanations given by the female guide, who uses a pointer to draw attention to the individual items. The faces of the audience usually register pride and satisfaction at China's ability to produce these things, but at times they also show discontent and dissatisfaction that it will probably be a long time before they will be able to buy these desirable things for themselves.

It may be some consolation to the inhabitants of Shanghai to know that they have the highest standard of living in China, even in comparison with Peking. There are more goods in the shops and the people are better dressed. The Western observer may think the differences are trivial, but they count.

Many of the young intellectuals, of whom there are a particularly great number in Shanghai, are looking forward to a rapid resurgence that will restore the city to a place in the front rank of the world's great metropolises. "It won't be long now, you'll see," an official told me, his eyes flashing, over an opulent meal in the Peace Hotel, formerly the luxurious Cathay Hotel. "We are already building our own ships, our industry is expanding by leaps and bounds and the harbor is being modernized." Was this said ironically, or was it the product of the self-deceit that comes from a diet of propaganda—or was it naïve conviction? I cannot tell. In no other city in China does the population appear to include so many ambitious and fanatical intellectuals living peacefully side by side with critical and ironic fellow intellectuals. This is the legacy of a unique and exciting past which is unlikely ever to be repeated.

Chapter 4

HANGCHOW

I had been looking forward with pleasure to my visit to Hangchow. After Shanghai's matter-of-fact industriousness and gray ugliness, Hangchow seemed the appropriate counterpart. Its very name conjures up visions of beauty and contemplation and delights every Chinese who hears it. Despite Communist rule, the history of Hangchow and the legends that are interwoven with it are still alive in the hearts of the people.

In their descriptions of the imperial city of the Sung dynasty, the medieval chroniclers and adventurers tried to portray a place that overshadowed even the brilliance and the glory of Venice. "The finest and most splendid city in the world," wrote Marco Polo and Brother Oderic, "with palaces, gardens, the mausoleums of art-loving emperors; a city of lagoons, with twelve thousand bridges, three thousand public baths fed by warm springs, with streets brimming with turbulent life, as smooth as the floor of a ballroom and so wide that they could take nine coaches side by side."

The tide of a cruel history destroyed the erstwhile greatness of Hangchow, "the heavenly city of the Chinese Graces." It began with the onslaughts of the Mongols in the thirteenth century, which reduced the libraries, the walls and the monuments to rubble and ashes; and ended with the destruction wreaked by the Taiping rebels, the Chinese Anabaptists. In the spring of 1862, these took the town, burnt it almost completely to the ground and murdered 600 thousand people. The remainder of the population perished from starvation and disease, and those who still survived, as a contemporary chronicler tells us, drowned themselves in the canals, which were soon choked with corpses, or in the West Lake, so that "a man could walk half a *li* across the corpses as if he were on a footpath."

Hangchow never recovered from this dreadful atrocity. The town dwindled to the level of a large village, with close-packed houses, twisting alleys and the atmosphere of any other Chinese town. The West Lake remains, completely cut off and isolated from the rest of the town and framed by three ranges of green hills. Misty vapors roll like phantom shapes across the water as far as the hills, then dissolve or loop themselves together in snakelike coils to form clouds. On the banks, brightly colored temple roofs, monasteries and pavilions can be seen peeping through luxuriant foliage.

In the bamboo groves and thickets of mulberry trees, reached by means of steps cut into the mountain paths, in the midst of garish subtropical flowers, lie the four most celebrated monastic colonies in the southern Orient. The most important is Ling Ying, "the sanctuary of the spirits," the loveliest monastery of the Sung period. To the cheerful babbling of a brook, one goes down to the monastery under a canopy formed by the branches of giant trees. In niches in the walls of the hillsides, surrounded by mimosas and climbing plants, stone statues of Buddha, overgrown by tangles of iridescent plants in hundreds of varying shades, look down into the ravine in silent meditation. The monastery itself, partly restored though not always with great skill, looks from the distance like a bastion of piety. Closer up, the inquisitive looks and slightly mocking expressions of the innumerable Chinese visitors, and the protestations of the "duty monk" as to the magnanimity of the Communist government "which has at last ensured us Buddhists a secure and worthy existence," reveal the present-day character of the place to be that of a purely tourist showpiece.

The main center of attraction for all Chinese visitors to Hangchow, however, is an imposing hemisphere of polished stone, located on the bank of the West Lake in a great memorial grave. This is the tomb of General Yo Fei, who was murdered in 1141. His fate is now part of Chinese history. His deeds have made him the Chinese national hero and his tomb a place of pilgrimage. For the foreigner, however, the most important experience is to see how the Chinese behave at this sacred place and how they reveal certain features of their national character.

To explain this it will be necessary to say a word or two about the relevant period of Chinese history. At the time of the Sung emperor Kao Tsung, the Mongols invaded the country, and Hangchow, the capital, was in serious danger. The young leader of a robber band from Honan, Yo Fei, came to Hangchow and tendered his services to the emperor. Kao Tsung accepted the offer and Yo Fei and his band of intrepid followers went off to face the enemy. There followed one Chinese victory after another, until the Mongol forces were surrounded. Then misfortune struck. As Yo Fei was getting into position to deliver the final blow that would annihilate the Mongols, the chancellor of the Sung Empire, Chin Kwei, forbade him to go on. Chin Kwei had wormed his way into the emperor's confidence and was intriguing against the victorious Yo Fei, whose influence was growing. The chancellor managed to bring about the dismissal of Yo Fei and the withdrawal of his army. Soon after this the Mongols were again threatening Hangchow. In his hour of need the emperor again installed Yo Fei at the head of his army and once more Yo was successful.

The chancellor now hatched out a further plot, using more brutal methods. He got from the Mongol leader the promise of a safe conduct and a liberal reward if he could engineer the removal of the Mongol leader's most dangerous enemy, Yo Fei. Chin's mistress, who was at the same time the Mongol leader's lover, joined in the plot. Yo Fei was accused of treason. At his trial, however, he was acquitted. Chin tried a different method. He found some corrupt judges, who threw Yo Fei into prison. Now Chin acted. Inside an orange, which, according to legend, had been sucked dry by his mistress, he sent to the jailer an execution order, purporting to come from the emperor but in reality sealed with his own seal. Yo Fei was put to death that same night in a remote corner of the prison.

It was not until twenty years later that, as a result of the insistence of the incensed people, Yo Fei was rehabilitated. He was awarded the title "Fearless Guardian of the Heir to the Throne" and posthumously ennobled. A memorial temple was erected on the banks of the West Lake. This is the place to which to this day, 750 years later, the Chinese throng to pay homage to their national hero.

The tomb is simple and dignified. There is no sign of any intention to present an emotional picture of the national hero as one of the virtuous elect. His image is only to be seen as symbolic decoration on a corbel of the temple roof. In the robes of a general, as the Peking Opera portrays him, with a luxuriantly flowing beard, furrowed brow and wearing a tinsel crown, with pennants projecting from a quiver at his back and with a sword in his hand.

It is another piece of statuary altogether that draws the people. At the entrance to the tomb there is a group of figures in bronze, kneeling, with their hands tied behind their backs. These are the ones who were responsible for the murder of Yo Fei, Chin Kwei the chancellor and his accomplices. Through the centuries the people have filed past the group and have given vent to their hatred with every imaginable form of uninhibited vituperation. At first astonished, then amused and finally thoughtful, I watched the comedy played out by one group of blue-clad pilgrims before the bronze figures. It was one of the rare moments during my tour when I completely forgot that this was a Communist China that I was in.

The events at the Yo Fei tomb seemed to show how deeply rooted remembrance and feeling for history are buried in the Chinese people. After all, the murder of Yo Fei took place nearly eight hundred years ago. And this was a remarkable way to commemorate a national hero. The distinguishing feature was not reverence, wide-eyed, naïve or insincere, but profound contempt for wickedness and hatred of those who personify it, contempt and hatred that are continually being revivified by the contrast between the national idol and his murderers. Can this affecting naturalness be kept alive in the people, even in the future?

On the way back to my hotel I saw signs of a new era. Sanatoria, workers' holiday homes and tourist parties. Routine, order and tedium have penetrated a landscape unequaled for fairy-tale beauty and easy lightheartedness. I walked along the footpath over to the West Lake, where rowboats can be rented. People were standing around, gossiping, chewing candy, laughing and larking noisily about. It was a unique picture of carefree gaiety. These Chinese are unlikely to lose their spirit of humanity as easily as all that.

Chapter 5

THE CENTRAL PROVINCES

It has been raining for days in Hunan. A dense blanket of cloud has settled over the landscape. The gleaming surface of the Changsha streets reflects the multicolored, varnished umbrellas of the passers-by. The Siang River, which divides both the province and its capital, is bathed in a diffused silvery light. Dozens of junks with perforated gray sails glide silently by, reminding one of unmanned ghost ships sailing into the infinite. Outside the city walls, work on the harvest has been stopped. Peasants, barefoot boys and girls in clothes of traditional black, splash through the red mud, carrying into the sheds and mills baskets of rice suspended from poles balanced on their shoulders. Everywhere there is an atmosphere of constraint, which does not at all fit in with the picture of the Central Chinese province of Hunan that I had had in my mind.

Hunan has always been said to be the cradle of revolt. "If there were no emperor, the people from Hunan would invent one, so as to be able to revolt against him," runs a saying that has been current in China for centuries. The people are hot-blooded and temperamental. Their dialect has the shrill, mordant tones of defiance. The food prepared in the kitchens of Hunan is the most pungent in the country after that of Szechwan. The red-pepper pod is as symbolic of the province as is the reputation of the people for hard work, bravery and honesty. It is said that they have always furnished China with her best soldiers and her wisest sages. Nowadays they provide the nucleus of the Communist Party leadership. More than a quarter of the members of the Central Committee of the Communist Party of China (CPC) were born in Hunan. President Liu Shao-chi comes from here, and, more important still, so does the undisputed leader of China, Mao Tse-tung.

The scenery and the inhabitants reflect the characteristics attributed to the Hunanese. The settlements of this province of lakes and wooded hills are less compact than those elsewhere. Everywhere there are sturdy farm buildings between the rice fields and on the hillsides. The people are stocky and their hard but open countenances are chubby, with broad foreheads. Strikingly thick, black hair and particularly dark eyes are characteristic. The young people are better-looking and more attractive than those of the same age in the neighboring provinces.

But it is precisely here, in the interior of China, far removed from the commercial hustle of the big cities like Peking, Shanghai and Canton, that the traveler feels the traditional Chinese art of "living slowly and enjoying slowly." They work hard, certainly, but they also possess the gift of enjoying that quiet happiness which is in such sharp contrast to the hectic lust for life, outwardly rich but often inwardly hollow, of many other peoples possessing more advanced civilizations.

There they sit on narrow wooden benches in the countless teashops of Changsha, at plain wooden tables lit by weak, flickering kerosene lamps: they sip their tea and are never at a loss for something to say. What they do have to say, with a wealth of descriptive gesture, is attentively listened to. There is joking and laughter, but there can also be discussion, as serious as if it concerned the settlement of world problems. They squat in the small, idyllic eating houses and cook shops wreathed in steam from batteries of cooking pots, smacking their lips, enjoying their food, belching and conversing with their neighbors.

Out in the countryside there are similar scenes. In the People's Commune "Yellow Flower," not far from Changsha, the atmosphere was not the cold impersonal one which usually characterizes a large machine. This was simply because the people had very little actual direct contact with the mammoth organization. As far as they are concerned, everything happens on a small scale, in the working group in the fields, in the friendly company in the teahouses or in talking over their troubles within the circle of the family.

For me also the formal ceremonial or the unnatural friendliness of the receptions at the guest houses or in the board rooms of the commune directors did not represent real contact, but rather the incidental unplanned meetings which, despite the distance that was clearly maintained, hinted at a degree of human warmth that one often thinks is long gone and forgotten, to judge by the methods and propaganda of the leaders. It was shown, for example, in a conversation I had with an old woman, who explained to me in detail how she worked the spinning wheel she was using; or in the talk I had with a peasant family when I was shown their house, in which I was pressed to stay while the kettle sang on the quickly laid fire and they entertained me in their smoke-filled best room with witty talk about the everyday things of their life.

But when one turns in the direction of one of the great city centers, the scene changes once more. In Wuhan, only a couple of hundred miles from Changsha, I caught my first glimpse of the Yangtze Kiang, called "The Father of Rivers." It is over three thousand miles long and feeds nine provinces of China and their 250 million inhabitants; in other words, a third of the Chinese nation. It is the king of all the rivers of Asia and has many times demonstrated its power. Between the time the first records were made, in 246 B.C., and 1948, it had overflowed its banks altogether 979 times. The most recent floods are recorded in the old customhouse in Hankow, the town which, together with Wuchang and Hanyang, makes up Wuhan. The highest level attained by the 1931 floods stands at six feet six inches, the highest that anyone could remember at that time. But the mark for the level of the 1954 floods stands at nearly eleven feet. In 1931 the streets of Hankow could only be traversed in boats. In 1954 the town's million inhabitants were only saved from disaster thanks to the superhuman efforts of hundreds of thousands of people.

Even today, more than ten years later, the saving of Hankow ranks as a modern Chinese epic. Three hundred thousand people streamed into the nearby Shen Mountains with wicker baskets and bamboo yokes and, working day and night, carried earth down to the riverbanks to shore up the dykes and reinforce the threatened weak spots. Many a story is told in words and pictures of the heroic deeds performed by individual men and women who sacrificed their lives for the general good in one courageous exploit or another. A national heroic epic has grown out of the sacrifice of the people who, when the river burst its banks, massed themselves shoulder to shoulder in the raging storm, trying to hold back the surging waters until the gaps could be sealed up behind them.

The eyes of the inhabitants of Wuhan light up with pride as they speak of "their" bridge, the imposing two-tiered structure that was thrown across the Yangtze Kiang with the help of Soviet engineers, creating a direct, uninterrupted thoroughfare between North and South for the first time in the history of China. They are also proud of "their" giant steelworks, which employs forty thousand workers and is becoming an independent township far outside the city gates of Wuhan.

Do these manifestations of selflessness and pride portend a new sense of social awareness? Do they indicate a consciousness of the kind of unity the Communists are striving to create? This feeling is admittedly to be found in the larger cities, but I had the feeling that it has still not taken root in the remoter parts of the interior. People who know China well have told me that in the years immediately following the Communist takeover there was a certain naïve enthusiasm for the new regime. The spontaneous urge to action such as was displayed by the people during the catastrophic floods in 1954 was genuine and convincing, they said, but the terrible setbacks caused by the plan for the People's Communes and the 1959 natural disasters had brought disappointment and disillusion. As far as possible, the individual was once again withdrawing into the narrow, intimate sphere of life that had existed since time began. The regime knew of this and allowed for it.

I seemed to get some confirmation of this assessment when I visited a workingmen's club in Changsha. It was by no means a palace of culture, just a modest place for spare-time activities such as can be found everywhere in China. The factory to which this club belongs produces rubber shoes, a product unlikely to stand high on the list of priorities in the Great Plan, so there was all the more reason to suppose that this was an ordinary workingmen's club without special privileges.

The workers seemed to be engaged in their normal pursuits. The biggest crowd was in the table-tennis room and the room where cards and chess were played. In the reading room and library, on the other hand, the men looked as though they had been detailed to be on hand and they no longer showed the simple naturalness I found so likable. A check through the library index soon revealed that the club members were not exactly falling over themselves to get at the great political works. I pointed out to the club director this discrepancy of interests and he admitted that he was not satisfied with what had been achieved so far. He frankly said, "The progressive worker is something we still have to produce."

It would be wrong to generalize on the basis of this reply, which testifies to the ironic realism that I often came across among the junior officials, who seemed quite willing to abandon the standard clichés when they talked to me. In the younger people, however, I found many indications, even in Central China, of idealism and the kind of faith which corresponds to the ideal the progressive worker is trying to achieve. I well remember, for example, a meeting I had with three young workers in charge of a pumping station for the irrigation of the rice fields I was shown in the course of a cross-country journey through Hunan Province. Their faces were filled with huge delight at being able to talk to a foreigner for the first time in their lives. With glowing enthusiasm they showed me what they had to do.

There was no feeling of routine, no superfluous words of extenuation such as I had so often had to listen to in the course of pre-planned inspections. Their flashing eyes made it clear that they firmly believed in what they were doing. When I ventured the opinion that twenty-four to twenty-eight yuan (nine to eleven dollars) a month was very low pay, they replied, "Oh, but we are still young, only twenty-two. One day we shall certainly be earning more than that."

Again, in the Wuhan steelworks, unobserved and from a distance, I saw some men coming off shift, young men, laughing and joking, lined up in their overalls and safety helmets. On a command they suddenly burst into the "Workers' Solidarity Song." Despite eight hours of grueling work at the furnaces, I could see no sign that they felt any reluctance or ill-temper at this extra requirement. They, too, seemed to believe in what they were doing.

In Wuhan, one evening, in the company of the Norwegian Sinologue, I visited a privately run teahouse away from the main streets. The place was full, with dozens of men sitting around. With a friendly gesture the owner put us at a table at which some customers were already sitting. Then, telling his wife to serve us, he excused himself and went back to his other occupation, that of shaving the customers, which was carried out just inside the entrance to the teahouse. The people we were sitting with were laborers and artisans, plain and outspoken. They had never heard of Norway, and knew nothing about the division of Germany. They listened intently to us when we spoke and asked many questions. One of them introduced his sons, lads of about twelve to fourteen years of age. "What do you want to be?" I asked them, and like a shot they replied, "Steel workers!" The men smiled, proud and content.

The modes and rhythm of an ancient traditional way of life still predominate in Central China, but new ideas and concepts are beginning to take root, particularly in the towns and especially among the younger generation.

Chapter 6

"CHINA'S SORROW"

The Northwest is the cradle of China. Here lay the capital cities of the old imperial dynasties, the Chou, the Han and the Tang. Sian, now the capital of Shensi Province, was the center of the Chinese empire throughout eleven dynasties. Twelve hundred years ago the city already had more than a million inhabitants.

Many of the relics of Sian's glorious past are still in existence. As in Peking, broad streets divide up the town into squares. The center is surrounded by massive walls interrupted at different points by immense gates, the finest in the Middle Kingdom. Rising above the sea of houses stand the Bell Tower and Drum Tower, from which in olden times the hours of the day were announced. The Temple of Confucius, now a splendid art museum, radiates dignity and nobility. A hundred or so miles to the east lies Loyang, once the residence of nine imperial dynasties. Buddhist monasteries and the tombs of famous generals and feudal overlords are to be found all over the town area, and not far away are the famous cave temples of Lung-men.

The glory of the two ancient imperial cities has long since faded. They have melted away and declined into poverty. In the seventh century, Sian was six times as big as it is now, and had a circumference of nearly twenty-three miles. Twenty years ago Loyang's population had dwindled to less than eighty thousand, which made the town, by Chinese standards, an insignificant provincial small town. It is only recently that these two venerable towns in the Northwest have begun to revive. Industrial areas have brought new life to them. Sian again has a million and a half inhabitants, and Loyang more than 600 thousand.

Yet my visit to the two towns was one of the most depressing experiences of my whole tour. The standard of living is far below that of other parts of the country. The inhabitants are not so well dressed and their expressions are more serious. The people are being worked more intensively here than elsewhere. In spite of the building of enormous new housing estates immediately adjacent to modern factories, the shortage of living accommodation for the masses is frightening.

The landscape is the clue to understanding the problems and the backwardness of the Northwest. Yellowish-brown hills, barren and dreary, stretch as far as the eye can see. The hills, standing like extinct volcanoes or the stumps of sawn off trees, are grim and repellent. The unexpected ravines gaping in the level ground are full of ragged fissures.

Since remote times the people here have lived in caves which can be easily cut out of the earth mounds or the walls of the ravines. Those who can manage it also build a fenced forecourt, behind which there will be the door to the cave, traditionally painted blue. There are no villages. The caves are cheaper and more durable, warm in winter and cool in summer. But they have also been the cause of the death of thousands of people when cloudbursts have undermined the hills and caused the cave dwellings to fall in.

The Northwest is a sad and unspeakably barren landscape of loess, that mixture of clay, sand, quartz dust and chalk. Erosion is the greatest power here. The ground will not absorb water, which runs off the surface, taking with it seeds, young plants and any humus that may have formed. It eats away the soil and hollows out the valleys and ravines. Down below in a vast basin waits the Hwang Ho, the Yellow River, like a voracious animal lying in wait for the prey being driven toward its fangs by the rain. After the Yangtze Kiang, "China's Sorrow," as the people call the Yellow River, is the greatest and most dangerous life-giver the Chinese people have. Three thousand miles long, it is the muddiest river in the world. Recent research has shown that an average cubic meter of its water holds seventy-six pounds of mud. More than half of the mud flows into the Pacific, but the remainder is deposited on the river bed, which is continually rising as a result. The dykes on the banks have to be raised accordingly. The lower reaches of the Hwang Ho make their way through the Chinese provinces like a wall of water as high as a house, contained by laboriously constructed embankments.

But the Yellow River has not always been willing to submit to the restraint men put on it with their dykes and embankments. It has broken out, seeking a new and deeper bed, twenty-six times in the last three thousand years, inundating vast areas, slaying millions of people, laying waste fields, villages and towns. And even when it is not the search for a new channel that causes an eruption but merely flooding due to the higher water level, the victims it claims and the damage caused are still inconceivable. In the last hundred years there have been more than two hundred such catastrophic floods caused by the Yellow River.

As long as men can remember, millions living in the Hwang Ho area have been dreaming of the day when the vicious giant will be tamed. The traditional rites intended to appease the dragon god of the river brought no relief. Only by using modern technical methods might it be possible to achieve their objective. The first plans were worked out by American engineers, but the Kuomintang authorities had other interests at this time, and it was the Communist government which finally got down to serious work on it. A tremendous plan for the systematic control of the Yellow River was worked out. The principal element of the plan was the building of the San-men Dam, which, backed up by fifty-nine smaller dams in the upper reaches, was to hold back the water before it plunged into the broad eastern plains. When this dam had been completed, it was thought, the

Yellow River would at last be tamed, its waters would be crystal clear and the river would never again afflict the people of the surrounding areas. Not only that, the control system would also supply 110 million kilowatts of electricity a year to the growing industries in the adjacent towns.

But since then the original optimism has begun to waver. The mighty San-men Dam was completed in 1960, and Edgar Snow, the American writer, who was proudly shown the dam shortly afterward, reported on the immeasurable expanse of shimmering water, "as blue as the Aegean." Four years later foreign journalists were no longer permitted to visit San-men, a fact which gave rise to much speculation and a large number of rumors.

There have been a number of official hints that suggest that things did not go as expected. Chinese experts had always been skeptical about the possibility of using dams as the main means of controlling the Yellow River. But Soviet experts, who played a decisive role in the planning and construction of the project, pooh-poohed these doubts. Now it is becoming clear that the Soviet experts were wrong. Both in Sian and in Loyang, which lie close to the San-men Dam, when I asked about the state of things regarding the control of the Yellow River, officials gave evasive replies to my questions. It was clear from what they said that there had been "structural faults" because too little allowance had been made for the river's wild unpredictability. In particular, the destructive natural forces at work in the world's greatest erosion area had been underestimated. However many dams and reservoirs you build, it turned out, they are pointless without simultaneous radical measures to check erosion in the areas adjacent to the river, without which silting up of the reservoirs and obstruction of the sluices by mud or sand will be inevitable. This is exactly what seems to have happened at San-men. The fact that I was not allowed to go and see the project might add weight to the suspicions arising from official statements and the hints contained in conversations with functionaries; and the fact that the 1964 reissue of the *Concise Geography of*

China makes no mention of the San-men Dam, which had been highly praised years before, only reinforces this supposition.

Right from the start the planning authorities in Peking must have been aware that if the unique problem of the Yellow River was to be overcome, the building of the dam would have to be accompanied by a gigantic program of reforestation and soil conservation. A "new greenery" campaign was launched all over the country. "Great green walls" were to be erected. This project, costing millions, was taken so seriously and success seemed so certain that in 1956 the Chinese Minister of Forestry claimed that, "in twelve years China will be a green land." To combat erosion, forest belts hundreds of miles long were to be laid down along the northern frontiers, and tree plantations and orchards were to be established in the river areas. During my journeys through the provinces of Shensi, Honan and Inner Mongolia I often enough saw some very considerable results. But in other places there was no mistaking the failure. Vast tracts of dried-up, withered or damaged young trees served to illustrate that overhasty mass campaigns alone will not do the trick, but need to be combined with systematic, careful and expert work.

The overhasty soil conservation measures seem to have worked out even more unfortunately. Armies of peasants were set to building terraces, ditches, wells and canals, putting up embankments, creating irrigation ponds and constructing earth defenses. Along with all these measures there was to be an immense plan to connect up the three great rivers, the Yangtze Kiang, the Yellow River and the Hwai Ho. The creation of a network of canals, some large, some small, would not only provide an extensive reservoir system but would also enable the South to divert some of its more than ample water supply to feed the parched North.

It soon became clear from official statements, however, that all these very difficult measures, which would have required the most careful coordination, had been launched without sufficient expert advice and preparation. In the areas in which the underground water level was high, the ground dried up, drained of water by the deep canals. The situation was even worse in the areas with a low underground water level. Seepage from the canals caused the underground water level to rise, carrying harmful salts and alkalis to the surface, which, when the water evaporated, became encrusted with them. In 1960, the very year in which the San-men Dam was ceremonially completed, the official ideological newspaper of the Chinese Communist Party said that the irrigation and drainage installations had been laid out completely haphazardly and that as a result of using incorrect methods, the country had suffered damage.

Anyone who spends any time on the upper reaches of the Yellow River today must feel that the assault on "China's Sorrow" has failed, at any rate for the present. On all sides there is dead land and dried-up fields covered with a network of fine cracks. The original enthusiasm for the reforestation project has died away. Many of the groves of trees, which the individual People's Communes have to plant according to the plan, look listless. Out in the countryside, too, it looks as if the saplings which were planted are getting little more care and attention than they did during the furious mass action. The strange lunar landscape of the Northwest will retain its peculiar character for the time being.

Have the Chinese leaders learned their lesson from the mistakes they made through overhastiness in recent years? Judging by the talks I had with officials of People's Communes and provincial administrations, I think they have. The time is gone when they thought that all that was needed to banish the specter of "China's Sorrow" was the lavish expenditure of millions. Now everyone thinks more modestly, is soberer and more ready to pay attention to something less imposing but liable to be more profitable in the long run—the creation of a sound agricultural policy. There is much less illusion about dam-building, reforestation and water conservation these days. All the talks I had with responsible authorities about the extraordinarily difficult problems of the Yellow River basin were marked by an absence of cheap propaganda slogans. The faces of the people of the Northwest still display anxiety and despondency today, just as they have throughout the centuries. It is still possible that not only the face of this part of China but also those of its inhabitants may one day change.

Chapter 7

MANCHURIA

Manchuria is still the great industrial center of China. In the large towns one sees row upon row of factory chimneys, manufacturing plants and slag heaps. Streets and houses are covered with a layer of dust and soot, whose metallic smell stings the nose. The traffic is heavy, especially when shifts are changing over. The people here live better than in many other provinces. The wages here are the highest in China.

I had often wondered why Chinese officials are so very keen to show Manchuria to foreign visitors. It is true that the province is China's industrial base, the country's technical showpiece. But with all due respect to the postrevolutionary achievements of the Communists, the real basis for Manchuria's economic boom was created by other people altogether. Czarist Russia, for example, when she covered northeast China with an extensive railroad network; or the Japanese, who began building modern plants, factories and steelworks in the twenties. What the Chinese Communists did after they came to power was at bottom nothing more than the continuation of a recognized development, the extension and renovation of what was already there. In other regions of China there were achievements that took the people with one bound from medieval conditions into the technical age of the twentieth century. Some of these things were sensational performances, yet not half so much fuss was made about them as about Manchuria, even though they could in fact have been used to very great propaganda effect.

The reason the Chinese are only too willing to let the foreigner travel to Manchuria, in my opinion, is not so much that they want to show off their economic achievements as that they want to demonstrate a political fact which already is having its effects and will do so in the future. What Peking seems to want to do is to prove China's territorial integrity, including this part of the Middle Kingdom as well. Manchuria is Chinese and is to become even more Chinese. This was also the reason why they changed its name. "The Three Northeast Provinces" is what Manchuria is called now; and it is not by chance that the change of name also meant the disappearance of the name of the Manchus, the last foreign imperial dynasty, who ruled China for nearly three hundred years.

It is less than twenty years since a neighbor country last cast a covetous eye on Manchuria. This sparsely populated country, with its terrifyingly vast plains, its rich woodlands, its priceless mineral wealth and favorable climate had always attracted the powerful countries of the northern Far East. First it was czarist Russia, which, after her conquest of the Far East, tried to enrich herself at the expense of the utterly defeated Chinese. Then the Japanese had the same idea. The Russo-Japanese War gave the Japanese a juicy prize when Russia was defeated and had to give up her rights in Southern Manchuria by the Treaty of Portsmouth in 1905. In the decades that followed the Japanese set about exploiting Manchuria, which they renamed Manchukuo. The Japanese defeat in 1945 put an end to their ambitions and Soviet troops took Manchuria.

There is strong evidence that to begin with Stalin also looked upon Manchuria as an area ripe for colonial exploitation. He got Chiang Kai-shek to sign agreements granting the Soviets long-term use of the Manchurian railroad system and consenting to Soviet occupation of Port Arthur. The promised speedy withdrawal of Soviet forces after the end of the war was postponed again and again. In the meantime extensive dismantling was taking place, and whole plants and most of the available rolling stock had been removed to the Soviet Union before National

Chinese troops could reach the Manchurian towns. Edwin Pauley, who headed a United States reparations commission in the Far East in 1946, estimated the value of the dismantled machinery and equipment at 858 million dollars and the cost of replacing it at two billion dollars.

When the Communists achieved their victory in China, the Soviets had no choice but to surrender their last remaining rights in Manchuria. The long-drawn-out negotiations in 1950, for which Mao Tse-tung personally flew to Moscow, were evidence that the Soviets were giving up their position with the worst possible grace. The Chinese received no compensation for the dismantling the Soviets had carried out, and had to put up with it. As a consolation Stalin promised them economic aid and credits at low rates of interest. From this time on China had to pay in full for every single one of the many items of plant and machinery which she imported from the Soviet Union.

Actually, it was not until the Russians withdrew from Port Arthur on May 31, 1955, that Manchuria finally became Chinese territory in the full sense of the word. So it is not surprising that the traveler still sees indications of recent colonial or half-colonial status wherever he goes. The city center of Shenyang, formerly Mukden, is still un-Chinese in character. The style of the public buildings and house fronts in the main streets could be described as "early Japanese." In the coal-mining center of Fushun the endless slums are reminiscent of the former days of Japanese exploitation.

But the Soviet neocolonial era has also left some typical traces. The name plates on the stations, still showing Cyrillic letters with the Chinese characters under them even today, may be acceptable; but in front of the station at Shenyang there is a massive war memorial surmounted by a tank. It was erected to the memory of the Soviet soldiers who fell in the fight against the Japanese, and who died "for freedom and independence, for the honor and victory of the Soviet Union." On the freedom and independence of the Manchurian part of China there is not a word.

1. The Great Wall of China, used for two thousand years as a defense against invading barbarians, runs along China's northwest frontier.

2. "Working masses" detailed to greet foreign visitors arriving at Shanghai Airport.

3. An orchestra welcomes foreign sight-seeing visitors to the Summer Palace in Peking.

4. Meals are available at all railroad stations and cost only a few cents.

5. Enormous passenger boats ply on the Yangtse Kiang, the father of Chinese rivers. The two-tiered bridge at Wuhan is seen in the background.

6. On the dusty road to Inner Mongolia.

7. Bridges are still scarce in China and rivers usually have to be crossed by ferry.

8. Typical Peking shopping street.

9. Changan Boulevard, Peking's public assembly and parade ground.

10. The Temple of Heaven in Peking, one of the most beautiful and graceful structures in China.

11. The Bund, imposing waterfront boulevard of Shanghai, runs along the Hwang Pu.

When I was being shown plants and factories in Manchuria, the officials, engineers and directors seemed mainly concerned with bringing out the native ability of the Chinese and their achievements in reconstruction since the Communists came to power. What was surprising was that at a time when the Sino-Soviet dispute was at its height, they not only said nothing about the Soviet dismantling activities in 1945 and 1946 but in fact, with one single exception, point-blank denied that there had been any. And this despite the fact that in 1957, during the "Hundred Flowers" period, the unsuccessful attempt at domestic "liberalization" in China, these matters had been publicly and heatedly discussed.

I repeatedly asked the same questions about the losses due to the Soviet dismantling and was always told that here in this factory there had not been any, or that in this town nothing had been taken away. Only once, in a coal mine in Fushun, did the managing director admit that he remembered hearing that the Soviets had removed the conveyor-belt machinery and equipment from a nearby mine.

It is possible that this strange unanimity on the part of officials has its origin in tactical considerations. Perhaps the Chinese want to keep a particular trump card up their sleeve in their dispute with Moscow. Or it may even be that the Chinese leaders fear that even though the facts are known to the world, to admit them officially would cause the Chinese to lose face, seeing that in the decisive negotiations in 1950 they failed in their attempts to get compensation.

Puzzling as the denial of the immense damage the Soviets caused after World War II may be, it is the losses in industrial wealth caused by the Kuomintang and the Japanese that are being given increasing prominence. An official of the Shenyang municipal administration told me in vivid detail how the National Chinese had let the Shenyang factories go to rack and ruin. Instead of putting them in order, they had made barracks out of them. In Anshan the director of a steel combine told me that in the years 1945 to 1947, during the National Chinese occupation of the works, nothing had been done, and by the time the Communists took over the plant, birds had built their nests in the smokestacks and the factory grounds looked like a meadow. Moreover the Japanese had also carried out destruction even before this. For example, they had let molten iron go cold inside the furnaces. Japanese engineers had prophesied in 1947 that it would take twenty years to build up the works again. They had said it would be better to raze the whole plant to the ground and use the area for agriculture and raising cattle. This piece of advice, said the director, clearly showed the extent of the destruction and the prejudiced belief of the Japanese that the Chinese had no technical ability.

A good part of such statements as these is probably grossly exaggerated, but it is certain that the consequences of World War II and the chaos brought about by the civil war did in fact destroy much of the foundation necessary for industrial reconstruction in Manchuria. Consequently, the achievements of the Communist government must be admitted to be considerable. Manchuria's industrial potential has increased enormously. Shenyang, with its suburbs and satellite townships and its population of more than four million, has become the Chinese equivalent of Bochum or Essen, with machinery and textile plants, cable works and innumerable factories producing consumer goods. Fushun, with a population of one million, is still the coal-mining center, but in addition possesses modern refineries. Harbin, with a population of 1.6 millions, is proud of its manufacturing facilities for making electrical machinery, ball bearings and measuring instruments. Changchun, the capital of Kirin Province, had 1.8 million inhabitants and has built its reputation on its automobile manufacturing plant. The port of Dairen has a population of 3.6 millions and has factories for making locomotives and cranes. Anshan has China's largest iron- and steelworks, with twenty blast furnaces and twenty-five open hearth furnaces. Including the dozens of auxiliary undertakings, the Anshan combine employs a total of a hundred thousand workers of all grades.

There is no doubt that Manchuria is still the nation's industrial home. Although the province's population of sixty million is not even a tenth of China's total population, it produces about a third of the country's industrial output. It has the most experienced technicians and engineers. Students from all over the vast country are studying at Manchurian technical universities.

There is no evidence that the leaders in Peking are planning to cut back Manchuria's economic position. The area is still underpopulated by Chinese standards. It has eighty million acres of fertile, arable land and the mineral wealth is incalculable.

There are also sound political reasons for allowing Manchuria's economic power to continue to develop. The leaders in Peking are anxious to make the northeastern provinces an integral part of the total Chinese economy after all the years of separation from the mother country. An economically healthy Manchuria might in fact act as a spur in other directions. There are still territories that once belonged to China but are now in foreign hands—the neighboring Soviet territory on the Amur River, for example, and the Soviet Far East. The name Vladivostok, "Ruler of the East," will always be for the Chinese a permanent reminder of humiliating periods when their country was under alien rule.

Chapter 8

ON THE EDGE OF THE

GOBI DESERT

In 1962 I had traveled in Outer Mongolia, and the first on the list of proposals I put to the Foreign Ministry in Peking was a trip to China's Inner Mongolia. I was looking forward to renewing my acquaintance with a fascinating landscape, in which one's gaze extends into the infinite distance across chains of delicate blue-green hills, and to meeting again the proud nomad people, rich in tradition and loyal to their old customs and usages. But I was also looking forward to the opportunity of comparing conditions and examining the possibilities that might arise in a Central Asian border area of political, territorial and racial contrasts.

Once the train has left the rugged mountain country northwest of Peking, across which the Great Wall of China winds like a giant snake, the traveler sees the Mongolian plateau open out before him. In those southern regions of the home of Genghis Khan's descendants, however, both the landscape and the people have long since changed completely. It is no longer the white tents of the nomads which come into view on the horizon, the nostalgic view so familiar to me from Outer Mongolia. There are no longer the grazing grounds on which the Mongol herds moved about in freedom. The endless silent emptiness and the spell of the vast rolling plains have completely disappeared. The land has become Chinese. They are Chinese towns and villages and the fields and meadows of a peasant people that glide past the train window. The smoking chimneys of the numerous factories, the brickworks and small iron- and steelworks which have sprung up all along the railroad tracks signify a new era. Everywhere people are building and working. The Chinese are toiling with energy and determination to change the age-old face of the country.

Huhehot, the capital of the "Inner Mongolian Autonomous Region," has also become completely Chinese, with only the name to remind one of its Mongolian origin. The streets, the noise and the teeming crowds in the marketplace and the alleys are all Chinese. Even the mosque belonging to the Muslim community lacks the familiar characteristics of mosques in the Middle East or the Central Asian republics of the Soviet Union. The roofs and even the minarets are gracefully curved and covered with green glazed tiles in traditional Chinese style. One rarely sees the typical Mongolian dress, the felt hat, the long silk robe tied with a colored belt and the riding boots peeping out below.

In the Mongolian national museum in Huhehot, the foreigner sees the transformation process very effectively illustrated. In this museum the Inner Mongolian era begins with the setting up of the Chinese People's Republic in 1949. There are displays illustrating all the great achievements, the reforestation program to prevent the desert from encroaching on the habitable areas; the irrigation projects, particularly in the bend of the Yellow River; and the industrialization, culminating in the great Paotow steelworks and the Huhehot rolling mill. But about the history of the Mongol people the visitor is given no information. In an out-of-the-way corner of the museum is a model of the Iksao Meng mausoleum, the colossal edifice constructed by the Chinese at the place in the northwestern territories where Genghis Khan is supposed to have died. When I asked the guide in the museum the purpose of this magnificent building, she replied unemotionally, "In memory of a certain Genghis Khan."

The area of Inner Mongolia is 540 thousand square miles, making it almost as large as the Mongolian People's Republic. The Mongolian population is also roughly the same. Inner Mongolia is estimated to have 1,340,000 Mongols and Outer Mongolia about 1,200,000. The important difference between them lies in the fact that the Mongols of Inner Mongolia, along with many other nationalities, are in an absolute minority. Of the total population of twelve million, nine million are Chinese. This explains the completely Chinese character of the towns and industrial centers. Nowadays, anyone who wants to see Mongols in their ancient character of nomad herdsmen must travel far into the northern border area of Inner Mongolia.

From Huhehot I traveled two hundred miles north by jeep, at first over good roads, then over rough tracks in the steppes and finally across country over the plains on the edge of the Gobi Desert. My first objective was a small town in the border area between Inner Mongolia and the Mongolian People's Republic. The road led over mountain passes, through broad valleys, small townships and new village settlements. I always had a feeling of being in pionoor torritory. Yard by yard the tough and hard-working Chinese had wrung arable land from the sterile Mongolian steppes. The fresh, reddish-brown soil of the fields had been pushed forward in enormous squares as far as the hills or into the river lowlands. Groups of new, Chinese-style houses stood like silent guardians over the bare landscape. The farther north I went, the harder became the faces of the people I saw, and the more forsaken and lonely they seemed to be.

Night had fallen by the time we reached our destination. Mongolian officials in colorful national dress welcomed me in front of the guest house. I was offered a tent to sleep in and the evening meal included all the curious dishes I had already met in Outer Mongolia. At last, I thought, I had arrived in a purely Mongolian settlement. However, the long discussion with the municipal functionaries over buttered tea and oversweet candies showed me I was wrong. This particular border district, they said, took in nearly eight thousand square miles and was based on nine agricultural People's Communes and ten stock-raising communes. It was only with difficulty that I managed to get population figures out of my hosts. Sixty-eight thousand inhabitants lived in this district, they told me, made up of some dozen nationalities. I asked if I could not get some more precise details.

"Well," explained the chairman of the district council in a roundabout fashion, "we have five hundred Muslims, thirty Tibetans, fifteen Dahoyans, seven or eight Koreans, five Manchus, five Miaos, five Üwenküs, two Tus and eight thousand Mongols."

"And the rest—they are Hans?" I asked.

"Yes. We have over fifty thousand Chinese" was the reply.

So the "rest of the population" of this border area was in fact the overwhelming majority.

Next morning, at last, my wish was to be fulfilled. We drove thirty miles to the Chang An-bao commune, "The White Cairn," named after a nearby ancient shamanist shrine. This is one of the ten stock-raising communes of the district. Grazing ground accounts for 85 per cent of the whole area of the district, only 15 per cent being devoted to agriculture. The proportion of inhabitants, however, is exactly reversed. Eighty-five per cent live in the agricultural areas (and of these again, 95 per cent are Chinese) and only 15 per cent, almost entirely Mongolians, in the endless grasslands. Will it stay this way? I was told that in this district the productive arable land had been trebled, from 320 thousand *mu* (50 thousand acres) in 1949 to 920 thousand *mu* (152 thousand acres) in 1964, all as the result of Chinese diligence.

Even at a distance the Mongolian character of Chang An-bao was plain. Atop a flat hill stands a Lamaist monastery with a gilded roof. The commune administration buildings crouch in the temple quarter. There are still monks here. In the whole district, I was told, there are still seventeen Buddhist temples and monasteries, inhabited by 150 lamas. This is an amazingly large number considering that the official figure for the whole of the Mongolian People's Republic is only 110. Mounted Mongols came galloping up to greet us. The jeep forced its way through herds of horses, cows, camels and sheep. The people assembled in front of the buildings had put on their ceremonial national costume to welcome the unaccustomed foreign guest.

Everything in this commune is tailored to fit Mongolian conditions. The commune is 120 square miles in area, but has only 280 families, with a total of 922 members to tend the commune's forty-eight thousand head of cattle. Speaking to me through two interpreters, one from Mongolian into Chinese and one from Chinese into German, the director told me that right up until 1956 all the herds were privately owned. Then, between 1956 and 1958, the state began to "buy them up gradually." Since 1958, when the communes were established, all the herds have belonged to the state, except for 5 per cent left in private hands. Every worker is entitled to a horse and even the children ride to school on sturdy Mongolian ponies.

The faces of the Mongolian functionaries glowed with pride as they showed their visitor the commune's social amenities. One part of the Lamaist monastery had been made over into a hospital. I saw a good number of rooms, an operating theater, nurses, a doctor in a clean white coat, two Lamaist doctors who are allowed to practice the old Mongolian quack methods, and lots of drugs and medicines—but no patients.

In front of the small primary school, Mongolian children, wrapped up in thick quilted jackets, played basketball in the icy wind from across the Gobi Desert. There was a veterinary station, a repair shop, a workshop for making tools and implements, an astonishingly large general store and even a savings bank. All these things had been specially spruced up for the foreign visitor, obviously, and the tour went off like an inspection of a recruits' company by the commanding general. Still, all these things, which no Mongol could even have imagined only a few years ago, were undeniably there, however primitive and makeshift they might seem to Western eyes.

I was invited to lunch by the leader of a horse-breeding brigade. A whole sheep, roasted on a spit, was served up on an enormous dish placed in the center of the tent. The guests, each armed with a knife, set to work to carve themselves pieces of succulent meat, which was accompanied by milk wine, a kind of vodka and many strange-looking side dishes. Everything went

on in typically Mongolian fashion, with loud smacking of lips
and little conversation. Only when the meal was over was the
brigade leader ready to answer my questions, which he then did
willingly, about the conditions of life for his people. His answers
revealed the mentality of a self-assured people who have no love
for servile words and kowtowing gestures.

"You have seen our amenities," he said. "They did not exist before. Until 1949 we made our living by barter. For a sheep, for
example, we would get one block of brick tea. For a steer we
would be given nine yards of white cloth. A horse would fetch
a pair of boots. Now we sell our products to the state, get the
money for them and with the money we can buy what we need
from the commune stores. To give you an idea of the difference,
we now get five and a half blocks of brick tea for one sheep,
two hundred yards of white cloth for a steer and eighteen pairs
of boots for a horse."

Toward the end of my visit to Chang An-bao I tried to guide
the conversation into less serious channels. I told my hosts how
almost exactly two years before I had camped in a place a hundred miles away, in the middle of the Gobi on the territory of
the Mongolian People's Republic. They listened intently as I told
them about the deep-rooted desire for Mongol unity that I had
found in Outer Mongolia.

"There is no such movement here," they told me, tersely and
decidedly. "The Mongolian People's Republic is an independent
state which we recognize *de jure* and *de facto;* and we want to
have friendly relations with it. Since the end of 1962 the frontier
has been clearly defined by treaty. The boundaries of our district have also been newly fixed. Generally speaking there has
not been much change. There is little movement of herds and
only occasional frontier traffic, which is governed by detailed
agreements. We are only sorry that the First Secretary of the
Communist Party in Ulan Bator, Tsedenbal, is fishing in revisionist waters." The features of my hosts, though inscrutable,
seemed to be hinting that there was much more that could be
said on this subject.

Back in Huhehot, under the influence of the tremendous industrial expansion in the completely Chinese southern areas of Inner Mongolia, I could not help but think back to what I had been told about the Mongolian question in the Foreign Ministry in Peking. It was very similar to what I had heard from simple, lowly officials up there in the north of Inner Mongolia. But the Peking officials were bearing in mind the wording of an interview Mao Tse-tung gave to Japanese socialists in the summer of 1964, in which he charged the Soviet Union with regarding the Mongolian People's Republic as a Soviet satellite. One seemed to detect in this a long-term objective, one that Mao Tse-tung had already put quite clearly not quite twenty years before, when he had said that China's immediate mission was "to recover all the lost territories and not only to plead for sovereignty on this side of the Great Wall." This would, however, also imply regaining Outer Mongolia, which used to belong to China.

There is not the slightest indication that the Chinese intend to try to achieve this by force. When this subject came up, responsible officials in Peking told me, "Everything will stay as it is, but let us wait and see what the future brings. At all events, if there are any changes, they can only come about through peaceful negotiation." These words also indicate a long-term prospect based not on conquest but on inducement and persuasion.

The signs of such a program had been evident years before. It was no accident that Mao Tse-tung restored to Inner Mongolia the administrative autonomy which had been broken up by his predecessors, the Kuomintang. Nor was it by coincidence that in 1954 the capital of Mongolia was given the Mongol name of Huhehot in place of the previous Chinese Kweisui. It was again not by chance that the great mausoleum of Iksao Meng was built, with a flourish of trumpets, to honor the Mongol national hero, even though his descendants once subjugated China. It is even less of a coincidence that a mighty industrial area is being built up in southern Inner Mongolia. The new social order, the technical advances and the economic boom conditions in Inner

Mongolia are intended to exert an attraction on the Mongolians who live in an independent state on the other side of the frontier, an attraction which, it is hoped in Peking, may one day have its political effects.

Chapter 9

THE FAR SOUTH

To move from Mongolia in the Northwest to the far South of China is not merely to travel a few thousand miles. It is to enter a region which might almost be in another world. In the North the inhabitants have the stamp of the raw climate and rugged scenery, which have given them hard features and tall and robust bodies and made them laconic in speech. In the South, life is conditioned by a tropical climate and luxuriant vegetation. The South Chinese are the nation's bantams, small and wiry, excitable and restless. The permanent humid heat has dried out their bodies, exaggerating their typical racial characteristics.

When one speaks of South China, most foreigners think of the city of Canton and the area surrounding it in Kwangtung Province. The metropolis on the Pearl River is the center of the South, the place where all roads meet. No other city in China is so full of pulsating, hectic bustle and so much perspiring activity and restless hurry. The alleys in the old quarters of the town are like the maze of streets in an Oriental bazaar. Bamboo mats, cloths and washing hung out to dry keep off the dazzling light that beats down from the sky and the people hurry past one another in dim twilight, an eddying mass of pale silhouettes always on the move.

In the main streets there is a tangled mass of people, pedicabs, buses and bicycles. There stand the flashy fronts of the department stores, and shop after shop stand cheek by jowl under covered arcades, on the columns of which the tropical rain has left the signs of impermanence. The goods offered for sale still overflow onto the sidewalk while the sellers sit in the shady background like idols on the altar of business.

Canton is also the center of China's foreign trade. When the international trade fairs are on in spring and autumn, the city puts on its finery. This is the time when a new element makes its appearance, the towering figures of the white executives with their bulging briefcases and serious faces looking like creatures from outer space among the seething mass of the business quarter. Sleek cars convey them like royalty from their hotels to the trade exhibition buildings, where they gravely bargain with the representatives of Chinese commercial organizations sitting at large tables, sip tea, leaf through catalogues, scribble on bits of paper and do deals.

Canton, this symbol of Chinese vitality, Chinese diligence and Chinese business acumen, represents only one aspect, albeit a most important one, of South China. The South has others, to be found in the provinces of Yunnan and Kwangsi, the gateways to Southeast Asia and once the Cinderellas of the Middle Kingdom. I began my journey through China in Kunming, the capital of Yunnan Province in the far Southwest, and my last stop was Nanning, the capital of Kwangsi Province in the central South.

Both of these provinces are the homes of many different peoples. In Yunnan about one third of the inhabitants, about twenty-two million, are not Chinese; and in Kwangsi the proportion of non-Chinese is even higher. (According to the 1958 census, of the twenty million inhabitants of Kwangsi, the Chuang people alone accounted for seven million.) The non-Chinese races of the South have strange-sounding names—Chin Po, Chi, Miao and Chilao in Yunnan; Chuang, Shiao, Mulao and Tung in Kwangsi. They have their own styles of dress and in figure, features and gesture they resemble the races across the frontiers in adjacent countries, Thais, Burmese Shans or the people of Laos, more than the race of Han, the Chinese. Most of them live in the impenetrable jungles which cover the mountains. They were the original inhabitants of this part of China until, with the passage of the centuries, they were driven into the mountains by the advancing Chinese.

They can be met with in the exotic marketplaces of Kunming or Nanning. They have carried their wares, mostly fruit or artistic handicraft work, a long way. The girls are graceful and shy and seem to compensate for their feeling of insecurity by a cultivated aloofness, although much of this may be traditional. For centuries now the mountain people and the Chinese have disliked and mistrusted each other, the original inhabitants regarding the Han as interlopers and the Chinese regarding the queer little people as primitive barbarians. There was little intermarriage, each race keeping itself to itself, the Chinese mostly staying in the few towns and on the plains, the minorities in the mountains or the jungle.

It was only recently, with the advent of the Kuomintang era, that any attempt was made to draw the mountain peoples into the official Chinese state organization, and the process has been carried on by the Communists in their particular fashion. A complicated system of autonomous regions and districts was introduced. The Chinese were careful to allow for the national feelings of the minorities and to give them their own status in administrative and cultural affairs. For example the majority of key positions on the administrative councils of the autonomous regions and districts are held by members of the minorities, even when the Chinese population is very much larger. "It is, after all, their homeland," someone said to me in Inner Mongolia when I expressed surprise at finding that the twenty-one-man district council comprised thirteen Mongolian functionaries and only six Chinese, even though 85 per cent of the population were Chinese.

On the other hand, the Chinese have also been careful so to lay out the autonomous regions that the minorities can never make themselves independent or break out of the great national framework. Typical examples of this can be seen in Inner Mongolia, which used to have a population in the ratio of 800 thousand Mongolians to a million and a half Chinese, but which, through the addition in 1955 of some districts from purely Chinese provinces, now has a much greater proportion of Chinese. Another method is the breaking up into a number of autonomous regions of any compact areas with a non-Chinese population. There are, for example, ten separate Tibetan districts. In the autonomous regions of the Muslim Ninghsia Hui there are esti mated to be a million Chinese as against 600 thousand Hui. The remaining half million Hui, although they live in the same area, belong to Kansu Province, where they form an insignificant minority.

The Communists are pursuing the same policy in the South. Has it been successful? Has the government managed to win over the peoples concerned while at the same time retaining firm control over them? The foreign visitor who has only spent a short time in the country can hardly give an answer, particularly since the cities and industrial centers are populated almost entirely by Chinese. The minorities are scattered over almost inaccessible territory. The overland route from Kunming to Yunnan's second-largest town, Paoshan, for example, follows the beginning of the famous World War II Burma Road. The 620-mile serpentine journey takes four days by bus (by air the distance is less than 125 miles). The areas where the mountain peoples live can be reached only by jungle roads and paths branching off from this arterial road.

Notwithstanding the occasional propaganda claim to the contrary, it seems unlikely under these circumstances that the traditional enmity and reserve felt by the minorities in the southern border regions for the Chinese can be completely dispelled. I was given a clue to this by an opera I saw in Kunming. The play was a revolutionary drama and the scene was the settlement of the Ching Po clan. The heroine, Dai No, after whom the opera is named, joins up with the advancing Communist army. Through the play there runs the motif of the reproaches of the members of her clan that she has betrayed her own people. The Han, they argue, are conquerors and oppressors and have come only in order to exploit her country. Needless to say, the play ends with the victory of the Red Chinese and the dawn of an era of freedom, justice and happiness for the Ching Po.

On the other hand, however much the minorities in South China may foster nationalist traditions and the desire to keep alive their own way of life, it cannot be denied that the Communists have done great and beneficial work in this area. Only a decade or two ago Western journalists and missionaries were bringing back reports of unbelievable conditions in this part of Asia. Crime, opium smuggling, child labor in primitive tin mines, slavery and slave traffic were all quite normal. In the interior, the rice trade and commercial traffic were menaced by bandits. Anyone who wanted to traverse the region with a caravan had first to hire an armed bodyguard if he wanted to be reasonably sure of getting through. Life may be less colorful, exotic and exciting today, but for the great mass of the people Communist rule has brought order into their daily existence, an existence that may be poor and shabby but is at least better and safer than it was.

In Kunming, the town "south of the clouds," which lies nearly sixty-five hundred feet above sea level and has an eternally springlike climate, there live some 600 thousand people. From the Buddhist temples at the Dragon Gate on the steep sides of the West Mountains there is a wonderful view over the town and the surrounding district. Through the broad valley there billows the smoke from numerous factory chimneys. This is where the Chinese are exploiting the province's natural resources, the enormous deposits of coal, iron ore, tin, copper, zinc, phosphorus, manganese and mercury. The types and varieties of goods already being produced in Kunming, including buses, generators, textile machinery, cranes and drilling machinery, is astonishing.

Nanning, the capital of Kwangsi Province, with its 400 thousand inhabitants, makes an impression of equal vitality. The town is dominated by a gigantic chemical combine, and there are factories for refining the sugar and canning the fruit of this tropical area. As in Kunming, the visitor is pleasantly surprised by the difference between the broad, modern districts here and the new districts in other industrial centers of China. This is most probably due to the richness and abundance of the vegetation. The trees grow bigger and faster and the avenues, parks and gardens are a blaze of brilliant tropical shrubs and flowers. The ugliness and standardized monotony are hidden under glorious color and vivid green.

The symptoms of backwardness and poverty cannot be overlooked. There are still slums in the towns. The markets are full of barefooted, ill-clad people jostling around the stalls which sell the poorer-quality, cheaper fish or vegetables. A drive of even a mile or two outside the towns brings one into contact with the depressed standard of living in the villages, which often enough look as though they have hardly changed in the last thousand years.

And there is another thing which strikes the visitor to the towns in the South: the existence and preparedness of an enormous army. Throughout my travels in China I had always found it surprising that one seldom saw the military in town or countryside, considering that China is supposed to have two and a half million men under arms. But the population is so colossal that the soldiers simply seem to be swallowed up in the masses. Another reason is that the greater part of the army is stationed in areas into which the foreigner never penetrates, in Tibet, Sinkiang, Fukien (opposite Formosa) or in the southern frontier areas, near to the vital troublespot of Vietnam.

One does, of course, see soldiers in the larger cities and provinces of the interior. Sometimes they are out in columns, sauntering relaxedly along; sometimes tightly packed into trucks, a mass of khaki out of which the young faces look down puzzled or smiling at the foreigner; in the museums, where companies of them are being lectured and where the way through the rooms is sometimes blocked by the hundreds of squatting soldiers listening intently to their officers; but above all out in the countryside, when entire battalions are put to work in the fields.

Apart from the units specially trained for parades and the well-drilled militia sections, who are marched past the gaping crowds on important holidays and festival days, the army does not make a very martial impression. The soldiers look slack and flabby. Their features show none of the arrogance one sees in so many of the jackbooted figures in Europe. The officers are reserved and hardly distinguishable from their subordinates. I never saw—except on parades—tramping columns of marching men proclaiming their military ardor in martial song.

The modesty with which the military comport themselves is quite remarkable, considering the special position the Chinese army occupies in society. The army is considered to have inherited a great tradition. The revolutionary past is zealously expounded and the army is held up as a shining example, second only to the Communist Party. I was told by some young officials that they would have liked to go into the army, but that the army would not take them. "It is now an honor to be a soldier," I was told. In another case the main reason seemed to have been material benefit. An NCO, I was told, gets a hundred yuan, which, taking into account free food, uniform and accommodation, would be a third more than the average wage of a Chinese industrial worker.

But little as one is aware of the presence of the army in Central China, all the more noticeable is it in the South. The streets of Kunming and Nanning are full of infantry, artillery and air-force uniforms. Massive barracks stand on the outskirts of the towns. The airports in both towns also serve as military airbases. Dozens of jet fighters are lined up along the edges of the runways like enormous glistening dragonflies. In Nanning the crest of the nearest hill was completely removed in order to prevent it from interfering with planes landing and taking off. The mountains are dotted with anti-aircraft guns. Columns of military vehicles are to be seen on the cross-country roads. From time to time the sounds of military exercises can be heard.

Only in the South did I come to realize that the many impressions to be gathered in the course of a journey through China would include the experience of seeing an enormous army in a state of constant alert.

Part Two

MISFORTUNE IN NUMBERS

Once, as the Master was passing through We, he said to the pupil who was driving the carriage, "How numerous the people here are now."

The pupil asked, "What can one do for the people now that they have so increased in number?"

"Help them to prosper."

"And when they are prosperous, what could one do for them then?"

"Educate them," replied the Master.

—Confucius (c. 551–479 B.C.)

Chapter 10

A SOCIETY IN TRANSITION

China is in a period of transition, the transition from a society still largely characterized by the peculiar features of a deep-rooted traditional structure to a society which will reap the benefits of a modern economic and social order. This development had its first beginnings a long time back. The first cautious steps were already being taken more than a century ago, but the resistance to change was so strong and tradition was so deep-rooted at that time that the forces of progress made only slow and painful headway. Further barriers to progress were created by the inroads of Western imperialism, with its ruthless profiteering and the political humiliations it inflicted on the Chinese. The Chinese had recognized the correct road to progress and were striving to follow it, but historical events in the East Asiatic sphere in the first half of this century did nothing to make the road less painful. Chiang Kai-shek's Kuomintang foundered because of its ineptitude and its failure to create the minimum essential conditions for the difficult transition process.

The experiences of modern industrial nations show that one of the fundamental requirements for a nation's advance is a new elite exercising firm political control from the center. Only this will be able to break down the economic, social and political regionalism which is an essential part of an underdeveloped society. Only strong, centralized political power will be able to bring about the radical alteration in the traditional methods of production, the social concepts and the scale of values which is essential for the nation's revival. And only strong, centralized political power will be able to take on the task of guiding the driving force of nationalism—an important element in any transition from a traditional to a more progressive form of society—into the channels which will serve to increase the standing, the welfare and the wealth of the nation.

The Communists were the first to turn the China which had suffered decades of political impotence both at home and abroad into a powerful national state and thus create the preconditions for modernization. It was now possible to make a start on the problems which had to be solved in order to clear the road to emancipation. These are the problems which face any society in a phase of transition to a modern and more fruitful form of association, although in China's case there are additional difficulties to be overcome.

In his book *Stages of Economic Growth*, Walt W. Rostow, the economist and sociologist and influential adviser to the United States government, has convincingly delineated the possibilities and requirements of social and economic progress in a traditional society. These are particularly valid as regards China. Rostow places particular emphasis on the limitation of population as one of the most important problems. In all backward societies it is regarded as a blessing to have a large number of children, who are thought of both as a form of security in one's old age and also as an assurance of immortality. A society whose real income, measured against the population figure, is far too low cannot advance without a drastic reduction in the birthrate, or, in other words, without some alteration in the traditional scale of values and concepts of security.

This is closely linked with the problem of transforming a primarily agricultural society into one in which industry, trade, distribution and services predominate. Only in this way can the rate of capital investment be increased to a point at which "the increase in real income regularly, basically and perceptibly exceeds the increase in population, although this is not to say that capital investment is regarded as the ultimate objective" (Walt Rostow).

For a country such as China, this principally means that agriculture must be so encouraged and expanded that it will be able not only to feed the increasing population—which itself becomes a problem because during the transitional period the urban population grows at a disproportionate rate—but also to provide capital resources for the purchase of capital goods for the building up of industry and for paying for the import of any additional foodstuffs which may be required. From this basic thesis Rostow concludes that "the rate of growth in the production of agricultural commodities determines the extent to which the transition to industrialization can be carried through."

Simultaneously with this a third precondition must be created. The traditional standards for evaluating the individual, based primarily on membership of a certain class or social grade or on whether or not he belongs to the educated elite—or on whether or not he has connections with the seat of power— must be replaced by the evaluation of his suitability as an individual for a specific function within the structure of the projected new society. This means a complete reorientation of existing values and in particular the creating of a new attitude toward science and technology. This is where education has an important part to play.

Economic, population and educational policies are thus among the most necessary components of the efforts of a backward society to advance. China is no exception. This had already been recognized long before the Communists came to power. The new regime is carrying on with the work already begun, using different and more rigorous measures. What is the result? How far have the Communists succeeded in dealing with China's fundamental problems? In short, how much progress has been made along the thorny path of a society in transition?

Even while he is still in the airplane on his flight to China the traveler is given a demonstration of something which staggers

the imagination of people outside of China: the incredible population density in every part of the country that can be made
even halfway productive. Immediately the rugged, empty mountain country and untamed jungles of Burma have been left
behind, the traveler sees the landscape of China open out below
him. Countless settlements huddle between the endless terraces
which bespeak intensive rice cultivation. No one knows their
names and no map gives their details, but their number reveals
a dizzying concentration of human beings, and this number grows
as soon as a town of any size comes into view. The sea of
glistening roofs broadens out and the villages press nearer together until they are inextricably linked and interwoven. Rivers
and canals, covering the land like a network of silvery veins,
hint at pulsing life. Ponderous junks with unwieldy sails glide
over them like sinister dark moths, with myriads of tiny boats
darting nimbly around them. From this great height everything
seems very tiny and one cannot make out any people. They
remain hidden from view as if they were deliberately keeping
themselves out of sight of foreign eyes.

The minute one lands on Chinese soil, however, the scene is
transformed. The sprawling settlements are seen to be overflowing with humanity; the streets resemble an inexhaustible stream
of humankind; it seems that every vehicle must collapse under
the weight of the people. There is nothing to compare with this
in any other country.

Shanghai Airport was the first eye-opener. The runway had
to be lengthened to accommodate jet planes. Whereas this
would have needed weeks of planning and work anywhere else,
here it was completed in a few days. Twenty-six thousand
people were simply ordered to show up at the airport, where
they dug, shoveled and rolled with antlike zeal—massed human
power taking the place of machines, the rule which still obtains,
even in the modern China of today.

The same picture presents itself wherever one looks. The
sound of modern farm machinery is seldom to be heard, even
in the fields and meadows outside the large towns like Peking

and Shanghai. The brigades on the People's Communes work in tightly packed groups, using primitive farm implements such as must have exhausted the Chinese peasant of two or three thousand years ago. Oil presses of a type that might well have existed in the Stone Age are worked by hand in unchanging monotony. In the South the peasants squat in dozens on giant wheels and tread the water out of the irrigation canals into the rice fields. In the towns, when drainage canals have to be opened up, thousands of people stand in the mud and dig—as with the movements of a thousand-footed monster mole shoveling the earth away in spasmodic rhythm as he goes. On the country roads there is an unending stream of carts pulled by men, two, three or even more, depending on the size and weight of the load. Trucks are rare and very scarce, and when they are used it is less to carry goods than to transport people, who stand patiently in the open trucks, jammed together, men, women and children, with the wind whistling about their ears. The trucks resemble bunches of grapes composed of human bodies.

The large towns are bursting at the seams. Shanghai is said to have ten million inhabitants, Peking seven, Tientsin five, Dairen three and a half, Shenyang four, Wuhan two and some dozen others more than a million each. No one knows the exact figures. The visitor is at a loss to know how all these people can possibly find somewhere to live. European-style apartment blocks are still rare, and most people live in the traditional way in low houses in picturesque districts, in the shelter of walled-in alleys and inner courtyards, as in Peking, or in the overloaded, noisy highways and byways of the towns on the Pacific coast and in the interior. The street is a safety valve. People swarm on the sidewalks in endless columns. There is no oasis of peace where the individual can be alone. There is always someone else there. One is in permanent contact with one's neighbors.

Even the spacious parks offer no small corner for individual meditation. Here, as everywhere, there is an army of children. It almost seems that every second Chinese is a child, for wherever one goes, wherever one looks, there are always children, staring at the strange, unusual "long-nose," curious, amused or shy. Any who have reached the age of ten will certainly be carrying a little brother or sister. Those who can afford it boast a baby carriage, but not the usual type intended for one small occupant. In China there are only two-seaters and at a pinch they will accommodate three or even four.

The European finds the multitudes of people depressing. He perhaps does not mind when he is being taken by car or bus to see some tourist attraction in the solicitous care of the state organization. But when he gets there, despite all reserve, he will be swallowed up by the mass. Whether he visits the Temple of Heaven or the Summer Palace in Peking or inspects the venerable Great Wall or the Ming Tombs, whether at the revolutionary memorials in Canton or viewing the relics of a cultural golden age in Hangchow, he will always be accompanied by thousands of other people. If he wants to see some special attraction he will stand in line with them, packed together with them. He is constantly having to elbow his way through some densely packed crowd.

The perpetual masses really become a nightmare when some outstanding event brings onto the streets everyone who can walk, for example on the afternoon of May First or October First in Peking, when the entire population of the capital seem to have only one goal as they stream in from all directions: whatever happens, not to be too late to get a grandstand view of the monster fireworks display in front of "The Gate of Heavenly Peace" in celebration of May Day or People's Republic National Day. They roll on like a relentless stream of lava, in columns or in groups with bag and baggage; marching in disciplined order or riding in buses; with flags and banners; accompanied by orchestras and amateur theatrical groups; in uniform, in olden-day costume or even in fancy dress. Everybody is on the move, all going in the same direction, blocking the streets and alleys, taking up the whole width of the vast boulevard through the capital. Anyone who tries to move against the stream appears lost. The march past goes on for hours, until at last a million people are assembled, a heaving sea of humanity stretching as far as the eye can see.

It is not only the sheer numbers which are so impressive, it is also their appearance. All masses have a leveling effect, all the more so when every single member is outwardly practically identical with every other member. The *chung san kwan*, the standard blue clothing of the Chinese, has become the symbol of the new China. For the foreigner it eventually takes on an obsessive quality.

Clothes of indigo-dyed cotton have been the badge of the masses since time out of mind, but nowadays it is the uniformity of shape and cut that is so conspicuous. There are, of course, some variations, particularly in summer, when the women and girls wear colorful print blouses and the men leave off their jackets. The senior official wears the single-breasted tunic, buttoned up to the neck, and with patch pockets, black for evening wear and in lighter shades, sometimes of gray and sometimes of brown, in summer. But apart from these slight variations the average man—and therefore the mass of average men—wears only the one color: intense, cold, repellent blue. In addition there is the no less standard floppy cap, also in blue. The Spartan simplicity of the shoddy suits gives one the impression of a people eternally at work or a nation mechanically marching in step. For the foreigner there is something uncanny and alarming about the standardized uniformity of a mass composed of millions upon millions.

Every Fourth Person in the World Is Chinese

The exact size of China's population is still a mystery. It has never been possible to do more than make estimates of it, and even such a rigidly organized and centrally controlled state as the present Communist People's Republic, with its armies of officials and functionaries, has not been able to make much difference. At least, that is the impression the foreign visitor gets when he tries to procure some information about the size of the Chinese population from official agencies or by studying official Chinese publications.

Someone well versed in internal Chinese affairs told me that at the beginning of 1964 the government had ordered all lower administrative levels to establish and report the number of people living in their districts. The result of this direct census had been disconcerting; the total population of China at that time had amounted to some 750 million. Early in 1965 Mao Tse-tung said in an interview that some people were alleging that China had a population of 660 to 690 million people, but he did not believe it. How could the figure be so high?

Whenever I asked Chinese officials for their estimate of the size of China's population, they would shrug their shoulders: it could be 650, 700 or perhaps even 750 million. Official figures only increased the general confusion. The census of 1953 produced a figure of "more than 582 million," but the 1957 census (only four years later but admittedly including Formosa) resulted in a figure of 656 million. Also in 1957, the Minister of Health reported to the National People's Congress that the population was increasing by 15 million a year. So that at the time Mao Tse-tung was saying he did not credit even the figure of 680 million, the real figure—if one accepts official statistics—had already risen to more than 760 million.

Is there any explanation for this confusing difference in the statements about China's population or for the fact that even the highest official quarters seem to have no exact information to go on? There can be only one answer: the system for obtaining population statistics is simply not functioning. This will come as no surprise to anyone who knows conditions in the interior and the people's attitude there.

It ought, of course, to be easy to obtain reasonably exact population figures by taking those required for the country-wide distribution of ration cards for basic necessities such as rice or cotton. Furthermore, births, deaths and changes of residence must be reported, by law. Anyone who moves from one place to another must register himself with the authorities, in the towns within three days and in the country within ten days. Births and deaths must be registered within one week in the towns and within a month in the country districts. But all of these things are only on paper. The real situation is very different.

To begin, there is a shortage of trained statisticians at all levels of the administration. Where they are available, they are mainly engaged on production statistics, which possibly seem more important to the regime than census data. At the very lowest levels the task of counting the masses is left to low-grade officials, for example brigade leaders in the communes. These officials are naturally more interested in the figures of productive workers than in the number of children or old people, which they very likely simply guess at. In any event, however, the lower-grade official will not be familiar with the uses of population statistics or the reasons for compiling them.

The biggest stumbling block of all lies in the mentality of the peasants. Mao Tse-tung confirmed this early in 1965, when he said that the peasants had "occasionally confused the picture." It is not difficult to guess what he meant. The peasants have always been suspicious of officials who seemed to them to be interfering in things which were none of their business. Also, Chinese country people still have a propensity for deceiving the authorities and leading them astray. Nowadays, there is a further, more concrete reason for not telling the whole truth. Deaths are often left unreported for as long as possible, simply in order that the survivors can continue to draw ration cards for the deceased persons.

All these reasons make it likely that for the present the situation will stay as it has been for centuries: the exact size of China's population will remain a matter for academic speculation.

At the beginning of 1965 the consensus of expert opinion put the total population at about 700 million people, which means that every fourth person on this earth is Chinese.

Fifteen to Twenty Million New Chinese Every Year

The figure of 700 million is not in itself so very alarming. China is huge and there are still wide areas completely uninhabited. In spite of the intensity with which the people work, especially in agriculture, there is little underemployment. On the contrary, the army of those working on the land has been steadily reinforced for some years now, so great is the shortage of workers.

What is alarming, on the other hand, is the rate at which the population is increasing. Experts have worked out that by 1980 there will be one billion Chinese, and by the turn of the century 1.2 billion. Figures such as these automatically conjure up visions of "the Yellow Peril."

Reliable figures on the population increase are as hard to come by as precise data on the size of the total population. As has been said, the increase was reported in 1957 to be at the rate of fifteen million a year. Later it was officially stated that the annual increase was of the order of 2.1 or 2.2 per cent, but it was expressly pointed out at the time that this figure was valid only for the towns (where the authorities presumably have enough reliable data to go on). Moreover, the increase can fluctuate from year to year. Refugees, for example, were unanimous that there was a very considerable drop in the birth rate in China in the disastrous years 1959–61. Today the rate of increase is believed to have risen again to slightly above the previous normal rate of more than 2 per cent.

How different the rate of increase can be was illustrated during my visit to a People's Commune in Hunan Province. The Party secretary explained that it was just this problem that was worrying him most. "My commune has about eighteen thousand people," he said. "In 1963 the population increased by about eight hundred, but only 10 per cent of these came from outside the commune." In other words, allowing for the newly arrived settlers, the rate of increase for this commune was 4 per cent in a single year!

The high national rate of increase is certainly not due mainly to an increased birth rate. Indeed, it is safe to say that there are fewer births in China today than ever before. The death rate has been considerably reduced and there is every reason to believe that it has fallen more than the birth rate. An additional factor is that child mortality is very much smaller than in previous decades and that the average expectation of life has risen. I was told in Peking that whereas the life expectation of the average Chinese used to be about thirty years, it has now risen to something like fifty years. This may be exaggerated, but there is doubtless some truth in the claim.

The main reason the death rate is lower than it was in the past is the Communists' introduction and rigorous enforcement of an extensive scheme of hygiene measures. Sometimes the foreigner finds it difficult not to smile when he sees the deadly seriousness with which the instructions on cleanliness are obeyed. On one occasion, while taking a meal in the dining car of an express train, I was obliged to wait a long time for the next course because someone had discovered a fly in the dining car. The entire kitchen staff, armed with fly swatters, went into action to dispatch the troublesome intruder.

The cleanliness of the streets in the towns has become almost proverbial. Columns of street sweepers are on the move at all hours of the day and night. In the houses and apartments, too, responsible functionaries see to it that everything is kept in scrupulous order. Much that one sees may be down-at-heel, neglected and shabby, but one never sees the kind of filthy quarters, crawling with vermin, that one encounters in other parts of Asia. The same applies to people's clothes. They may often be scanty, faded and worn, but they are always clean. Out in the provinces I often came across peasants wearing shirts whose original color could no longer be even guessed at, they were so covered in patches, but I never saw clothes that were tattered or crawling with vermin. Here too the officials see to it that the rules of hygiene are unfailingly obeyed.

Along with the effects of this unexampled and fanatical campaign of cleanliness in every sphere of life, the regime's achievements in the field of medical attention were among the things that impressed me most forcibly. There are still not enough doctors, of course, and many of the hospitals and clinics are still primitive and inadequate, but the whole country is now covered with a network of medical institutions for the treatment of illness on a scale far greater than before. In many places, too, there is at least some provision for dealing with those aspects of health which do not demand specialized medical training or equipment but which may be of the greatest importance for the general health of the public; for example inoculations, mass examinations, midwifery, infant care and much more in the sphere of prophylactic medicine.

I was given an impressive example of the effects of such medical activity in "The White Cairn" commune in Inner Mongolia. In common with their compatriots all over the Central Asiatic Mongolian grazing areas, most of the descendants of Genghis Khan in this district were infected with syphilis, which used indeed to be referred to as the Mongolian national disease. Between 1951 and 1956 a massive team of doctors made an all-out assault on this dreaded disease. Some seven hundred cases were found and treated in the neighborhood of the present White Cairn commune. Thereafter there was an annual inspection of all those who had ever contracted syphilis. Within a few years, there were signs that the operation had been an outstanding success, and today the figure of the infected has dwindled to twelve.

The improvements in hygienic and sanitary conditions, the establishment of an extensive health service and the sending of doctors and trained medical auxiliaries into the provinces thus contributed to an unprecedented increase in the population. It seemed imperative to apply the brake in the only way it could be applied; namely, by working out a program of birth control and family planning.

Birth Control—"The Fragrant Blossom"

A Communist government considering introducing family planning comes up against insuperable difficulties. Any form of birth control is apt to be regarded as an idealistic or bourgeois concept like the one once propounded by Malthus. Karl Marx ridiculed Malthus and maintained that it was only in a capitalist society that the population could, in certain circumstances, increase more quickly than society's ability to feed them. A Communist planned economy, on the other hand, in which all the means of production belonged to the proletariat, would always be in a position to produce proportionately more than the increase in the population. This was the principle on which the Russian Communists acted when they came to power and in the early stages the Chinese Communist leaders followed the same principle. "Birth control," the official Peking Party paper was still saying as late as 1952, "would simply be a bloodless method of killing off the Chinese people. It is nothing but a poisonous growth."

Only a few years later, however, the Communists were obliged to abandon ideological objections. The rapid increase in the population was out of step with agricultural production, which was expanding much more slowly than had been expected, and this gave rise to serious anxiety. Suddenly, in 1956, it began to be said that "to be a great people is good, but family planning is also good." The leading speaker in the debate on birth control was the Chancellor of Peking University, Professor Ma Yin-chu, a Yale graduate, an outstanding scholar and an independent thinker. He evolved a new theory, which he claimed had nothing to do with Malthusianism, and which embodied a two-pronged warning. In the first place, he said, a rapid increase in population would be the main obstacle to China's balanced economic development. Secondly, it was dangerous to force industrial expansion at the expense of agriculture. In 1956 and 1957 Professor Ma succeeded in winning over the high-level officials to his point of view. In the official propaganda, what had been the "poisonous growth" of birth control now became a "fragrant blossom."

However, it soon emerged that the Communist leaders had not merely ideological barriers to overcome. Much more formidable was the resistance among the people. With their birth-control and family-planning program, the Communists were intruding into a sphere which the Chinese regarded as the most personal and intimate of all, on which nobody had any right to speak but the family's senior members. More important still was the deep-rooted, centuries-old feeling that a large family offered the best security in old age. The people, especially those in the countryside, refused to go along. Despite an extensive propaganda campaign, the attempt at educating the masses bore little fruit.

It may have been a feeling of resignation which caused the Communist leaders to execute a complete about-face in their population policy in 1958. But there was another factor which seems to me to be more important. Nineteen hundred and fifty-eight was the year of unbridled optimism. The Chinese leaders believed they had discovered the key to progress. The ambitious Second Five Year Plan, the Great Leap Forward as it was called, and the establishment of the People's Communes were proclaimed simultaneously. The ideologists prophesied that with a single one-time burst of energy from everyone it would be possible to reach the final goal, the Communist era, within a few years. Everybody would have to be harnessed to this effort. The Peking *People's Daily* said at the end of 1958, "There were some people who were worried about China being overpopulated. That idea is now out of date. Our problem now is not overpopulation but a shortage of labor."

It is only too clear that at a time when millions upon millions were being concentrated into armies of workers to dig canals and irrigation ditches, to build dykes or produce steel in miniature furnaces, the idea of birth control for the purpose of reducing the population must have seemed downright paradoxical. There simply could not be enough hands to achieve the realization of the gigantic patent solutions that the leaders had laid down as the costly next stage on the road to Communism.

This remained the situation until the concept of the Great Leap Forward was revealed to have been an illusion. The set-backs of the years 1959–61 brought disillusion. The plans and methods for effective birth control suddenly became all the more urgent. Consequently, family planning has once again been an important item on the Communist leaders' program since the beginning of 1962.

Methods of Family Planning

Generally speaking, three roads are being followed in the effort to slow down the increase in China's population. First, the propagation of the idea of late marriage, secondly, contraceptives and thirdly, abortion or sterilization. The campaign for late marriage is by far the most intensively promoted of the three. This is the principal item in Communist family planning and is the most promising because of the many different possibilities of influencing the people concerned.

Legally, men may still marry at twenty and women at eighteen in China, but official publications preach the desirability of a higher marriageable age. Until recently, however, there was no sign that a common line had been adopted, and the recommended ages varied between twenty-two and thirty years, according to sex. But from a large number of discussions which I had with officials all over the country I had the impression that a standard policy had now been worked out for the district officials to follow, laying down that wherever possible the men should not marry before attaining the age of thirty and the women not until they were twenty-five.

In order to achieve the objective of getting the principle of late marriage generally accepted, the usual methods of education and instruction had been adopted. The advantages of late marriage are urged in radio talks, newspaper articles and pamphlets, at meetings and during school instruction. The arguments are logical and are similar to those one also hears in the non-Communist countries of Asia. Between the ages of twenty and thirty, it is said, for example, the human is in a decisive period of his development. It is the period when he should be principally concentrating on developing his gifts and faculties. In family-planning exhibitions I repeatedly saw eloquent posters depicting the disadvantages of early marriage in stark black-and-white style. On the one side the young mother was shown working her fingers to the bone and exhausting herself with housework and the care of the children; on the other, a girl student was portrayed sitting at her books or in class, completing her education. On this side everything was untidy and chaotic and the sky was full of dark rainclouds. On the other, there was gleaming cleanliness; the sun was shining in through the window and lighting up the road to a successful future. Moreover, the women are emphatically warned that bearing children while young is prejudicial to their health and may make them prematurely old.

An important part in the effort to persuade young people to put off marriage as long as possible is the deliberate creation of a climate in the relations between the sexes that might be called a "de-erotization" of public life. We know from the great classic Chinese novels that the Chinese were by no means averse to eroticism and sensuality. Today, exactly the opposite seems to be the case. Fashions, cosmetics, chic and sex appeal are words which seem to have been banished from the Communists' vocabulary. Morals must be kept pure, and the definition of morals is interpreted very widely. Entertainment for young people such as we know it in the West is taboo. According to reports by foreign students who were studying at Peking University in 1960 and 1961, Soviet and Western song hits were very popular and the young intellectuals were fond of dancing to them. But today these "bourgeois excesses" have been done away with. "Modern dances are bad for the health," the editor of the official Chinese theatrical magazine told me. Even the accordion, which grew quickly in popularity in the first ten to twelve years of Communist rule, is being rapidly driven out, to be replaced by traditional Chinese instruments and dances.

During my travels I asked a number of girls what they thought of love and when they intended to marry. The answer was always to the effect that they thought work more important for the present and that they wanted to make something of themselves and devote their energies to "the building up of socialism." There would be time enough for marriage later on. Such comments as these echoed the official slogans, which probably went against the grain in many cases. Nevertheless, it is undoubtedly not without significance that one seldom sees young lovers in public, even bearing in mind that it has always been "not done" in China to make a public display of one's feelings. Nor does one come across those clubs and other localities one finds in many Eastern European Communist countries, not excluding Russia, where the *jeunesse dorée* let off steam and generally imitate their Western idols. The life of the young people in China is puritanical, respectable and sexless.

Naturally, this state of affairs is not solely due to understanding and inner perception on the part of the young. The Party organization has limitless opportunities for influencing people. In the schools, universities, youth organizations and places of work the Party functionary finds opportunities to guide and persuade, or, if there is the occasional tendency to go against the official Party line, to apply a certain amount of pressure. In the old days it was the parents who decided who should marry, and when. Today, although the Party does not actually lay down who should marry, the functionary at the ground level is in a position to dictate the course which will best serve the Chinese population policy and the policies of the Party, too.

Nevertheless, the functionaries' power and influence are not always availing. As foreign students at Peking University have related, their Chinese fellow students have very different opinions about young love from those of the Party officials, ideas which are not perhaps discussed in public but are certainly held in private for all that. At all events they act like it. The same sources told me that many a young couple get around the Party's instructions by bringing a baby into the world before the wedding, in order to ensure that permission to marry will be granted. All the same, one had the impression that such cases were the exception rather than the rule. Generally speaking it does seem that the Party has gradually succeeded in getting the principle of delayed marriage largely accepted by the young people, even if this has sometimes been achieved by means which would never be tolerated in the West.

A second element in the Chinese population policy is the propaganda culminating in the slogan "Have fewer but healthier children!" Using almost the same arguments as are employed to propagate late marriage, the Communists try to persuade married couples to keep their families as small as possible. This, they argue, is better for the parents, who not only can devote themselves more intensively to their work, but will also be financially better off and thus contribute to the development of their country. Moreover, a small family is better for the children themselves, who can develop more fully and receive better training and education. Once again a particular appeal is made to the women by reminding them of the dangers to health that must follow too many births in too quick succession. As far as possible, they are told, there should be an interval of from three to five years between children.

Official publicity media commend the family with two or, at the most, three children. The reality, however, is vastly different, as the traveler discovers after even the shortest stay in a Chinese town or village. The popular belief in the desirability of a large family will not be eradicated for a long time to come. Even functionaries are not immune, although they in particular are urged to lead the way and set a shining example. I came across many an official who had many more children than was pleasing to the Party because he could not rid himself of the atavistic notion that he must produce male progeny at all costs. It is only among the young and highly ambitious Party officials that the idea of the small family has developed into an acceptable ideal.

Nor has the intensive campaign of education on contraceptive techniques had much obvious effect on the large families which are still being produced and which people still consider so desirable. In the larger towns there are exhibitions in which uninhibited models and demonstrations are used to show the different types of contraceptives and the methods of using them. In the country, meetings are held, with educational diagrams and models, and clinics offer a large selection of contraceptives at low prices.

Nevertheless, I continually had the impression that the people were not very much interested. In the Park of Culture in Canton I came across a permanent exhibition of contraceptives which few people visited, whereas it was significant that in the next-door building there were roars of laughter and applause from thousands of people watching a performance of the traditional Chinese puppet theater. Similarly, when I visited corresponding exhibitions in the country districts, I usually found that they were in an out-of-the-way corner of the building, and neglected.

It was explained to me that shyness and modesty had a great deal to do with this, especially in the country districts (although this still seems to be the case in the towns, too). And there is, of course, a certain contradiction in preaching sexual puritanism on the one hand while at the same time demanding that the people should be progressive and open about the most intimate matters.

The contraceptives offered for sale in China are of the same kind as those found elsewhere. I heard in Peking that a contraceptive pill was being developed but that so far the results had not been satisfactory. Delegations of Western doctors have been to China to exchange views and give advice on these matters, and Chinese experts have been to Japan to study the methods used there to bring about the phenomenal reduction in the rate of population growth to less than 1 per cent. All these things are clear indications that the Chinese leaders are beginning to take the problem of birth control increasingly seriously.

In contrast to the publicity given to the education on family planning and birth control, propaganda on behalf of legalized abortion or sterilization hardly appears at all. Indeed, generally speaking, people are warned against abortion, unless undertaken on medical advice. The experience of recent years seems to have been unfavorable: it has happened all too often that the women concerned have suffered deleterious aftereffects. It is possible that with improved medical techniques the practice of abortion will increase in importance, as has happened in Shanghai, where there are comparatively advanced clinics and experienced doctors, and where abortion is being increasingly recommended as a means of family planning. But in this, as in so many other things, Shanghai is an exception.

Sterilization has been much commended lately, but for understandable psychological reasons the effort seems to have met with little success. There is no official pressure or compulsion and the propaganda is directed almost exclusively to the men, for whom the operation is simpler and more straightforward. From publications and conversations I learned that a small number of husbands who already had large families have occasionally volunteered to be sterilized.

China is still a long way from compensating for the drop in the death rate by a corresponding reduction in the birth rate. The danger that the enormous population growth will imperil the nation's existence will remain for generations to come, even if it turns out to be possible to create economic and nutritional conditions far beyond what has been achieved up to the present. If there has been a certain amount of success in the field of family planning, it is still not sufficient to warrant undue optimism in the Chinese leaders.

Chapter 11

ECONOMIC PLANNING ON
TWO LEGS

If anyone asked me what made the strongest and most abiding impression on me during my tour of China, there could be only one answer: the indescribable poverty. The standard of living is low, and wages are minimal and entirely disproportionate to the amount of physical work the people do. I vividly remember the scenes each morning at the assembly points of the local transport brigades, which I saw all over China, where thousands and thousands of handcart men and coolies are allotted their day's work. From then on until late evening they are on the streets, pulling or pushing loads of food, fuel, industrial goods, motors, even enormous concrete telegraph posts, from one place to another. I remember, too, seeing on a country road a seriously ill child being transported at a swaying jog trot by its relatives on a makeshift stretcher to the distant hospital in the next town. And I also remember a rail journey along the Yellow River after the end of the harvest. Tens of thousands of people were toiling away in the fields, plowing, hoeing and digging. For hundreds of miles I saw no tractors, no horses, no oxen: only gangs of human beings clustered together, dragging the plows through clayey soil at the end of a rope.

There is something else which cannot escape the foreign visitor. Unlike other underdeveloped countries, which receive economic aid and credits from East or West—or sometimes both —the greatest underdeveloped country in the world is left to fend for itself. There is no sign of fraternal assistance from the socialist camp. Even the transactions which took place before the outbreak of the Sino-Soviet conflict were mostly kept within the framework of normal trade and credit relations, in which the Chinese were granted no special privileges. Even their political and ideological allies were not prepared to give the Chinese something for nothing. Economic collaboration with the West is sporadic and rudimentary: it, too, is on the basis of un-emotional reciprocity.

There is no indication that the grinding poverty and economic isolation which characterize China's economic condition have led to resignation in the people. On the contrary, the feeling of being pitied, ridiculed or written off by the world as "have nots" has done more to create a feeling of solidarity and to spur the nation on than any amount of ideological, hypothetical argu-ments could have done. There can be no other explanation of the vitality, the willing self-sacrifice and the natural cheerfulness of the ordinary Chinese that the foreign observer sees almost everywhere. It is this same reason, and not just exaggerated racialism, which leads the people to believe they must go along with the government in its demand that the Chinese should make common cause with other nations living in poverty, and whose independence is also threatened.

In China, as in every other developing country, the watch-word is "industrialization." If backwardness and poverty are to be overcome, then the country must become an industrial country; and this is the objective the Communists have pursued ever since they came to power. From the start they were well aware that this would entail great difficulties. What applied in the case of the modern industrialized states at the time of their transition from the old order to a more modern form of society applies still more in China. The Far Eastern colossus is an agricultural country and will remain one for many years. For the foreseeable future, therefore, only agriculture will be able to provide the means for expansion and growth.

Not only that, there is yet another problem. The agriculture that is supposed to produce the capital resources to invest in industrialization must simultaneously provide sustenance for a rapidly growing population which already amounts to something like seven hundred million. This was the problem which nearly brought about the downfall of the regime a few years ago. There is at present no danger of famine in China, it is true, and a regular supply of foodstuffs for the whole country seems assured. Yet the question remains, whether this holds good for the foreseeable future. On the answer to this question depend the policies and indeed the very existence of the Communist regime. Only when the food supply has been stabilized and made secure will it be possible to indulge in surmise and speculation about the possibilities of industrialization.

The Agrarian Problem

The Chinese have not put out any official production statistics for years, so that in dealing with both industrial and agricultural production one has to fall back on estimates, as corroborated by occasional hints and suggestions. As regards the production of the basic food products, rice and wheat, official statements have hitherto been confined to vague assurances such as that "the harvest this year is better than last year's." At the beginning of 1964 some more detail was given by Anna-Louise Strong, the American journalist who lives in Peking. According to her figures, the 1963 grain crop amounted to 180 million tons. Chou En-lai also asserted during his 1964 African tour that the yield had been under 190 million tons. As the 1964 harvest, according to official statements, was not bad but not exactly abundant either, it must be assumed that the yield had for 1964 lay between 180 and 190 million tons. But even if one were prepared to accept the optimistic estimates of some Western experts and to assume a yield of something in the region of 200 million tons, the outlook for the future is still bleak. According to the last reliable figures from official Chinese sources in 1957, one year before the introduction of the Great Leap Forward and the

People's Communes, the harvest in that year amounted to 185 million tons. In other words, the total yield cannot have risen very much since then, a menacing symptom considering that since 1957 the population of China has increased by at least 100 million people.

The planning staffs in Peking realize, of course, what a delicate matter the future food supply of the country is. There is no getting around the fact that in China more than 60 per cent of the soil lies more than sixty-five hundred feet above sea level. Another 15 per cent is completely unworkable for geographical or climatic reasons. Moreover, one cannot ignore the overcrowding in the fertile areas. In North China this amounts to nearly 850 people to the square mile. In the cultivated areas of Szechwan and the Yangtze Kiang delta the figure is almost thirty-two hundred to the square mile.

But the responsible officials are optimistic. Whenever I brought the conversation round to this difficult question, the Chinese would always be ready with the comparison with the Japanese, who have shown that they are able to solve the food problem under similar circumstances. If the arable acreage stayed the same as at present, and assuming one employed the same intensive cultivation methods as the Japanese, it ought to be possible to quadruple the yield. If the arable acreage could be increased to the extent the Peking planners intend, then it must be possible not only to satisfy China's domestic requirements in basic foodstuffs but even to export considerable quantities of grain.

"There is no cause for anxiety," I was told in responsible quarters in Peking. "We have 275 million acres of arable land, which is after all three times as much per head of population as the Japanese have. Furthermore, we can increase this acreage by another 137 million acres, in other words by 50 per cent, any time we like." With equal composure, the planners point out another circumstance. "The yields per acre are extraordinarily varied. The highest is around three tons an acre and the lowest is six-tenths of a ton. You can see from that what possibilities there are. The problem in our agrarian policy is not that we have too little land available or that we are already producing from it all that can be produced. Without any question, we are potentially able to produce more than enough grain and other foodstuffs. Our real problem, our only problem, is how to find the state investment capital we need to achieve the larger yields that our agriculture is undoubtedly capable of producing."

Here in those words lies the root of the problem of China's economic development. In order to ensure the supply of sufficient food for the whole country, agricultural productivity must be increased. In order to achieve this increase there must be capital investment. Moreover, every responsible Chinese realizes that the objective of socialist planning, industrialization, is not merely an ideological hypothesis but the only possible way out. But here again, only agriculture can provide the means required to achieve it.

In the early years of Communist rule, fully realizing the conditions in the Chinese economy, the Peking planners embarked on an economic course completely different from the Soviet course. The money for investment was not diverted directly from agricultural yields, but was obtained indirectly, by extracting it from the profits made by the industries which processed agricultural products. These industries bought the agricultural raw materials at comparatively low prices and sold the finished products at high prices. According to Japanese estimates, more than 93 per cent of the Chinese state revenue in 1960 consisted of profits and yields from state factories, 80 per cent of which were engaged in processing agricultural products.

Within a few years, however, it became clear that this way of doing things would only allow a very slow increase in industrialization. If large sums were to be obtained, this indirect method demanded that there should first be a considerable increase in agricultural products and a great expansion of the light industries which processed them. Yet neither of these conditions seemed ideologically acceptable or easily feasible in practice. Thus the one-sided preferential nourishing of heavy industry with investment capital automatically brought about a state of ominous imbalance in the economy. To make matters worse, most of the increasingly large imports from Communist countries of capital goods needed for industrialization had also to be paid for in agricultural products and raw materials. So it was that the last official statistics for 1957 clearly revealed not only stagnation in industrial production and revenue but also a fall in the volume of trade with the Soviet Union and the satellite countries.

This stagnation was also bound to have an automatic effect on the heavy industrial sector which the Communists were giving priority. Together with political and ideological motives it was an essential reason for a new economic policy, which was called the Great Leap Forward. The Communists did not completely lose sight of the fact that agriculture must provide the resources needed for industrialization, but it was believed that a colossal and far-reaching effort would enable both industry and agriculture "to be developed at one and the same time," as official statements put it. Even if capital resources were scarce, even if it was extremely difficult to create the funds for investment by any of the usual—or even by unusual—methods, China still had one asset, an asset possessed by no other country in the world: one billion Chinese hands, ready and willing to toil and to build, provided one knew how to direct their efforts correctly. What the Chinese leaders were proposing to do was to convert this undeniable asset into hard economic cash. The setting up of the People's Communes was the main feature of this new policy. The establishment of back-yard furnaces all over the country for the making of steel on "do it yourself" lines was another of the many experiments intended to lead to the rapid attainment of ambitious objectives.

At this time the Chinese Communists were filled with unbounded optimism. With considerable Soviet assistance, the first stage in the expansion program for heavy industry was already completed. Thanks to unusually good weather, the 1958 harvest prospects seemed better than ever before. But above all, the leaders thought themselves justified in believing that the people

would spontaneously fall in with the idea of a concentration of
effort unprecedented in world history. There began a period of
gigantic "battles for production." Carrying fluttering banners,
to the sound of drums and gongs, millions of people moved out
into the fields, created irrigation installations, built dykes, rolled
out millions of tons of earth, smelted iron and steel, built rail-
roads on wooden tracks, collected fertilizer or destroyed flies
and sparrows. "The heroic upsurge of a nation" the official
propaganda called it. The working day of twelve to fourteen
hours became standard. Some brigades stayed out in the fields
or at their places of work night and day and did not even go
back to their towns or villages to sleep. There were women's
brigades that worked through without a stop for three days and
nights. Communal feeding and communal care of children and
old people were the rule. The organization of the mammoth
multitudes of workers was carried out by the army and the
militia.

But the Great Leap Forward as originally conceived turned
out to be a failure. Official propaganda puts the blame for the
fiasco on the natural disasters of the years 1959 to 1961 and the
cancelation of Soviet economic aid after the Sino-Soviet conflict
came out into the open. It is certain that these events did in fact
greatly aggravate the economic distress of that period. But it is
equally certain that the demands made by the Great Leap
program went far beyond China's capacity. The radical com-
munizing of people's lives met with a great deal of resistance.
Many operations had turned out to be pointless and had led to
the neglecting of other tasks which, although they might not have
promised spectacular results, would have been more profitable.
The "miniature furnace campaign" had soon been shown to be
an absolutely useless undertaking which had only resulted in a
waste of time and energy.

The Great Leap had been made in too much of a hurry.
Lacking detailed preliminary preparation and disregarding the
limits of human performance, it had taken the wrong road and
produced results which bore no relation to the efforts and the

sacrifices which had been made. In general it seemed as though
the whole thing had been determined not so much by the need
to work along rational and economical lines as by amateurish
procedures, wasteful of both labor and capital, on purely party-
political principles.

So there came about another change in economic policy. In
the spring of 1962 it was decided to give priority to agriculture
once more. "The development of agriculture as the basis of our
economy, with industry as the deciding factor" or "Henceforth
walking on two legs" were the official slogans of the Chinese
planners. The lives of the peasants were made easier. The communes were "liberalized" and their number increased from
twenty-six thousand to seventy-four thousand in order to enable
more rational methods to be introduced. The new policy also
included increased inducements for the individual peasant. More
land was made available for private holdings, the prices the
state paid for agricultural products were raised and the peasants
were promised more consumer goods to buy with their extra cash
in future.

Changes in the Communes

The change in the People's Communes is very striking. Up to
a few years ago these Communist Chinese institutions aroused
alarm in the West and scorn and sarcasm from the officials in
Eastern Communist states. At that time, in 1958, the year of
Sturm und Drang, they were described by Peking as the genuine
basic units of Communism. The peasants were brought together
into enormous communities in which the state administration
was practically one with the commune administration. The
entire life of the inhabitants, and particularly their working lives,
was organized on military lines. Pay was no longer in accordance with the results of the individual's work but in accordance with his "needs." These were laid down in so-called
"guarantees"—food, clothing, shelter, education, marriage, mater-

12. Street scene in Shenyang, the capital of Manchuria.

13. Chestnut vendors in Chengchow.

14. Peking ducks, one of the finest Chinese delicacies, are still bred on special farms near the capital.

15. A rice grower in the South.

16. A vegetable vendor in a Peking Street.

17. Since cotton fabric is rationed, many Chinese mothers do a good deal of knitting.

18. A woman of the Miao tribe comes to market from her mountainous jungle home.

19. The splendid Chi Hing-yen Gate near Chaoching in Kwangtung Province.

nity care, medical attention and burial. There was little pay in cash; everyone received what was in effect pocket money. A campaign was begun to persuade people to surrender their right to private proverty, in order to hasten on the attainment of the desired goal of full Communism.

Worst of all was the attempt to communize the private lives of everyone. Meals were henceforth to be taken only in canteens. There were some cases in which every single item of kitchen equipment in the peasants' houses, down to the last saucepan, had to be handed in, and where the sight of smoke rising from the chimney of a farmhouse, giving away that some private cooking was being done, called down punishment. Crèches and kindergartens were hurriedly put up in order to ensure that the services of the women, down to the last mother, would also be available. Old people were put into "Happiness Homes" or given light work to do. Barracklike sleeping quarters were erected, in which, in some places, husbands and wives were accommodated separately. Often enough the newly built houses had no kitchens or lavatories of their own. In the North, functionaries proposed that the ancestral graves, which were strewn all over the fields, should be assembled in one place—an unheard-of suggestion for Chinese.

In the course of my visits to communes in various parts of the country, I discovered that it was just those elements of the commune concept which had horrified the West that were least put into effect at this time. What had been exhibited by the propagandists as a particularly fine example of genuine Communist thinking had stayed mostly on paper. Excessive interference with people's private lives happened only here and there, just as it is not true that there was ever a uniform commune structure everywhere in the country. The main reason for this was that each commune was practically a state within a state and it mainly depended on the responsible Party officials how far and how quickly they wished to push on toward the goal of total communization. There were some officials who took senseless and stupid measures in an attempt to make a name for themselves.

Others planned carefully and did not start a new project until the necessary preliminary steps had been taken. But different as things may have been in the individual communes, there was one unfortunate consequence that soon made itself apparent everywhere. The overhasty propaganda, the fanatical energy of countless untrained officials and the universal frenzied determination to achieve success, no matter what the cost, very soon led to a state of hopeless confusion, so that in a short time even the leaders lost control.

I was given a detailed description in the communes of the lines along which measures were thereupon taken to cool off the overheated ardor of the Great Leap. Wherever personal property had been sequestered, it had now to be returned or replaced. The use of canteens, crèches or kindergartens was to be a matter for individual families to decide. Excessive compulsion was to be dropped. The barrack experiment was stopped. New farm buildings and apartments were to be laid out in such a way that all the members of a family, both young and old, could live together. Working hours were laid down for every worker; the peasant must be guaranteed twelve hours off, even at busy sowing and harvest times.

Further, the practice of organizing work in the communes along military lines was forbidden. What was now to be aimed at was the atmosphere of a large business concern, where planning and working methods can be worked out by discussion and not simply ordered from above without any possibility of argument, as in any army organization. The militia in the countryside were to have only the character of a potential defense force and not to be able to initiate and decide on methods of production. No one was allowed to be the militia commander and the head of the commune at the same time.

One of the most important innovations was the decentralizing of the communes. Three levels of property ownership were introduced. First, there was the property belonging to the commune, mainly consisting of the workshops, tractor depots, power stations, plants, public buildings and streets built by the commune; all the installations, in other words, paid for out of commune funds. Secondly, there was the property of the brigade, generally consisting of the things that a village community owns. The brigades were given back their land, farm implements, local business, public buildings built by the village community and so forth. Thirdly, there was the property of the so-called production community, usually comprising one large family or several families. The production community was allocated houses, personal belongings, private farmland, domestic animals and the like.

Concomitantly with the decentralization of property in a commune the administrative system was also changed. Nowadays the commune is actually nothing more than a superior organization which exerts little influence on the peasants' production. I was told that the commune administrative machinery had been heavily cut. When I asked a farmer in the Northwest what he saw of the commune leaders, he answered sarcastically, "Oh, those people! We don't have anything to do with them. We just carry on in our own way."

The basic component of the present-day commune is the brigade, and in fact I often had the feeling that there was a development afoot which might well end with the small production community, i.e., one large family or a group of families, becoming the central, basic unit in the agricultural productive process, similar to what it used to be in the old days. At all events, the People's Communes have lost their former dreaded Orwellian character. The commune has been pushed into a position from which, functioning as a central body, it can do useful work without having too much direct influence on the course of the daily work of the mass of the peasants.

Life in the commune has become more human. During my travels I seldom saw scenes such as those which used to conjure up in the West the specter of a way of life communized down to the last detail during the years of the hectic productivity campaigns. They still do occur, admittedly, as for example when pioneer groups move off into the fields with banners and drums to build an irrigation installation, or when the commune assembles an army of workers to do road repair work. But the normal farm work is done by groups of one or two dozen people. They are to be seen all over the fields in the North or along the terraces of the paddy fields in the South. They move off to their work at the universal steady jog trot without the noise and fuss of a frenetic mass action.

The villages and settlements breathe an air of country peacefulness. I very seldom saw mass quarters of the type that were held up as the ideal of the new development some years ago. New houses are now being put up in the traditional style, to suit the individual taste of the occupants. "We have dropped the idea of communal barracks," I was told by the head of the Manchurian commune Kao Tan, "The Plateau." "The commune members preferred the detached house with its *kang* (the traditional clay stove of North China), a vegetable garden and stables for their cattle. They want to live together with their families. So we have acted accordingly."

The tradition concerning ancestral graves, too, was something that could not be done away with in North China. In the "Red Star of Chinese-Korean Friendship" commune, near Peking, one of the best stockbreeding farms in the country—where the working methods, a group of visiting Canadian farmers told me, would undoubtedly stand comparison with those in Canada— I saw an enormous field of ancestral graves, lying, of all places, in front of the ultramodern byres which housed forty-five hundred head of cattle. I drew the attention of the head of the commune to the striking contrast between the modernity and advanced technique on the one side and the ancient tradition on the other. "It will be a long time before the peasants, even those living near the capital, get rid of their old ideas," he said with a self-confident air. "We are leaving them be for the present." I often had the impression, especially when visiting communes in the interior, that now that the excesses of the Great Leap have been eliminated, the people's way of life is not much different from what it always was. And yet the influence of the modern age can be felt everywhere—and not only in the bad sense. In conversation, of course, overzealous officials would try to make up for the obvious defects in the living conditions and performance by rhetoric and propaganda. And it is hardly to be supposed that the visitor will be shown the worst communes.

In Peking I pointed out to a senior official a fact which had struck me as very strange, namely, that in every People's Commune I had been to, I had been given loads of statistics according to which the harvest results in recent years had risen rapidly as a result of the setting up of the commune. On the other hand, in an interview which he gave in early 1964, Premier Chou En-lai gave a figure for the total 1963 harvest yield which suggested that there had not been much improvement on the results for 1957. So the communes which the foreign visitor was allowed to see could not be regarded as representative. The official frankly admitted that there were great differences in the yields per acre of the individual communes, depending on their geographical position and the stage of development. But I must also remember, he went on, that "every year there are always some areas in the throes of natural disasters." The conclusion to be drawn from these remarks is that while the communes the visitor gets to see may not necessarily be models of efficiency, they will at any rate be communes that are functioning as the leaders think they ought to function. I think it is important to be aware of this and not to regard the dozen communes the visitor is shown as a yardstick by which to measure the rest of the seventy-four thousand.

Nevertheless, it can still be maintained that much has been done to bring about a widespread improvement in living conditions. Primary and secondary schools, hospitals and clinics with operating theaters, X-ray departments, maternity wards and dispensaries are more or less taken for granted in every commune. But the main effort is still being devoted to the field of production, although in a different sense from that of the original People's Commune concept. The exclusive competence of the commune as an institution no longer covers the daily work in the fields, but is reserved for projects of general significance, of the kind the smaller working unit cannot handle. This embraces, in addition to small plants, irrigation projects, road building, pumping stations and so on, efforts to make industrial production part of the commune's operations.

Almost every commune of any size has foundries, brickworks, forges, repair shops of all kinds, workshops for making agricultural implements and even plants for making necessary electrical equipment—for example, transformers. The purpose of these plants is clear. As much as possible of the commune's requirements is to be produced by the commune itself. This sometimes leads to what appear to Western eyes to be wasteful procedures, as when nails are made one at a time, agricultural implements laboriously put together by hand or containers cast in processes that seem almost medieval in style. Cylinders and bearings for farm machines are made on lathes, one item taking half or three-quarters of an hour to make. Western experts told me that in the industrialized countries automation enabled similar items to be turned out at the rate of four to five hundred an hour.

In the "Horse Bridge" commune near Shanghai I saw young girls laboriously assembling transformers. This may seem amateurish and hardly likely to stand up to safety tests by professional experts; and in any case this method would be far too expensive by Western standards. But in saying this it is very easy to overlook the fact that more modern and practical methods could be employed only if the country already had an industrial basis. Since Communist China does not have it, the Chinese have to resort to improvisation and the use of technical methods which may appear primitive to Western eyes but which, given the conditions existing today, do help the Chinese economy forward.

Two reforms introduced and realized after the failure of the Great Leap have principally affected the living standard of the peasants—the handing back of private land and the revising of the wages and income system. As far as the return of private land is concerned, the area released for the peasants' private cultivation is still very small. In most of the communes I visited, it amounted to about 5 per cent of the commune's total arable acreage. In others it rose to 7 per cent and in some of the more remote and poorer areas it is said to be as much as 10 per cent. This may seem surprising at first sight, since this makes the arable area available for the private use of the peasants greater than in the "revisionist" Soviet Union, where the peasants' own land is estimated to be about 2 per cent of the total; only in the collective farms is it 3.5 per cent. But responsible officials in Peking pointed out that this was the wrong way to look at it. One must not forget that the population of China was very much greater. The area of private land per head was much greater in the Soviet Union than in China, and in some instances, in fact, it assumed "capitalistic" proportions.

Nevertheless, the return of land for personal cultivation gave a great lift to the peasants, for whom it meant a stimulus to the production of vegetables and dairy produce and the raising of cattle. Not only did this lead to an easing of the supply problem in the country areas, but the urban population benefited as well. The peasants were allowed either to sell their wares to the state or to offer them for sale in the markets. In 1963, for example, sales to state purchasing authorities of privately produced pork and eggs in some areas are said to have amounted to 40 per cent of the total state purchases.

The supplementary income which the commune members receive by this means varies from region to region. In the Horse Bridge commune I spoke of above, the peasants' extra earnings were very high, probably because of the proximity of the great city and its millions of inhabitants, and amounted to 20 per cent of the total annual income of the members, I was told. At the Yellow Flower commune in Hunan, on the other hand, I was given a figure amounting to not more than 6 per cent of the annual income of the members. In general, however, the private land seems to produce about 10 per cent of the owners' annual incomes.

The overhauling of the wages and incomes system meant

abandoning the original concept of the Great Leap years, by
which each would be paid according to his needs, and returning
to the principle of payment by results. Basic pay and all kinds
of bonuses make up a complicated wage-computing system. The
intention is to give the peasants material incentives and also to
bring about a redistribution of the labor potential by a system
of special rewards for work which the regime regards as beneficial
to the community, but which no one wants to do. This seems
a more acceptable way than the former system of using harsh,
semimilitary discipline.

The result of the system of differentiated payment by results
can be seen in all the communes today. Incomes vary within
the same commune but there is one respect in which the pay
is the same for all members: payment in kind. What the individual receives depends on what the commune happens to be
producing and on the state of the harvest. An example will
illustrate this. In the "Red Star of Chinese-Korean Friendship"
commune near Peking, each member was allotted 450 pounds
of grain, which the head of the commune explained would
correspond to the individual's requirements of rice and flour for
three months, corn for five and a half months and sweet potatoes
for two weeks. In addition, each member received an average
of 330 yuan in cash.

There can be very great differences in the cash payments
made in the individual communes. This provides the clearest
illustration of the transformation in the wage structure after the
Great Leap period. I found a particularly striking case of this
in a commune in Manchuria. The lowest cash payment here was
300 yuan a year and the highest about 1000 yuan. From what
I could gather, this seemed to be exceptional. In most cases
the difference between the highest and the lowest cash payments was about 200 yuan.

In the course of my travels I was able to see what great
differences there were between the wage structures of the different regions and provinces, just as there were in so many
other things. For example, the annual cash income of the mem-

bers of one commune in Shensi Province was around 200 yuan, in Kiansu Province about 250, in the Peking area about 350, in Hunan Province 400 and in Manchuria 525; while in one stock-raising commune in Inner Mongolia it went as high as 600 yuan a year. These are figures taken at random and are admittedly by no means representative. Every province could doubtless quote quite different figures. But however incomplete and scanty these figures may be, they at least show how far removed the Communist China of today still is from having a uniform, leveled-out Communist order in every respect.

More Consumer Goods Are Made Available

Even outside the communes the liberal agricultural policies produced effects surprisingly quickly. The produce on sale in all the markets in the provinces I visited during my journey through China was varied and plentiful.

Eggs, vegetables and spices of all kinds are piled high. In clean market halls and at stalls belonging to cooperative organizations, salespeople in white coats, many of them wearing gauze masks over nose and mouth and gloves on their hands, offer the traditional Chinese meats, pork and poultry. Near rivers and in the coastal regions fish is also on sale. As to the rest, all the markets make the same impression: a variegated throng of prudent housewives out shopping.

Only rice, corn, flour and cotton material are generally rationed. I was assured by a senior official in Peking that the present rationing would continue for the foreseeable future. Should a shortage of certain commodities arise in any particular part of the country, ration cards are issued for these commodities on a regional basis. "Incidentally," he adds, "we have rationing not only because of shortages, but also for social reasons, to stabilize prices and to prevent hoarding."

The ration of rice and other basic foods is about thirty-three pounds a month per person. The annual entitlement of cotton material was recently raised to four yards a person. My interpreter tried to persuade me that these quantities were quite sufficient, and assured me, for example, that he normally consumed only thirty pounds of his thirty-three-pound ration. But if one asks an unprejudiced citizen, his answer will be quite different. Not only is the ration of basic foods too small, but the rationing of cotton materials and the general shortage of money are felt to be particularly oppressive. The normal consumer tries to make up for these defects by buying more of the abundant vegetables and by the purchase of wool. Women and girls are to be seen knitting everywhere—while taking walks and even during the performances at the Peking Opera.

Although it is possible to make up on the rations, the food supply for the vast majority of the Chinese people is anything but lavish. The peasants rely on their own gardens for the essential items and the city dwellers are not much better off. A good meal in a "coupon-free" luxury hotel in Peking costing five to ten yuan is beyond the reach of all but a very few privileged industrial workers, the average wage being sixty to eighty yuan (twenty-five to thirty-five dollars). But a simple meal at one of the stalls that stand on practically every street corner costs only a few cents. There is an astonishing difference between the meals in the commune canteens and those in the factories. The working man in the towns has to pay about ten yuan a month for all meals every day in his factory canteen.

The government is trying to parallel the boost they gave to increased output by the "liberalization" of the communes by increasing the supply of industrial consumer goods. The foreign visitor finds the variety of goods on sale in the Chinese department stores astonishing, compared with those in many another Communist country. In Peking I was told with pride that it was estimated that some fifty thousand different items were available in the stores in the capital, and in Shanghai the total number was even higher, about seventy thousand. The desire to provide a stimulus to the consumers, both in the towns and in the country, sometimes produced effects which I found strange in view of the general economic situation in a Communist-controlled developing country run on strictly utilitarian lines. For example, in a large department store in Kunming in South China I saw on sale in the drug department what was alleged to be a highly effective traditional restorative for men, made out of ground-up tigers' bones. In the toy department of the same store there were mechanical walking dolls and plastic goldfish that wriggled.

Admittedly, consumer goods in China are extremely expensive by Western standards. A yard of standard cotton material costs one and a half to two yuan, a pair of canvas shoes three yuan, a pair of leather shoes twenty to thirty yuan, a simple shirt twenty, a pair of pants twenty, a plain raincoat 120, a transistor radio 150, a bicycle 200 and a television set with a tiny screen 500 yuan. These are exorbitant prices considering the average income of the ordinary Chinese worker or peasant. As a result, conversations always contained the same complaints about the prices of goods, however plentiful the supply. But no less characteristic were the statements of the officials who pleaded for understanding for the high prices because the state needed a high profit margin "for the time being," this being the only way to get hold of investment capital.

Western and Eastern observers who have lived in China for many years, however, were unanimous that the supply position in the country had not only become more stable but had actually improved. There is no longer any starvation, and the individual can now begin to think about ways and means of achieving relatively greater prosperity. This makes itself chiefly apparent, of course, in the large towns. In the main department stores in Peking and Shanghai the people come in droves and buy. In the working-class homes the modest stock of possessions is increased by some newly bought item that satisfies the small man's esthetic values. On the streets the number of bicycles grows from month to month. The clothing of the women, and especially of the children, increasingly displays colorful indications of individual taste and fashion sense.

Anyone who has a good deal of money can even buy luxury items. I had already noticed the numerous fur shops in the main shopping streets of Shenyang, and at first I had connected these with the icy Manchurian winter. But then I also found a row of fur stores in Hangkow on the Yangtze Kiang, even though the winter temperatures in these ports of Central China do not make fur clothing an absolute necessity. A number of women's fur coats were on display in the shop windows, in styles that were the height of fashion in the twenties and thirties. To me the prices seemed horrendous. Out of curiosity I went into one of the shops and was shown a collection of finest and costliest fur coats. I asked why such high-cost things were made and who would dare to wear them. "Oh, anybody can buy them, and people do," the salesman said evasively, with a sardonic smile. "Of course you will never see them worn in public, but many a one is quite satisfied just to be able to show off her precious possession within her own four walls."

Consumer goods also find their way to the countryside. The goods available in the village stores I visited corresponded roughly to what one would find on sale in one of the smaller department stores in the city. Not only the peasants' curiosity has been aroused but also their desire to buy. Eastern European observers in Peking thought in fact that this tendency was worrying the government, which was afraid that what had originally been intended as a stimulus might develop into something that could not help but lead to the drawing of conclusions, and might then become a hindrance to the fulfillment of the over-all Communist plan.

As yet, however, the officials in the country are still proud of the peasants' growing prosperity. They carefully note the increase in possessions and take pleasure in telling the foreign visitor about them. In the "Plateau" commune in Manchuria, for example, I was shown a detailed list of all the "luxury goods" that the peasants had bought within the last year or two. The families in the commune, not quite three thousand in number, possessed 1170 radio sets, 745 wristwatches, 411 bicycles,

143 sewing machines and, believe it or not, more than a thousand alarm clocks. The satiated Western visitor may find the presenting of this kind of information absurd, but to the official, and to the individual Chinese peasant also, this increase in material possessions is indicative of a rise in living standards which only twenty or thirty years ago would have seemed inconceivable.

Private Business in China

There is another phenomenon which is characteristic of the general relaxation and rationalization of the Chinese economy. This is the more indulgent attitude of the regime toward the private business sector, whose role in China is generally underestimated in the West even today.

From the beginning the Chinese Communists pursued a different policy with regard to privately owned firms and businesses than was, for example, pursued in the Soviet Union. "Capitalism" was not immediately stamped out, root and branch, not liquidated with Bolshevik thoroughness. The Peking regime clearly distinguished between those industrialists and businessmen whom the leaders regarded as "antinational" and those who, notwithstanding the class struggle, had behaved "progressively" and were "pro-fatherland." All those who belonged to the first category, representatives of foreign firms, "counterrevolutionaries" who had fled abroad, collaborators with the Japanese, "usurers" and "exploiters," were dispossessed completely. Those in the pro-fatherland group of capitalists were initially allowed to carry on running their businesses. The official view at this time was that during the period of transition to a purely socialist economy, a mixed form of ownership might have its uses.

As the years went by, however, these capitalists were subjected to heavy pressure. Many of them were tried on charges of corruption, tax evasion and similar crimes. Thousands were bankrupted and "sold" their businesses to the state. In other cases government controllers soon took over the running of the business and the position of the owner became intolerable. Very few of them managed to hold out against the systematic campaign designed to persuade them to convert their businesses into mixed "state-private" concerns. The end of capitalism in China seemed to be in sight.

Then, in 1956, the leaders decided that 5 per cent interest was to be paid on all shares still held by private businessmen, without regard to whether the businesses made a profit or a loss, and that these payments should continue for seven years—that is, until the end of 1962. What happened after that was regarded in the West as a grotesquerie without parallel. Capitalists sorrowingly submitted applications for their businesses to be taken over by the state as soon as possible. When this had been done, the businessmen concerned organized "joy parades" to thank the Communist government for the favor they had granted them. But however much of a farce all this seemed to us, it had a completely realistic background. After the years of "transition," the private entrepreneurs had lost all hope of being able to continue their former business activities. The "interest" payments for a limited period were small consolation, but they were gladly accepted in the conviction that one would at least be able to survive.

Even today the Communist propaganda machine still has a number of prominent capitalists on tap, who will enthusiastically tell the foreign visitor about their present, much happier existence. They live in luxurious villas, have refrigerators, costly antiques and cars. They receive millions in so-called "interest" every year. One of them, a former businessman named Loh, managed to escape to Hong Kong. What he had to say there revealed the heart of the matter. The capitalists paraded before the foreign visitor were nothing but puppets and propaganda showpieces. They neither had any authority nor dared to say a word which had not been approved by Party officials beforehand. He himself had helped the state to entertain foreign visitors more than eighty times, he said. (During my journey I always deliberately declined to be "entertained" in this way.)

Still, the question arises of why, fifteen years after their seizure of power, the Chinese Communists still keep up the pretense of the existence of a "capitalist class." It cannot be for the sake of the propaganda value alone, since after all that has become known in the meantime, that must be quite worn away. Of course there are still some simple souls who let themselves be carried away by the hocus-pocus, such as the French industrialists who, after a visit to one of the show capitalists in Shanghai, were moved to exclaim that if the French Communists would follow the same policies as the Chinese Communists, they would have no objection to Communism. But in my view the leaders in Peking are too hardheaded to base their expectations on the illusions of a few simpletons.

Another reason might be that there are still eight so-called "bourgeois-democratic" parties in existence, recognized, at least formally, by the state. The existence of a "capitalist group" is ideologically consistent with the claim—which the Chinese, in contrast to their Soviet comrades, still maintain even today—that basic class differences exist in a socialist country. But this argument does not seem to me to be valid, either.

The deciding factor seems more likely to be the government's desire to retain qualified persons in the Chinese economy. There is still a widespread shortage of experienced staff, especially in the big concerns. The capitalists used at one time to occupy responsible positions and managed to attain success and wealth. They possess organizational and technical abilities which cannot be easily or quickly replaced. Why should the country refuse to use their advice and assistance, especially since the reins of control and decision are firmly in the hands of Party officials?

To me, therefore, it seems to be no coincidence that in the hour of need the projected ending of the "transitional phase" in the Chinese economy was postponed. The payment of "dividends" to the capitalists was to have come to an end in 1962. In other words, from then on they were to be left to their fate. It was thought that by this time it would be possible to dispense with their services and to rely on the abilities of the

Party officials. But following the catastrophic years of the Great Leap, the top men changed their minds. As I was told in Peking by the former Deputy Chairman of the State Planning Commission, Yung Lung-kwei, "the 5 per cent dividend payments to the remaining capitalists will certainly continue until the end of 1965. And we are still considering what is going to happen about this in 1966."

It is not only the relatively small group of former capitalists that are affected by this new "liberal policy." Much more important for getting the Chinese economy on its feet is the more tolerant attitude toward the large number of small businessmen and independent craftsmen. In March 1962 the Party decreed that private ownership in the trades and crafts was permitted, and that "for a long time to come it will have to coexist side by side with state cooperative small businesses and craft associations."

Trades and crafts have a long tradition in China. The skill of the Chinese craftsman and the business acumen of the Chinese tradesman are nothing less than proverbial. The function of the independent owner of a small business in so backward an economic structure, leaning so heavily on agriculture, has always been important. Naturally the Communists tried to combine the small businesses into cooperatives or even to nationalize them, just as they did in the case of the bigger concerns. Many a time it looked as if they were determined to get their way in this sector also and to find a new place for this vital component of the Chinese economy. "Use, economize, convert" was the motto in the first years of Communist rule.

Yet there are a number of signs to suggest that from the beginning the leaders trod more cautiously in their efforts to realize their aims in this sector than in other sectors of the economy. There are no figures of small independent businesses in China. Only once, in the summer of 1960, did the Chinese Minister of Trade, Yow I-lin, make an astonishing statement: he claimed that there were almost one million people running small private businesses in Peking alone. With this figure he meant all those who labored to earn their bread as independent artisans, coolies, rickshaw men and tradesmen.

There is little doubt that the new economic policies that have been in effect since 1962, which were intended to consolidate the entire economic structure, to bring about the smooth functioning of interdependent agencies and to create incentives, began to attach particular importance to this traditional sector of a solidly built structure. The slogan "We must walk on two legs" implies acknowledgment of the fact that in circumstances like China's no good can come of one-sided preferential treatment of certain areas of the economy, for example the industrial sector. This was shown clearly enough at the time the Communists thought agriculture could be neglected. Today agricultural policy stands at the head of the list. But this again should not mean ignoring other areas of the economy.

The view which now seems to be taken in Peking is that craftsmen and tradesmen also have a contribution to make to industrialization. It has now become urgent to foster and encourage them, because economic progress in China can only be achieved on the broadest possible basis of production, embracing every facet of manufacture and service. A leading economics official told me in Peking, "The Soviet revisionists nowadays reproach us for neglecting the building up of heavy industry and thus offending against the canons of socialism. That is wrong. It is wrong because these comrades do not grasp the special problems of this country. We have learned to regard economic development as a single whole. With an enormous population like ours we cannot afford economic disproportion. All, and I mean *all*, sectors of our economy must be developed, even if not at the same rate."

The meaning of the formula "development of all sectors of the economy" becomes clear to anyone who travels about China. One meets these independent artisans everywhere, especially in the interior, in their little stalls and in the markets, always busy, always working, the pinmakers, the basket weavers, the toymakers and the stocking makers. (A stocking maker in

Changsha, the capital of Hunan Province, told me that he produces one woolen sock an hour on his primitive machine.) The whole colorful spectrum of traditional Chinese manual skill is represented.

Even private producers of "luxury goods" can be found. In Shenyang I talked with two musical-instrument makers, who went around peddling their artistically made Chinese fiddles. In Chengchow, the capital of Honan Province, I discovered a young maker of picture frames right on the main square. He told me business was excellent. The peasants came in droves to have their family pictures, the portraits of uncles, nephews, aunts and grandmothers, framed. This enterprising young man was making more than half as much again as the average pay of a qualified skilled worker.

And then there are the hundreds of teashops still in private hands. In the evenings they are full to overflowing. Most of these places are sparsely furnished, with plain unvarnished tables and benches. Compared with the much better furnished cooperative-controlled restaurants and cafes they show up very badly. Nevertheless, this is where the ordinary man in the streets feels at ease. The owners are friendly people, who obviously get a great deal of pleasure out of a visit from a foreigner, probably because of the publicity this gives their place. I never heard any complaints, but in the faces of many a small businessman was written the anxious question of how long the state of "general encouragement of the economy," especially official permission to run a private business, would last. Everyone seemed to realize that the Communist leaders in China will tolerate no institution for long if it conflicts with their ideological concepts.

Industrialization in the Service of Agriculture

My observations concerning the transformation in the People's Communes and the official tolerance toward private businesses might lead to the conclusion that the Communist regime had suddenly become anxious to encourage consumption. Not only are there more provisions on the market today than in previous years, not only has the state plan allowed for the allocation of raw materials for artisan businesses for the first time in the history of Chinese Communism, but the consumer-goods industries have gained themselves a respectable position in the country's total production.

One of the sporadic statistical statements at the end of 1964 said that the value of the forty-one most important types of light industrial products had increased by 15 per cent over 1963. Not only had the volume been increased, but new production methods had made possible a more varied selection. Man-made fibers now play an important part in the textile industry and the improved cotton harvests of recent years also created more favorable conditions in the clothing industry. The government proudly announced in the fall of 1963 that the allocation of clothing material could now be trebled, so that the annual ration per person is now four yards. Plastic products now provide splashes of glowing color in the showcases in all the Chinese department stores. Plastic sandals in many different shades are very fashionable and foam rubber for linings for winter clothes is regarded as a sign of technical progress.

However, the dominant theme of Chinese economic planning is still the expansion of all sectors of heavy industry. All the measures which seem to indicate an intention to increase consumption are only a means to an end. They were urgently necessary in order to get rid of the unfortunate psychological effects of the failure of the Great Leap and to provide material incentives for the workers and peasants, so that they would set to work again more cheerfully and more enthusiastically. Another reason why the stabilization of agriculture and the encouragement of light industry were also necessary was to obtain the means essential for the main target—industrialization. Once again, as in the first decade of Communist rule in China, light industries principally concerned with processing agricultural raw materials must now bear the burden of a "socialist accumulation of capital," even though this task has been made more difficult by the fact that the prices of agricultural products have been increased.

This manipulation of the consumer-goods sector is intended to secure the development of heavy industry, still the fetish of every Communist official, and likely to remain so. An extremely significant sign of a new and more realistic economic understanding, on the other hand, is the obvious shift in the current aim of Chinese heavy industry, which can be best described in the words of a leading Chinese economist: "A few years ago heavy industry was being developed for the sole purpose of serving heavy industry. Today it has been put into the service of agriculture."

Only a general outline can be given of the way in which industrial policies have changed in recent years. As in almost all other sectors, no figures have been published for this sector. Even the targets of the Third Five Year Plan, which was supposed to be starting up in 1963, have never been published. In Peking, I was assured in responsible quarters that the plan was "not yet finally settled." But the basic outlines were completely in accordance with the new principle of developing all sections of the economy at the same time, the principal result of which would be that more attention would be paid to agriculture than had been paid in the past.

This does not only apply to investment in the agricultural sector. No less profound has been the realization that planning from year to year can be done only on the basis of the probable harvest yields. The three bitter years of natural catastrophe forced the planners to realize just how much the whole of China's economic position depends on agricultural output. The slogan "Agriculture is the basis of our economy" is therefore no empty formula. The leaders have learned their lesson and are now more cautious. They no longer publish grandiloquent target figures which may be made to look foolish because of unforeseen natural disasters in the following year or two.

As a result, Western experts have had to fall back on "academic estimates" of the figures for the new course in industrial policy. As far as the extent of investment is concerned, there can now be no doubt that there was "overinvestment" during the Great Leap years. Even if there had been no natural disasters or if the original concept of the People's Communes had not turned out to be a failure, it is probable that it would still have been necessary to alter the overoptimistic investment policies of that time. It transpired that between 1958 and 1960 some important industrial sectors had fed the economy with too many capital goods, too fast, and that industry and agriculture had been unable to absorb them profitably under the conditions existing at the time. The precipitate nature of the investment policy bore no fruit and merely represented a waste of resources.

The leaders drew the conclusions from all this. During the First Five Year Plan (1953–57) capital investment, according to official statements, amounted to an average of 23 per cent of the annual gross national product. American economic experts estimated an investment ratio of 28.8 per cent in 1958, 35.9 per cent and no less than 43.7 per cent in 1960. In the following years, however, the investment ratio decreased rapidly to 21.6 per cent in 1961 and 21.3 per cent in 1962. In 1963 it is believed to have fallen even more and to have been in the neighborhood of 18 per cent; and it is estimated that the industrial investment ratio for 1964 will also prove to be far below the standard of the fifties.

Heavy industrial output followed a similar pattern. For example, official figures gave the total 1957 steel production—the yardstick of successful industrialization in all developing countries—as 5.35 million tons. In 1958 it was 11 million tons, in 1959 13.35 million tons and in 1960 it rose to 18.5 million tons. (None of the figures given here includes the quantities produced by the "miniature furnace process.") But by the summer of 1959 the Chinese steel production target for 1962 had already been drastically revised and the target figure was now only 12 million tons. Western experts are agreed that this target was not reached and today the annual Chinese steel production is estimated to be from 8 to 10 million tons. Official agencies in Peking decline to give any information, and in the steelworks both at Anshan and Wuhan senior officials expressly told me that they were not allowed to give foreign visitors any figures of the total production of their steelworks.

In general, therefore, it can be said that in 1965 the whole of Chinese heavy industry, except for the chemical industry, has failed to attain the level of 1958–60. This much is indirectly admitted in the statement that efforts are to be devoted not so much to quantity as to quality and variety. It is not the level of production which is now important, it is said, but variation in production for the purpose of furthering technical development and achieving economic self-sufficiency.

Admittedly, this cutting back of heavy industrial production does not by any means signify that the lion's share of the state budget will not find its way into this sector of the economy, or that no new factories, equipped with the latest plant and manufacturing new products, will be built. The situation is rather that the Chinese Communists' industrialization policies are now guided by criteria which have radically shifted the emphasis in "socialist construction." Smaller resources are to be used but used more profitably. Apart from the munitions industry—which no foreigner is allowed to see but which can be assumed to consume considerable amounts of capital, particularly now that the Chinese have been promoted to the exclusive circle of atomic powers—heavy industry is being largely employed to modernize and rationalize agriculture. Fertilizers, irrigation, mechanization, electrification and the improvement of transport and distribution, these have been the Party's demands for 1964 and 1965. And it is intended that these shall not remain merely a matter of fine words. All over the country there are innumerable indications that these propaganda demands and targets will in fact be realized.

Visits to factories and plants in China give a clear indication that industrial expansion has been generally slowed down. Everywhere I went I came across immobilized plants, half-finished

buildings and installations, and in the factories which were
working I saw the occasional department in which the machines
had been stopped or which was not working to full capacity. I
was given a number of reasons for this—for example, that it
was the consequence of the exodus of Soviet specialist advisers
in 1960 and the cutting off of Soviet economic aid, both of which
are still keenly felt in China. Then there is the universal shortage
of trained staff, engineers, specialists and supervisory staff. Even
newly constructed factories in China give the visitor an impression of improvisation. Unskilled handling also causes an enormous amount of wear and tear. Technical knowledge and understanding are still at a low level.

Many factory directors and engineers make no attempt to
disguise these things from the foreign visitor. Thus the director
of a chemical plant near Canton asked me at the beginning of
my tour not to be too critical. "The factory was only built last
year," he said, "but in comparison with similar factories in West
Germany we are at least twenty years behind. And don't be
surprised at the numbers of workers. What we need two thousand
hands to do, you would accomplish with a quarter of that number."

In my opinion, however, the reason for the slowing down of
industrial development is the realization that large-scale "investment leaps," such as were once tried out, do not pay. On the
same level is the recognition of the devastating results that can
also flow from a large-scale drain of agricultural workers away
from the land. In 1958 alone the number of workers in industry
almost trebled, going from 7.9 million to 23.4 million, in a very
short space of time. Such an abrupt shift in the components of
the economic structure could not help but have harmful consequences, particularly for agriculture. At all events these consequences were quite out of proportion to the gain in economic
efficiency.

This slowing down does not, however, apply to the sectors of
industry directly or indirectly serving agriculture. The factories
in this field are not only working to capacity but they are also

being expanded with fanatical energy. These are chiefly the firms producing agricultural machinery and farm implements, plant for irrigation projects, pumps, generators, oil refineries, vehicles such as carts or mechanical rickshaws, artificial fertilizers and insecticides.

The picture I was able to put together from my personal observations during visits to industrial plants and installations in China is reflected in the latest estimates of production drawn up by Western economic experts. The present situation in steel production has already been mentioned. It has fallen considerably in recent years. It is true that at the beginning of 1965 it was announced that steel production targets were to be raised, but I cannot help thinking that what was meant was that there was to be a cautious increase in production to correspond to the gradual rise in demand within the general framework of Chinese economic policy. This is all the easier to do in that particularly in this sector of heavy industry there is a good deal of unused capacity, which means that relatively small amounts would have to be invested. At any rate, a new Great Leap is unlikely for the present.

On the other hand there has been a significant increase in those branches of industry which have come to fore as a result of the new "two legs" policy being pursued since 1962. The production of electric power, for example, is estimated to have been thirty-two billion kwh in 1964, compared with just under twenty billion kwh in 1963. Chinese crude-oil production is estimated at six to seven million tons in 1964 as against 1.5 million tons in 1957. In this sector, incidentally, there has emerged a picture of steady increase. In 1958 production was 2.2 million tons, in 1960 4.5 million, 1962 5.3 million and in 1963 5.9 million tons.

Cement production in 1964 is estimated at 8 million tons compared with 6.8 million tons in 1957. The production of artificial fertilizers rose from 3.4 to an estimated 3.6 million tons, whereas in 1957 the figure was not even a million tons. Twenty to twenty-five thousand trucks were built in 1964 as against seventy-five hundred in 1957.

In contrast to these figures, coal production was less than 220 million tons, which means that the level of production has been practically unaltered since 1961, considerably below the figures for 1958–60. In 1958, for example, 425 million tons of coal alone are reported to have been produced in China.

In the fall of 1965 the Soviets also published estimates of Chinese industrial production. The Soviet figures, given in the *Great Encyclopedia Year Book* for 1965, ran generally parallel to the estimates of Western experts. The Soviets assessed Chinese steel production in 1964, for example, at 9.5 million tons, coal production at 209 million tons, crude-oil production at 8.4 million tons and electricity production at 55 billion kwh. The Soviets, too, conclude that the Chinese economy has not yet fully recovered from the deleterious consequences of the Great Leap.

On the whole, the observations and estimates of Western- and Eastern-bloc experts lead to the conclusion that Peking has learned much from the failure of the Great Leap. There seems to be a much clearer understanding than before that although China's "socialist construction" demands industrialization, the key to the realization of the plans for industrialization lies in putting agriculture back on its feet and encouraging its advancement.

Chapter 12

TRADE WITH THE WEST

The chief obstacle in the way of a speedy and systematic expansion of the Chinese economy is lack of capital. The country's efforts to make technical progress and achieve a higher standard of living are also impeded by the want of any kind of economic assistance from abroad. What the Chinese are trying to do is to lift themselves out of the morass by their own pigtails, so to speak. Not very long ago they were still hoping that close economic collaboration with their political and ideological allies would bring them some relief; therefore, nothing could have caused them profounder bitterness and disappointment than the abrupt breaking off of relations between China and her erstwhile allies.

In the Chinese capital they will not easily forget the scenes that took place in the Peking railroad station in the summer of 1960. The last days of July and the first days of August saw one special train after another roll into the vast, hectically bustling new station, where groups of Soviet specialists and their families waited on the platforms. Their suitcases and great bundles indicated a long journey ahead of them. Overnight, Moscow had ordered them to leave China, and this was the start of the exodus of the Soviet advisers. There was no ceremonial background of farewell speeches or demonstrations of friendship, such as were at one time customary among Communist brothers on these occasions. The events of those days were the first visible sign that there had been a change in Sino-Soviet relations. There were some official attempts to explain the departure of the Soviet specialists by putting it down to the expiration of the agreements on technical assistance, but experienced observers were already beginning to suspect that it might have another, deeper reason, and that it would produce unforeseeable effects in the future.

Until these memorable events took place it had appeared that Sino-Soviet collaboration was running without a flaw. Less than four years earlier, at the 8th Party Congress of the Chinese Communist Party, Anastas Mikoyan had emphatically declared: "Never in this world have there been such friendly relations as those that now exist between our peoples and our two mighty parties. With our assistance China will pass through the intermediate stages of economic development and will rise from being the technically most backward country to being the most technically developed country, and will attain the pinnacle of scientific and technical progress."

In many respects Mikoyan's thesis seemed near to being realized. The Soviet Union granted China credits, only two of which were officially announced, one of 300 million dollars at the beginning of 1950 and one of 130 million in October 1954. Short-term credits granted up to 1960 were estimated by Western experts at one billion dollars, but a statement in July 1957 by the Chinese Finance Minister, Li Hsin-nien, in which he gave the total amount of Soviet credits as 2.25 billion dollars, indicated that the real figure was much higher. All the economic aid agreements between Moscow and Peking, however, explicitly laid down that the Chinese government were to repay their obligations under the agreements "by the delivery of goods."

Moscow was also generous in the provision of technical assistance. Between 1949 and 1958, 10,800 Soviet technicians were sent to China, while in the same period the Chinese sent eight thousand engineers and ten thousand students to the Soviet Union for training. Western experts have assessed the equivalent cash value of this form of Soviet assistance at 460 million dollars.

Under these circumstances it was natural that China's foreign trade should have a bias toward the Soviet Union. In 1956 about 80 per cent of all China's foreign trade was with the Communist bloc, 70 per cent of that amount being with the Soviet Union alone. In 1959, according to her own statistics, the Soviets delivered to China machinery and industrial equipment to the value of 2.9 billion rubles, which means that in that year more than half, namely 51.2 per cent, of the entire Soviet export of machinery were delivered to China. There was a similar situation with regard to the delivery of complete industrial plants. In 1958 China received Soviet plants and installations worth 660 million rubles, whereas the Soviet satellites received less than a third of that, namely, 210 million rubles' worth. Totaling the value of all the capital goods delivered to China by the Soviet Union between 1950 and 1959, one arrives at a sum of ten billion rubles for machines and equipment and five billion for complete industrial plants. All of this makes it clear that in the first ten years of its existence, the Chinese People's Republic maneuvered itself into a position of complete dependence on the Soviet Union.

The picture has changed since 1960, and the withdrawal of the Soviet technicians is not the only manifestation of it. The level of trade between the Soviet Union and China declined from year to year. In 1962 the volume sank to 675 million rubles. In 1963 imports and exports amounted to 540 million rubles and in 1964 only 404 million rubles, Chinese imports from the Soviet Union in this latter year reaching a new low of only 122 million rubles. This compares with the volume of trade in the heyday of Sino-Soviet cooperation in 1959, when it amounted to almost two billion rubles. In considering this, it must be borne in mind that for years the Chinese trade balance had already been showing a deficit vis-à-vis the Soviet Union. The value of Soviet machinery and equipment delivered to China in 1962 had declined to less than twenty-five million rubles as against 538 million rubles in 1958. It was tempting to think that the main reason for this development was China's unfavorable economic situation in these years. The country was simply unable to keep up with its export obligations to the Soviets and their satellites. In 1961, for example, the Soviets found themselves obliged to grant the Chinese a five-year moratorium in respect of 288 million dollars' worth of debts which had accumulated in 1960 alone as a result of China's failure to deliver her due quota of agricultural products.

However, we now know that the main reason for the deterioration in Sino-Soviet economic relations was the intensification of the political and ideological conflict between Moscow and Peking. This has been openly admitted by both sides since 1963, each side trying to put the blame on the other. In their Open Letter of July 14, 1963, the Soviets declared that they had fairly and energetically done all they could to provide China with economic assistance. A total of 198 industrial plants had been put up by the Soviets in the course of their collaboration. The Chinese also had the Soviets to thank for the establishment of their automobile, tractor and aircraft industries. Twenty-one thousand scientific and technical documents for planned projects and fourteen hundred blueprints for large-scale industrial complexes had been handed over to the Chinese. Despite this generous assistance, the Chinese People's Republic had suddenly and unilaterally begun to cut down economic and trade relations with the Soviet Union and the other Communist states.

The Chinese reply to this in December of the same year was contained in a detailed exposition giving exactly the opposite picture. In July 1960, according to them, the Soviets had begun to put the Chinese under pressure. All the Soviet economic experts—at that time 1390 in number—had been withdrawn from China, 343 agreements and contracts were revoked and 257 joint economic and scientific projects canceled. Thereafter the Soviets had begun to make extensive cuts in their deliveries of capital goods and had "recommended" their Eastern European satellites to do the same. Moscow's actions had caused China great losses. They had not only seriously imperiled the original plan for the development of the Chinese economy: they had ruined it.

All the indications suggest that the Chinese arguments were

the more credible of the two. It must be regarded as extremely unlikely that China would feel herself impelled to take foolhardy measures against her most devoted trading partner just at a time when the regime was in the middle of a catastrophic domestic economic crisis.

The Chinese leaders have learned their lesson from their experiences with the Soviets. The conclusion has been repeatedly made clear in recent years: China is determined to make herself independent of the Soviet Union. The present state of the conflict between the two countries makes it seem unlikely that there will again be any extensive economic collaboration between them in the foreseeable future. The dissolution of the association between China and the economic community of the Eastern bloc therefore automatically paves the way for an intensification of China's relations with the industrialized countries of the West.

The Chinese leaders have not failed to make known their interest in increased trade with the West. Contacts with Western merchants and business concerns have been considerably strengthened in the last few years. The stream of trade delegations traveling to Peking is unending. The Chinese government's efforts were also reflected in the outward appearance of the traditional Chinese trade fair in Canton. Western businessmen who have been visiting the Canton Fair for years were all agreed that it has changed its complexion. The Chinese are adapting themselves to the foreign visitor. In contrast to the practice in former years, there is no offensive political agitation. The usual banners with such inscriptions as "Down with American Imperialism!" have disappeared from the streets. There is a much more relaxed atmosphere in the hotels in which the foreigners stay. The officials are friendly. Everything possible is done to satisfy the foreign businessman.

However, all the exterior trappings and all the intensive friendliness cannot alter the fact that for years to come China's trade with the West will be on a very limited scale. The widespread belief that China represents an enormous market for the highly industrialized countries of the West is as much of an illusion as was the vision many people used to have at one time of a "gigantic Russian market." The "China market" had become something of a beautiful dream for the West, particularly in the last few years. The prospect of suddenly gaining access to 700 million consumers is intoxicating.

There is occasionally a temptation to ignore the realities of life, as in the famous and macabre case of the German who had a small business making metal fittings for coffins. He had worked out that ten to fifteen million people must die in China every year. If he could succeed in getting even a fraction of the Chinese market in coffin fittings, he would be set up for life. But he had overlooked one little detail: a Chinese coffin does not have metal fittings. In any event, wood is so scarce in China that the supply cannot possibly keep up with the demand. But even if neither of these difficulties had stood in the way, very few Chinese could afford the luxury of a coffin with stainless-steel fittings brought all the way from West Germany. Finally, even if they could, the authorities in Peking would be very unlikely to agree to release precious hard currency for the purchase of coffin fittings.

China is the epitome of the developing country and will be so for many years yet. Not only are the basic requirements for extensive trade completely lacking, but the structure and methods of Communist economic policies also stand in the way. There can hardly be a more convincing demonstration of the unhopeful outlook for a great "China market" than the figures of total Chinese foreign trade for 1962—about two billion dollars. This means that in 1962 a country as small as Norway, with 2.3 billion dollars, had a bigger volume of foreign trade than China, and Switzerland, with 5.4 billion dollars, more than two and a half times as much.

There has not been much improvement in subsequent years, either. Western experts estimate the volume of China's total foreign trade in 1964 at not quite three billion dollars, almost exactly what it was in 1957. No other country in the world with such low import and export figures has given rise to so much excitement in regard to foreign-trade possibilities as China has.

The main problem with regard to trade with China is still the same—how can China pay for imports from the West? The country's reserves of foreign exchange have been seriously depleted by the large-scale purchases of wheat from Canada and Australia during the past few years and her gold and silver reserves are not thought to be high. The only possible solution, therefore, is payment in kind. For this purpose there are first of all China's traditional exports such as bristles, feathers, hair, powdered egg, soya beans, tung oil, silk and furs. Then there are a few more interesting export commodities which might more readily find buyers in Japan and the West: coal and various ores, including in particular tungsten and a few other nonferrous metal ores, together with certain chemical products. These used to go almost exclusively to the countries of the Communist bloc, but since the paralysis in Sino-Soviet trade relations they would be available to the West in greater quantities.

Meanwhile the Chinese are trying other methods to obtain the money to cover their foreign-currency requirements. They are steadily increasing the number of different export commodities, the main weight being laid on exports to other developing countries. For example, the Chinese metal-processing and steel industries are providing serious competition in Southeast Asia. China has been exporting sheet steel, steel wire and finished metal products to the countries bordering Southeast Asia for some time. Cement and coal go to Pakistan and freight cars to Ceylon. Cotton piece goods are also being increasingly bought by the developing countries. The Chinese are also skillfully trying to find markets for simple equipment produced by Chinese small industries and handicrafts. A Chinese-made wire-drawing machine, for example, is selling well in the African countries. Increasing attempts are being made to build up trade in consumer goods. The British crown colony of Hong Kong is another source of foreign currency which is generally underestimated.

Finally there is a further possibility which should not be left out of account. The visits paid by Chinese trade delegations to African countries suggest that the Chinese intend to try to start up three-cornered trade. Chinese products are already being bought in considerable quantities in the North African countries of the franc zone—one has only to think of the enormous quantities of green tea being exported to Morocco. In return, the African countries send China capital goods which they have acquired through their own trade with Western European markets. The result is that the Chinese get what they want without having to dip into their currency reserves.

Still, even if China can be expected to find a variety of ways in which to expand her trade with the West, the fact remains that the West cannot reckon on finding huge markets in China for many years yet. This situation could only be changed if the Western countries were willing to grant China generous credits. The prospects of this are remote, although the Chinese have been able to arrange favorable terms on a few occasions in recent years. For example the agreement with the Japanese for the delivery of a synthetic-textile plant worth twenty million dollars contained the following payment terms: 10 per cent on the conclusion of the agreement, 15 per cent on shipment of the plant and the remaining 75 per cent in five annual installments at 6 per cent interest. An Italian firm concluded a contract to supply two artificial fertilizer plants, with a capacity of 300 thousand tons a year, worth twenty million dollars. In this case it was agreed that payment should be at the rate of 20 per cent down and the rest in ten six-monthly payments beginning with each part shipment.

It will therefore be some good time before the West's trade with China can consist of anything more than isolated profitable contracts. Moreover, China's new domestic economic course is reflected in her foreign trade. The government is placing contracts in accordance with a clearly recognizable program of priorities designed to further the restoration to health of agriculture, directly or indirectly. Grain imports still head the list, amounting in 1964 to five million tons. I was told in Peking, however, that the Chinese government did not intend to go on importing grain forever; but the grain imports for 1965 and 1966 have already been planned for. Fertilizer and synthetic-fiber plants (the latter to help to overcome the difficulties in the textile supply) and crude-oil processing installations (to help ease the transport difficulties) are further priority categories in the Chinese import program.

That these imports can go only a small way to improving China's total economic situation, at least for the present, is demonstrated by the example of fertilizer production. At the end of 1963 the Chinese bought from the West three fertilizer plants at short intervals. These have a combined capacity of 1.2 million tons a year, which brings the total annual production of artificial fertilizer to almost four million tons a year. But the country's total requirements per year are twenty to thirty million tons. It would therefore be advisable to make a clear distinction between illusion and reality.

There is no doubt that economically speaking China has pulled up a great deal in the last few years. This, following the bitter period of political miscalculations, is certainly a success. In three successive years the harvests were sufficiently good to keep pace with the increase in the population. Dangerous scarcities in various areas have been reduced or, in some cases, completely eliminated. However, the improvement in the basic food supply and the gradual increase in the production of urgently needed raw materials and capital goods is only marginal. The results so far are not sufficient to permit the setting of any spectacular targets. The leaders have decided that they must be content with achieving the status of a modern industrialized country, traveling at a modest pace and taking a long time to reach it. The people will have to resign themselves to the prospect of slow progress.

Peking's new economic policies have taken on a more rational complexion, and the Communist planners have become more realistic. However, it should not be overlooked that in addition to the negative consequences of the Great Leap there were also some positive effects. There can be no doubt that disciplined organization and the planned use of masses of workers played a great part in warding off absolute disaster in the catastrophic years. Not only that, but self-sufficient economic units have been created all over the country, able to operate intelligently and rationally to meet the demands of the prevailing situation.

At the same time, there can equally be no doubt that the colossal problems of the world's greatest underdeveloped country are still there. They can be solved only if, above all, there is a dynamic and successful population policy to rid the country of its continual food supply difficulties and if the leaders can succeed in gradually increasing productivity and releasing both material and human resources for industrialization in the measurable future. When this stage is reached, then the Chinese people, with their industriousness, their toughness, their pragmatic sense and their natural intelligence, will be able to look forward to an economic expansion that will probably equal what the Japanese have achieved over the last ten or twenty years. But it will take years, perhaps generations, to reach it.

And there is always the possibility that the leaders, driven by impatience and the thirst for action, may again be moved to take violent measures, to do another about-face, even at the risk of having to go through another fiasco like the Great Leap and turning back the clock for years to come.

Chapter 13

EDUCATION IN THE SERVICE
OF THE REVOLUTION

China's younger generation is a generation of readers
and students. On warm summer evenings thousands of young
people sit in rows under the great street lights along the Changan
Boulevard in Peking reading, studying or discussing. During the
great parades on May First or the National Day on October
First, they make use of the long waits before the parades to read
books and pamphlets. All over the country, even in the smaller
towns, there are crudely built reading rooms. Magazines, illustrated papers and comic books (identical with the American
variety, except that the heroes are brave soldiers of the Red
Army or virtuous Party functionaries and the villains are capitalists or American imperialists) are displayed on sloping boards,
in front of which the hordes of eager bookworms spend hours,
sitting on narrow benches.

In the city center of Loyang, among food stalls and tiny
restaurants that filled the narrow streets with strange aromas,
shortly after midnight I came across an open-air reading room,
in which a couple of dozen tireless seekers after enlightenment
were still reading away, even at this hour. In the factories one
sees the workers sunk in technical textbooks during their meal
breaks. The parks and gardens are dotted with school children
and students, all with their noses buried in books. I heard in
Peking that the Party had decreed that there was to be less read-

ing in houses and apartments after dusk, because for a long time now only low-powered bulbs (twenty to thirty watts) have been allowed in living quarters, and it has been found that there is widespread eyestrain among young people.

One of the undeniably most impressive achievements of the Communist regime is the way in which they have attacked the problem of illiteracy. As recently as 1949 it was estimated that about 90 per cent of the country population and 70 per cent of the town dwellers could neither read nor write. Nine out of every ten Chinese were illiterate at that time. Within the space of fifteen years, these figures have been reduced to about 60 per cent illiterates in the country districts and 20 per cent in the towns. Among the children, at least in the larger towns, illiteracy is already a rarity.

This transformation is all the more remarkable in that every Chinese educational reform, Communist or not, has had to grapple with the special problem of the Chinese script. In the course of thousands of years there has evolved a system of forty to fifty thousand highly complicated and elegant characters, each of which may have a different meaning. In contrast to this multiplicity of characters and their connotations, standard spoken Chinese has only 470 syllabic sounds. A well-known curiosity is the syllable *li*, which may be written in a hundred different characters and has innumerable meanings. Even accepting that a knowledge of fifteen hundred characters is sufficient for an elementary understanding of the language (this total has now been made the standard figure in Chinese primary schools); and that with a knowledge of three thousand characters (the standard for high school graduates) a man will have attained a considerable educational level; there can be no gainsaying the very great burden the script represents for education in a modern world. It is not only that the expenditure of time and energy is a hindrance but it also causes a one-sided development of the power of memory at the cost of reasoning power.

No Romanization of the Script Yet

People had been thinking about reforming the language and the script long before the Communists came. The first proposal was that one universal spoken language should be used, Mandarin, the tongue spoken in Peking. Then there were attempts after World War I to create a phonetic script and particularly the possibility of using the Roman alphabet, an idea which the Communists enthusiastically took up when they came to power. In 1956 Peking officially announced the introduction of Roman script in place of Chinese characters and started a campaign to popularize this. But this quietly folded up, like so many other things, and during my travels I never got the impression that anyone was interested in the reforms which were being so wordily propagated only a few years before.

There are two main reasons for the Party's failure to press on with this important step. The first is a very practical one. There are a large number of dialects in China, some of them so different from the others that many Chinese have difficulty in understanding their compatriots from other parts of the country. The written characters, on the other hand, being symbols and not bound to any particular language, can be understood by anyone who can read at all. This means that the romanization of the script could be successfully carried through only if there were no longer any dialects or if every Chinese also spoke Mandarin without accent. But it will be a long time before this comes about—"some generations at least," as a philologist told me in Peking.

The second reason was the opposition of the nationally conscious Chinese intellectuals, who felt that the introduction of the Roman alphabet would represent not only a complete break with their ancient Chinese heritage but also an almost intolerable impoverishment of the language and of China's literary tradition. The critics pointed out that the many different possible meanings of the individual syllables, while they were recognizable in the Chinese characters, would no longer be distinguishable once the script had been romanized, and that this would result in the disappearance from the language of about three-quarters of the Chinese vocabulary. All the classical literature and even some of the simpler modern works would have to go completely, since there would be no way of transposing them into the new script. This argument may well have carried weight, especially in recent years, when there has been a visible return of a kind of Chinese nationalism. At all events, the emphasis today is no longer on romanizing of the script but on the teaching of Mandarin and the possibility of simplifying the Chinese characters. "The simplifying of the characters is a better solution than romanization," an official frankly told me in South China.

Thus for the foreseeable future the Chinese educational system will continue to labor under the handicap of the strange difficulties of language and script. This means increased exertions by school children and students, which must have its effect on the level and quality of education in comparison with peoples whose phonetic scripts make it easier for them. But perhaps this will prove not to be so serious after all. In the course of their long history the Chinese people have time and again demonstrated their capacity for overcoming very great difficulties by remarkable mental and technical efforts. What is more important is the Communists' educational policy, which a foreigner who had lived in Peking for years told me must result in "the breeding of a race of semiliterate illiterates."

To create "the unity of theory and practice" is part of the general line of all Communist educational policy. Among the basic components of the educational program are political indoctrination, propaganda and agitation. Any method of influencing the consciousness of the young and inducing in them the particular manner of thinking and acting desired by the Party is justified. This principle has been particularly thoroughly applied in China. On top of this, the educational authorities have been making great efforts to realize the principle of making "a worker of every student and a student of every worker." This feature of Chinese instruction has evoked in the West a terrifying vision of a supertotalitarian educational system.

One Hundred Million Primary School Children

The peculiar features of the Communist educational system are least visible in the primary schools. It is true that here, too, the theoretical principle is that the aim of primary education is both to provide a general education and to create socialist consciousness. Political and ideological training and so-called "productive manual work" by the children are supposed to help reinforce these two basic requirements, but in general the main aim in fact is to give the children as broad a basic education as possible. In practice political education takes second place. Accordingly the defects in the Chinese primary educational system arise more from circumstances ascribable to natural developments and are much less the consequences of a one-sided, party-political training program.

Every primary school I visited in China presented the same picture. During the recesses, crowds of children pour out of every exit in the standardized school building: the throng seems unending. A sea of shouting, screaming, laughing and playing children takes over the playgrounds. There is a chaotic confusion which nobody seems able to control. In the classrooms, on the other hand, the children sit obedient at their desks, packed closely together, with thoughtful and attentive expressions. Most of them wear the red neckerchief of the Pioneers, indicating their membership of the Communist youth organization. Many have badges sewn on their left arms to denote the ranks they have attained. But there are also a good number, even in the larger towns like Shanghai and Peking, who sit among the "party adherents" wearing neither neckerchiefs nor badges. In the midst of these masses of primary school children the teachers look like lonely oases of color in the desert sands. Most of these teachers are remarkably young, often quickly trained; and in many a conversation I had with them I was surprised to find how low their educational level was.

Nor are appearances deceiving. The Chinese primary schools are ailing as a result of the staggering number of pupils, for whom there are far too few schools, too small and with much too few teachers. Whereas in 1960, according to official figures, ninety-one million children were attending primary schools; today it is estimated that the total has passed the hundred million mark. (These figures probably include the adult beginners who are trying to learn to read and write in spite of their age.)

Before the Communists took over, China was extraordinarily badly off for schools. It was impossible, within the space of fifteen years, to create as if by the wave of a hand the technical preconditions and the requisite teaching staffs to deal with the masses of those who were—quite rightly—being encouraged to attend the primary schools. The regime committed some unforgivable blunders in the early years. The resources provided for education were too scanty and priority was given not to the training of teaching staffs but to engineers and technicians. In the spring of 1952 the Dean of Peking University complained that at the existing rate of teacher training, it would take more than a thousand years to train the teaching staff needed in China in the next five years.

As in many other fields, lessons were learned from the unfortunate consequences of the overhasty, narrow, ideologically based training program of the first ten years. Nowadays considerably more attention is being paid to primary school education, and a school building program is being energetically pushed through. Teacher training for both primary and high school teachers is being given priority. With some 35 per cent of all the students in China taking this training, it is the largest single subject being studied. Official statistics showed that in 1961 there were three million university lecturers and teachers to serve the needs of the hundred million students and school children in the universities, high schools and primary schools. In

1964 the total of primary school teachers alone was 2.6 million.

The necessity to find more money for education also explains the astonishing fact that in China fees are charged for school attendance and textbooks, exercise books, etc., must be paid for. Actually, the fees parents are charged for education and textbooks are not very high: in the Peking primary schools, for example, the education fee is five yuan (a little over two dollars) a year. Families with many children are exempt. Stationery and other aids are also very cheap. An exercise book, for example, costs ten *fen* (one tenth of one yuan).

In spite of this, I was told, applications for exemption from fees overwhelm the school administrations and overload the teaching staffs with ticklish bureaucratic tasks. When I pointed out to the headmaster of one primary school that in the "exploiting capitalist countries" education was free and in many cases books and other aids were also supplied free of charge, his reply was, "One day we shall reach that stage, too. We are still too poor. We need the money for construction."

In Peking I visited a primary school in a newly built workers' settlement. This was a model school, I am sure, and one that cannot be regarded as typical. But as against that it can be regarded as all the more characteristic of the regime's current educational policies. Although the principal began by explaining that in his school also education must serve the "aims of the proletariat," the school curriculum put the greatest emphasis on the provision of a broad general education. The timetable contained no periods for "political instruction." "We instruct the children in political patriotism in the course of general education," the principal explained. The real political and ideological training is almost invariably given outside the school.

For example, the classes are taken on regular excursions to "places of work" such as factories and agricultural complexes, and the program also includes visits to museums and performances by the "revolutionary theater," or film shows. There there are the so-called "Pioneer Days." "On these days our pupils make the personal acquaintance of heroic workers or revolutionary fighters from the old days," the principal said. "Recently we had a visit from a former Korean War volunteer. He told us how and why he had fought against the American imperialists. Then in the evening an old teacher told the story of his life, how his little brother starved in the Kuomintang years and how the landowner class exploited his poor family."

Topical subjects connected with international politics are also discussed. "We give talks on events in Vietnam and in the oppressed countries," the principal went on, "all in simple language the children can understand. Our aim is to get the young people to love the new social order and to learn to hate the old one."

The slogan about combining manual and mental work is not taken too seriously in the primary schools, at all events not in the schools I visited. The principal of the model school already mentioned, in Peking, explained that the children in the first three classes are excluded from any kind of "productive manual work" and are organized into singing and amateur dramatic groups and other musical and play groups instead. The children are not in fact compelled to do manual work until they reach their fourth year, the fourth to sixth years being the highest classes in the Chinese primary school. But even that work is fairly simple. The fourth-year children must put in one hour a week at productive work and the fifth- and sixth-years two hours a week. One school principal proudly informed me that in the previous school year his pupils had planted a thousand trees in the schoolyard. In the school's experimental gardens vegetables and flowers are grown. For the rest, the productive work consists of minor repair work and sweeping and cleaning out the school building.

Things are different in the junior and senior high schools, however. Here political instruction is a definite part of the curriculum, an important part, if only because the applicant's political attitude has a lot to do with his gaining admission to technical colleges and universities. Practical work, too, is given more attention here than in the primary schools. I often saw columns of students in the streets of the towns, each with a

blanket and a small bundle (out of which there regularly pro-
truded a bowl and toothbrush, as if to demonstrate that the
owner had learned his hygiene lessons well), on their way to the
next railroad station, to spend some time working in a People's
Commune. Here I would meet them again, in the fields, where
they would be very noisy and very busy and apparently finding
the whole thing great fun. On very many occasions I saw high
school students engaged on various kinds of heavy labor. Although banners on the site would proclaim their pioneer spirit
and their willingness to sacrifice everything in the "service of
socialist construction," they never looked like an army of down-
trodden slaves, and equally, I never had the feeling that they
were devoting themselves to the work in deadly earnest.

Why Must Young People Do "Productive Work"?

Whenever I asked what purpose this productive work by
children was supposed to serve, the reply would be that practical
manual work was necessary in order to give the young people
"the correct attitude toward work and working people." They
were to be educated to be conscious socialists, who would one
day be worthy to assume the mantle of the revolutionary proletariat.

But of course there is a more realistic intention than that behind these airy phrases. Since time immemorial the Chinese have
felt that once a man has joined the ranks of the "educated class"
he can never again soil his hands with common work. Anyone
who has been educated is destined for better things. The Communist educational methods are intended to counteract this feeling and to prevent the formation of an intellectual elite which
would despise the peasants and manual workers and thus bring
about the very conditions that stood in the way of both social
and national progress in the past.

Arrogance and presumption toward the common man are
widespread even among the Communist intellectuals. I was

given a small sample of this on my arrival at a hotel in a small
town in Central China. I was being looked after by a representative of the municipal administration and an interpreter, both
university graduates. We climbed the stairs to my room to the
accompaniment of a torrent of words from my companions, while
a little, fragile-looking, panting girl lugged my baggage along.
I could see, just as my official escorts could, that this small
person was about to break down under the load. But my "escorts"
seemed unconcerned. It was not until I hurriedly took the bags
from the girl that the two intellectuals in turn rushed to take
them from me with a thousand protests.

There is yet another argument which can also not be lightly
dismissed. In 1960 the Deputy Minister of Education, Tsui
Chung-yuan, stated in an interview that at the present rate of
expansion of the primary schools, it could be expected that there
would be more than fifty million students in the high schools
and universities in less than ten years. The result of this would
be not only that gigantic efforts would have to be made at the
personnel and technical level but also that practically fifty million pairs of hands which had previously been automatically
available for production, mainly in agriculture, would be missing.
From this undeniable fact the Minister concluded that in future
the idea of combining study and practical work would have to
put more rather than less emphasis on productive work if China's
economic development was not to be endangered.

In the event, developments did not take quite so drastic a
turn as the Deputy Minister of Education had tried to make out.
One reason was that the number of high schools did not increase
as rapidly as had been forecast in the optimistic years. Another
was that in the agricultural seasonal periods millions of people
from towns and schools are pressed into service to cope with the
work that has to be done. During the harvest I very often saw
whole armies of school children at work in the fields and on the
rice terraces. The millions of "unproductive consumers" must also
do their bit toward assuring the country's food supply. This in
fact became an urgent necessity in the years of the natural

disasters, when there was work for every single pair of hands to enable the existing damage to be kept as small as possible.

But even if logical and practical premises did play some part in evolving the idea of productive work for young people, the main purpose in the minds of the leaders was to use this method to educate the coming generation in the principles of revolutionary proletarian doctrine. The Party Secretary for Propaganda and Agitation in the Central Committee of the CPC, Lu Ting-yi, put it plainly and concisely in these words: "We believe that education must serve the policies of the proletariat; we believe education must be linked to productive work; and we believe that education must be directed by the Party."

The Crisis in the Chinese Universities

Great as the difficulties in the sphere of primary and high school education may be, there can be no doubt that the regime has made very considerable progress, especially when conditions in China are compared with those in other developing countries in Asia—India, for example. But the situation in the universities has caused the traders great anxiety in recent years. Things are in a bad way and the old dream of being able to overtake the great industrialized countries in this field has long since dissipated.

Since the Communists came to power there has been a very considerable transformation in university education. In the days of the Empire the only subjects a gentleman studied were literature, history and philosophy; and this belief still prevailed in Kuomintang times. Chiang Kai-shek was even then trying to persuade the younger generation that if China was to become a modern industrialized state her greatest need was for engineers and scientists. But his efforts had little success, and it was left to the Communists, with their forceful methods and gigantic campaigns of persuasion, to bring about a change. However, their inexperience and their fanaticism almost made them go too far the other way.

The Peking education officials uncritically took over the Soviet pattern of university education, which was directed to the production of technical specialists. They cut down the number of existing colleges and created new ones more suited to their preconceived ideas. Between 1950 and 1954 the number of universities providing general education was reduced from sixty-five to fourteen, their places being taken by thirty polytechnic colleges, thirty-nine teacher training institutes, twenty-nine academies of agriculture and forestry, twenty-nine medical schools, four law schools, six colleges of economics and finance, eight language schools, five art schools and five colleges of physical training. The highest academic organization was given a new title, the "Academy of Science," on the Soviet model, instead of the venerable "Academy of Fine Arts." A country whose idols had been philosophers and men of letters was now to be turned into a land of serious, practical and utilitarian technocrats.

One propaganda wave after another rolled across the country, informing the younger generation that only engineers and technicians were needed. Within a few years the first complaints began to be heard that no one was enrolling for arts courses any longer, although China needed lawyers, historians, philologists and political economists. The catchword that university education must primarily serve the needs of the state—in other words the building up of a technically advanced socialist industry—had taken effect. This was clearly shown by the last official statistics, published in 1957. At that time there were in all 434,600 students registered in the country's universities. Of these, more than 40 per cent were studying engineering, fewer than 20 per cent were taking teacher training and 12 per cent were studying medicine. The remainder, about a quarter of all the students, were divided among the other branches of science. From 1949 to 1960, 230,000 students graduated in engineering. An American expert calculated at the time that if this rate of progress continued, China would be able to turn out between 100,000 and 200,000 engineers a year from 1970 onward.

This general tendency continued in the universities for some good time. The number of colleges increased rapidly. In 1961 China boasted 61 universities, 271 polytechnic institutes, 174 teacher training colleges, 113 colleges of agriculture and forestry and 142 medical schools. Comparison with the 1954 figures given above is significant: absolute pride of place was given to the training of specialists merely for their utility, not for the sake of advancing knowledge.

The inevitable consequences made themselves apparent in a number of ways. In the science faculties, where the numbers of teaching staff were traditionally relatively low, the sudden enormous pressure meant that the standard of instruction was lowered. The establishing of the "Red Universities of Experts" in 1958, the first year of the Great Leap, made the situation much worse. These institutions, which were created by the hundred almost overnight in the provinces, were supposed, in addition to the normal daily work, to take Communist officials and turn them into agricultural and industrial experts in rapid-study courses. Instructors from the existing universities were detailed for this work and were thus completely overtaxed. However, the Party overrode the protests from the ranks of the teachers and professors, arguing that the industrialization projects had to be put into effect as quickly as possible on as wide a scale as possible. These "universities" remained more Red than educational.

Overspecialization also produced ill effects. Little attention was paid to general basic technical training. The cry was that specialists must be produced. It was not long, therefore, before there were specialists in a very wide range of subjects. But they could only be employed in the specific sectors for which they had been trained. A specialist in building railroad bridges, for example, knew only about building railroad bridges. If he was called upon to occupy a post requiring a knowledge of, say, ordinary railroad building, he was completely lost. The mobility of these trained engineers and technicians within their own fields was too low, a fact which made itself particularly felt after the collapse of the Great Leap, when so many of the advertised industrialization projects had to be abandoned.

By no means the least of the causes of this situation was the Party's belief that the important thing was the individual's revolutionary political attitude of mind, and that professional ability came second. The strain on the students resulting from their employment on productive work was a direct consequence of this belief. Political instruction and manual labor took first place in the training program and professional knowledge was pushed into the background. This had very unfortunate effects and it came to be realized that it was not sufficient merely to be Red, after all. Since 1961 university training has been developing in a more rational direction, one likely to be of more service to the country.

The change came in a speech made to students by the Deputy Premier, Chen Yi (also a member of the Chinese Politbureau and Foreign Minister), in Peking in August 1961. The political aspect should not always be the predominant one in all circumstances, he declared. It must take its place alongside technical and scientific knowledge. In the initial postliberation period it had been necessary to stress political education, but henceforth the emphasis must be on academic training. It was wrong for the technical colleges to spend too much time on political activity and manual work at the expense of technical training.

The impression made by Chen Yi's further remarks, in which he defended the politically inactive students, was nothing short of sensational. Too much distinction ought not to be made between "Red" and "white" technicians he said. Even those who did not bother much about politics could make a contribution to socialist reconstruction and they ought not to be criticized merely because they showed little interest in political matters.

Surprising as these remarks may sound, they still did not bring about any radical change in university teaching and the utilitarian character of the studies continued. Education officials repeatedly told me that university and technical college education had to be completely subordinated to the demands of national reconstruction. Professors could not simply be allowed to teach what they thought desirable or important, and there was a limit to the extent to which students could be allowed to choose the subjects that interested them most. The deciding factor was and would remain the state's intention to push ahead with industrialization with all possible speed. Basic research and study for its own sake were not allowed. What did China need systematic research for, when she had not even reached the world standard of academic knowledge and technical skill? This provides the key to the tasks which clearly lay ahead: only when the country possessed enough qualified engineers and technicians would it be possible to think about allowing education to take a different direction.

The shape of university training has accordingly not been changed. In Shenyang, the industrial citadel of Northeast China, I was given a detailed general view of the colleges there. The town has four academic institutions today, a university, a technical college, an agricultural college and a medical school, with a combined total of some twenty-three thousand students. Then there are twenty-four other technical and teacher training colleges with a total of ten thousand students. The purely utilitarian nature of Chinese higher education is obvious from these details.

Even if the aims and content of the studies have not changed, there have been some slight shifts in emphasis and methods. Political instruction and manual labor have been reduced. Much greater value is placed on academic standards than before. The Vice Chancellor of Peking University—still the most select in China, and mainly concerned with training teachers and research workers—told me that while the aim was still to produce "revolutionaries," at the same time "a higher standard of academic knowledge must definitely be attained." The proportion of time devoted to political instruction is now generally only about 10 per cent of the syllabus for the ten thousand students in the arts faculties (philosophy, political science, economics, law,

Chinese literature, history, library science, Slavonic studies, Western literature and Oriental languages) and in the natural sciences (mathematics, physics, chemistry, geology and geography, biology, geological physics and electrotechnology). The quota of productive work to be done in the factories or on People's Communes has been practically reduced to what can be managed during the vacations. The Vice Chancellor told me that the arts students do one and a half to two months of productive work a year, and the science students do even less, one to one and a half months.

These are first cautious steps on the road to urgently needed reforms in the universities. It is unlikely that the responsible authorities will have the courage to proceed more energetically. The government's gaze is still fixed on the vision of the rapid industrialization of the country, which they hope to attain by means of the largest possible number of specialists. Nonetheless, the number of those among the more intelligent Party functionaries who are pointing out the dangers of this course seems to be increasing. After the failure of the Great Leap it became evident that many of the specialists who had been trained in only one field could not be used in others when there was no employment for them in their own, and when the Soviet advisers were withdrawn so suddenly in the summer of 1960 it was also suddenly revealed how dependent the previous achievements in the sphere of modern industrialization had been on assistance from a foreign country. The Chinese "experts" were often enough incapable of carrying on with the projects the Soviets had started and were sometimes unable to competently maintain the plants already running.

The academic standard of engineers and technicians in China is still low. If the policy of specialization and neglect of broad basic studies and research continues, it will foster a tendency whose dangers have been recognized but which nobody is prepared to take effective measures to counteract, namely, the tendency toward the atrophy of original and independent thought, a mania for cramming and a propensity for uncritical imitation. Should China remain in the state of technical isolation she has been in since the break with Moscow, this one-sided educational system in the universities could one day have serious consequences for the carrying out of modern industrial and agricultural schemes demanding the exercise of independent and logical thought.

New Forms of Training for the "Working-Class Proletariat"

Merely to describe and analyze the traditional stages along an educational road, however, does not give a complete picture of educational methods in modern China. Government propaganda has been making much, especially recently, of a procedure which the leaders apparently hope will lead the country out of the dilemma of the present educational policies. On the one hand it has been realized that because of the lack of teaching staff and the tremendous pressure on the schools, conventional educational methods are not sufficient, either quantitatively or qualitatively, and that the university system will be forced to take a hazardous road if the previous system continues. On the other hand, it is felt, for several reasons already described, that it is not possible to give up the idea of linking study and practical work.

One way out might be to set up schools which would create a direct connection between study and work, leaving it to the conventional educational institutions to fulfill the purposes for which such institutions were universally created. The latest fetishes in Chinese educational policy are workers' universities and technical schools. The idea is a twofold one, the first that the workers shall study in their spare time, in addition to their normal work; and the second that there should be a weekly change-over, a week studying and a week at work in industry or agriculture. In this way it is hoped to be able to train up the requisite nucleus of industrial and agricultural experts, while at the same time taking some of the pressure off the traditional high schools and universities and allowing them to concentrate less on political work and more on theoretical basic studies.

This idea of providing further education for the workers has also been thought of before in China. As soon as the Communists came to power, the trade unions were given the task of working out methods of spare-time study in order to make up the enormous shortage of technically qualified men.

The Great Leap also brought a new impetus to this. A very large number of evening schools of all possible types were set up to give the people the rudiments of theoretical and practical knowledge. In August 1960 official Peking statistics said that of the Great Leap, 200,000 workers enrolled for spare-time instruction, a good percentage of them trying to reach primary school level. "Red Specialist Universities" were founded to bring the cream of the proletariat up to specialist level. But the failure of the Great Leap brought with it the collapse of the precarious structure of mass technical education.

This was illustrated by the Peking *People's Daily,* which gave some instructive figures. In the spring of 1958, at the beginning of the Great Leap, 200,000 workers enrolled for spare-time courses in Tientsin, the port and industrial city. By the autumn of that year the figure had risen to 420,000 and at the beginning of 1960 it had reached 800,000. In 1962 it had shrunk again to 70,000.

It is not difficult to see why the spare-time schools failed. In the years of want and distress the workers and the peasants had other things to think about than using the little spare time they had for studying. Apathy and disinterest became widespread, even among Party functionaries.

Apart from this, the leaders themselves had begun to have their doubts about whether the system, originally so full of promise, would in fact lead to the results they had envisaged. As long as the purpose was that of providing elementary education to combat illiteracy, the system might be good enough, but as soon as anything more advanced was demanded and the schools had to concentrate on providing technical knowledge, the results seemed to be questionable. "Generally speaking," the leading Chinese trade-union paper said at this time, "the students in the spare-time schools lack elementary theoretical knowledge."

Despite the fact that the Chinese economy had made a good recovery in the previous few years, the Party's propaganda no longer made spare-time study of the kind described above the central point of its educational campaign. No actual obstacles were put in its way, and where technical courses organized by plants and firms proved useful, they were allowed to continue. Today, however, the emphasis in official propaganda is now on another area, due to the realization that much more extensive and thoroughgoing spare-time study is necessary if the aims of long-term national economic planning are to be attained.

There are two main ideas. The so-called "Industrial Spare-time Universities" have already been running for some time. They were started in a number of Chinese towns in 1960, but for a long time they were completely overshadowed by other educational institutions. This kind of spare-time study takes four to five years and leads to the award of a diploma. Since the summer of 1962 there has been a great deal of press and propaganda publicity for the Workers' Universities. An official statement announced that within a very short time twenty thousand students from more than a thousand plants had been enrolled in the seven faculties of Shanghai Workers' University.

One noteworthy thing is the change that has taken place in the methods of study at the Workers' Universities. Formerly the idea was that of purely spare-time study, which the worker carried out after his day's work, although it was possible for students to attend some of the lectures during working hours. As a rule the amount of time spent on lectures during the working day was a third of the total time allotted to lectures. Today the proportions are exactly reversed. It is reported of the Workers' University in Shanghai that in general the students attend twenty-four hours of lectures a week, sixteen hours during working time and only eight hours in their own time. Nevertheless, I was told, the students still receive their full wages.

It is only a small step from the new method of study at the Workers' Universities to another type of technical college which is now being held up as a model by the propagandists. The students spend one week at work and one week at their studies, turn and turn about. This system is not new, either. Individual large works in China started this kind of school in 1958, at the beginning of the Great Leap period, but the idea was never given official backing and these schools almost completely disappeared in the course of time. It was not until the fall of 1964, following the disappointing experiences with other forms of spare-time study, that the Communist leaders saw the worth of this type of further education for the rising generation. In December 1964 Premier Chou En-lai particularly stressed its importance in his speech to the National People's Congress.

Since then the government has set up bureaus in many of the provinces with the job of persuading plants to establish this kind of technical school. Managements can get advice from them and the government will provide the teaching staff. The Central Committee of the CPC is believed to have passed a resolution in the fall of 1964, and to have distributed it to all lower Party levels, laying down that this new form of mass technical education was to be energetically hastened on. And sure enough, by the end of 1964 these schools had shot up like mushrooms in towns all over China. In the meantime Shanghai is said to have 350 schools of this type with fifty thousand registered students. It looks as if this form of education is going to be one of the mainstays of the Chinese educational system for the foreseeable future.

The demand by the Party for these two types of specialist schools is linked in the minds of the leaders with another thought. The new methods of providing theoretical and practical opportunities for a working class that has little or no education are completely logical and rational. An important factor from the Party's point of view is that what is involved here is the education of a section of the people whose interests, according to ideological theory, the Party represents, and whose sympathies the Party wishes to gain for power-political reasons. There is no doubt that the regime believes it will reap political benefit if it can manage to provide the members of the "working-class proletariat" with the chance of getting practical training and with it the opportunity of advancement in their jobs. In this way the Communists are building up a reserve of devoted and fanatical supporters who provide a significant counterweight to the intellectuals, the top men in the economy, who have less "proletarian consciousness" and who have come up the traditional educational ladder. It seems to me to be no coincidence, therefore, that the pattern of resolute and solidly based workers' education has been in the propaganda limelight since the middle of 1964. About this same time there were some other activities and campaigns by the Party leaders which made it clear that the aging revolutionary elite in Peking were becoming concerned about the fate of the revolutionary heritage in the generations to come.

Part Three

THE REVOLUTIONARY ROAD
TO NATIONAL REBIRTH

You aim to conquer the world, to mold it?
I have seen that this cannot be done.
The world is an insubstantial thing:
To touch it is to spoil it.
Try to grasp it and it is gone.
Things sometimes go before, sometimes follow,
Now breathing warm, now blowing cold,
Now strong, now weak,
Now floating on the surface, now below.
Therefore the percipient avoid.
The too many, the too much and the too big.

—*Lao-tse* (*c.* 604–531 B.C.)

Chapter 14

THE OMNIPOTENT SEVEN

The Chinese Communist Party (CPC) is the driving force behind the titanic efforts to overcome the apparently insuperable difficulties facing the Middle Kingdom, difficulties such as are faced by no other country in the world: the efforts to lead the Chinese nation out of its impotence and backwardness and to give the country standing, influence and secure prosperity. The party is omnipotent. It lays down the guiding lines of all policies, rules the army, directs the economy, controls the intelligentsia, rules in the spheres of art and science and has a finger in every detail of the public and private lives of the people. Its organization is said to number seventeen million members. A fine-meshed network of cells, ground-level organizations and district and provincial committees covers the land. Not even the remotest corner of the Chinese mainland can escape the Party's power, the Party's control.

The millions of Party workers are only functionaries. The decisions and resolutions are taken by the men at the pinnacle of the Party pyramid. According to the Party Statutes, the supreme organ of government is the National Party Congress, which is to be re-elected every five years. It is supposed to meet at least once a year to discuss outstanding questions. These provisions in the statutes have been ignored in recent years. The National Party Congress had its 8th Party Conference in September 1956. Since then it has met only once, in May 1958. There have been no elections for nine years now and there has been no mention of the convening of the 9th Party Congress for a long time.

The failure of the leaders to abide by the provisions of the Party Statutes is all the more remarkable in view of the fact that at the 8th Party Congress in 1956 the statutes were amended with the specific purpose of initiating regular mandatory meetings of the Party Congress. In his speech explaining the amendment, the Party's General Secretary, Teng Hsiao-ping, told the Congress that "the principles of internal Party democracy can only be kept alive if the Congress meets regularly and exercises to the full the functions assigned to it." If this rule was ignored, he went on, the consequences would inevitably be detrimental to "democratic centralism."

According to the Statutes, in the intervals between the meetings of the Party Congress, the Central Committee of the CPC is empowered to make any necessary decisions. But even this body meets only spasmodically, and not even the prescribed minimum of "at least two plenary sessions a year" has been kept up since the Communists came to power. For example, the Central Committee did not meet at all in 1960 and met only once in 1961 and once in 1962. As a result, the formation of national policy and the real power are in the hands of one group, the Politbureau of the CPC, and in particular its nucleus, the Standing Committee of the Politbureau. This is where the discussions are held, where attitudes on questions of the day are formulated, basic decisions taken and the nuances in the general line also laid down at this center are adjudicated.

There are only seven men in the Standing Committee of the Politbureau. These are the real wielders of authority; they are the ones whose hands manipulate the levers of unrestricted power. On national holidays it is their portraits which range alongside those of the great men of Marxism-Leninism—Marx, Engels, Lenin and Stalin—in all the city streets and the village marketplaces. Pictures of them are on sale in every department store in the towns and in every provincial general store, printed on plain paper, painted in pastel shades or woven in black and white or colored silk. The names of the omnipotent seven are above and clearly set apart from the others: Mao Tse-tung, Chairman of the Central Committee; Liu Shao-chi, the President of China and Chairman of the National Defense Council; Chou En-lai, the Premier; Chu Teh, the Chairman of the National People's Congress; Chen Yun, the Deputy Premier; Lin Piao, the Defense Minister; and Teng Hsiao-ping, the General Secretary of the CPC.

I twice had the opportunity to see the paramount chiefs of the Chinese Communists at close hand, once on the eve of May First, Labor Day, and once on October First, the anniversary of the founding of the Chinese People's Republic. On both occasions I had been invited to the banquet in the Great People's Hall. On these and similar occasions it is standard practice to dine five thousand guests of honor in the enormous building, the proceedings always following the same set pattern. The place is crowded with Chinese Party functionaries in Party gala uniform. It seems as if every car in the Chinese capital is parked on the vast car park on the west side of the Changan Boulevard.

In the great banqueting hall of the pretentious building, built in the forbidding Stalinist style, the international world is also represented. All the miscellaneous delegations who happen to be in Peking at the moment meet in a huge assembly, Africans, Asiatics, Latin Americans and Europeans, seated around massive circular tables. Serious blond Scandinavians are seated next to adventurous-looking Cuban revolutionaries; African girl students from Rhodesia and Tanzania in colorful robes are next to Pakistanis in sober black. The lavish buffet is laid out on long tables, with notices emphasizing the cosmopolitan variety of the dishes, Muslim, Chinese and European. In the gallery there are three bands taking it in turns to play military marches and Chinese folk music. The stage in the background is draped with countless red flags, the sole visible reminder of the political nature of the assembly.

Apart from minor variations, the proceedings at these performances always follow an unvarying routine. On the eve of

May First, shortly before the ceremonial banquet was scheduled to begin, the first group of Party dignitaries entered the hall to the accompaniment of loud applause. At the head of the procession was Premier Chou En-lai, followed by Marshal Chu Teh and the General Secretary Teng Hsiao-ping. Places had been reserved for them at the tables in front of the stage. The placings at these tables of honor reveal the demonstrative preference accorded to some of the guests. African dignitaries and Indonesian ministers are particularly courted, as are leading representatives of pro-Chinese factions in other parties in the world Communist movement, for example Ted Hill, one of the leaders of the Australian Communist Party and the leading figure in the pro-Chinese wing's polemics against the "modern revisionists"; members of the Politbureau of the Japanese Communist Party and a Mr. Manson from the New Zealand Communist Party, another "true Marxist-Leninist" in the eyes of the Chinese Communists all enjoying the honored treatment which the Chinese leaders publicly accord them. The Albanians, it need hardly be said, are also represented in the circle of honored guests.

At these May First celebrations the Chinese trade-union leader, Liu Ning-yi, gave the main speech of the evening, but his attacks on colonialism and American imperialism did not hold the audience spellbound. The climax of the evening's proceedings did not come until later, when the second group of leading personalities entered the hall. The applause this time was for Liu Shao-chi, the President of China and the heir apparent of Mao Tse-tung. Liu mounted the stage. The other members of the Politbureau and the special guests of honor followed. They stood and waved, raised their glasses in a toast and coolly accepted the frenetic ovation.

One person who did not take part in the official May First celebrations was Mao Tse-tung. Some whispered that he was on one of the inspection tours he was so fond of making through the country. Others explained his absence as due to his unwillingness to condescend to take part in monster propaganda demonstrations. He did appear, however, on the eve of China's National

Day, the fifteenth anniversary of the Communists' coming to power. This time the applause and the ovation far outstripped anything I had witnessed on May First. As the Party leader entered the hall among his faithful followers and delegation leaders from Africa, Asia and Europe, a tumult of applause broke out. Groups of people feverishly shouting greetings, excited cries, continuous clapping, the craning of necks and the popping of flash bulbs turned the Great People's Hall into a bedlam.

Mao Tse-tung seemed little moved by the tumult. Walking with unhurried steps and giving friendly waves, he went straight to his seat. He is stockily built. He walks slowly but holds himself upright. His suit seems more modest than those of the other prominent personalities. The usual too-long coat sleeves testify to his casualness. The round face has grown old and his hair is thin. Youthful elasticity is hardly to be expected of a man more than seventy years old, with a past as full of hardship as Mao's has been. His features show his self-possession. The chin with the famous wart testifies to his strength of will. His eyes reveal his sense of fun. Mao has a good sense of humor; he likes to laugh and his laugh is infectious. He has not the attitudes of a puritan. He helps himself generously at table, enjoys his favorite drink, the strong *mao-tai* spirit, and smokes a good deal. The cadres in the hall do not seem to be perturbed by these human traits. They are luxuriating in the knowledge that they are in the same room as the man who made them what they are and who is for them a legendary figure, indeed, nothing less than a superhuman idol. For there is no doubt that it was Mao Tse-tung who led the Communists to power in China.

He was born the son of a "middle peasant" in Hunan Province in 1893. He was interested in politics and philosophy from an early age, but he had a long and arduous road to tread before he attained the position of assistant librarian in Peking University in 1918, where he hoped to be able to slake this thirst for knowledge. It was only when he got to Peking that he came under the influence of the men who were later to found the Communist Party of China, and when it was founded, in 1921, he himself was present. But nothing indicated that a brilliant career lay ahead of him. For the intellectuals among the leaders he was always "that dumb country boy." His great moment came in 1927, when Chiang Kai-shek smashed the Communist Party in the towns. Mao collected together the wretched remnants in the peaceful shelter of the mountains in the area between Hunan and Kiangsi. Now he could apply himself to the task of realizing his belief that the revolution had to be brought about not by the struggle of the proletariat in the towns, as had happened in Russia, but by the efforts of the Chinese peasant masses.

Starting with a few hundred followers, he and Chu Teh, who was later to become a marshal, built up a partisan army. Mao started with nothing. He had no resources, no cannon, no airplanes, no industry—none of the things essential to an effective fighting force was available to him. All he possessed was strength of will, toughness, stubbornness and inflexible, unconquerable ambition which no amount of toil, sacrifice or loss of life could daunt. The small group of revolutionaries were under attack by the forces of the Kuomintang, fully armed with the most modern weapons and advised by foreign strategists.

In ten months they made the legendary Long March, six thousand miles from the far South in a zigzag line right across China and up to Yenan in Shensi Province in the far North. Here they lived in caves, destitute, hungry, in misery and continual hardship.

Despite their escape, the fate of the small band of Communists might have been sealed if Japan had not overrun China in 1937. Chiang was now forced to carry on a war on two fronts, and in fact to some extent to collaborate with the Communists. Mao made clever use of the Kuomintang's weaknesses. China's Red revolutionaries owe their final success to their leader's indomitable will and tactical adaptability. "Cow dung is more useful than dogmas. At least it can be made into manure for the fields," he once said.

Mao always knew how to adapt himself to the particular circumstances of a given situation and never wavered in what he had once come to believe, despite resistance from his own ranks, criticism from the Comintern in Moscow and the views of Stalin, who had never thought much of Mao's theories on guerrilla warfare from the beginning. Even if the many setbacks, the errors of judgment, practices such as brainwashing, labor camps and robotlike organization caused some individuals among the Communist cadres uneasy moments, Mao Tse-tung is and will remain their symbol. He is China's Lenin, the initiator and executor of an idea which, in the fight for power, has proved itself to be correct. Every functionary must fear that the fall of Mao Tse-tung would bring about the collapse of Communism in China.

President Lui Shao-chi is the second man in the state. He is a man who finds it difficult to force his features into a smile in public. In his black, narrow-fitting tunic and with his combed-back, silvery-gray hair he gives an impression of great dignity. His face is fuller and he is taller and better groomed than one would imagine from his photographs. He is always serious and never makes gestures for the sake of courting public sympathy. For all that, he is second only to Mao Tse-tung in the volume of applause given at the great functions in the Great People's Hall. Everyone present knows his position in the Party and in the state. Everyone knows, too, that he is Mao's closest confidant, the *eminence grise* of Peking.

Mao Tse-tung and Liu Shao-chi have been friends since boyhood. Liu was born in 1898 in a district near Mao's home village. They went to school together in Changsha, and they were together at the founding of the CPC in 1921. Since then their paths have never separated. It was Liu who forged the iron Party framework and rose to become the guardian of the "one true Law." It was he, too, who drafted the Party Statutes. His books *How to Be a Good Communist* and *On the Party* have become required reading for every ambitious Chinese functionary. Liu rules with a rod of iron over discipline, order and the proprieties among the cadres.

On the fifteenth anniversary of the Communists' coming to power, Liu Shao-chi gave the main speech in the Great People's

Hall. It was one of the rare opportunities to hear this pillar of Party orthodoxy. His voice is incisive, the grating Hunanese dialect allowing no emotional inflection. His words diffuse a feeling of icy cold. His sentences are short, authoritative and logical. One can well believe in the selflessness, the lucidity of thought, the purity of political belief and the unfailing realism which are attributed to him. Unyielding determination in the realization of his political ideas is as much a part of Liu Shao-chi's makeup as the undeviating directness of his thinking. Liu is the abbot among the red monks of Peking. Mao Tse-tung well knows why he can trust Liu and why he can safely leave him to take over when Mao's hour comes.

Premier Chou En-lai comes next in order of precedence. The difference between him and Liu Shao-chi is patent. Chou is smaller and slighter and he looks positively elegant in his light gray suit. His features are relaxed, his eyes display wit. He moves with agility, sometimes even hurriedly. On another occasion I had a chance to hear Chou in conversation in a smaller company. For all his flexibility, he is no maker of epigrams. He is friendly, ready to listen, yet reserved. Chou controls every discussion with natural charm.

Born in 1898 the son of a rich mandarin of Chekiang Province, Chou is the Party's diplomat. He broke away from his family at an early age and became a revolutionary. At the beginning of the twenties he was both studying and earning his living in France and Germany. In the card index of the Renault plant near Paris there is still a card bearing the note: "Not to be re-employed—a revolutionary character." His star first began to rise when, in 1927, after the failure of a Communist revolt he had organized in Shanghai, he just managed to escape being put to death and joined Mao Tse-tung, who had founded the first tiny Communist soviet republic in the mountains of Hunan and Kiangsi. Thereafter Chou won his spurs as a negotiator and a nimble-witted diplomat. During the civil war he negotiated with the Americans and with Chiang Kai-shek, who called him an "upright" Communist.

After the Communist seizure of power, Chou made his appearance on the international scene. He represented China at the Geneva Conference on Indo-China, traveled through the neutral countries of Asia as the prophet of peaceful coexistence and was one of the leading personalities at the Bandoeng Conference. He has a winning smile and the ability to assume a dignified bearing. A boyhood friend of his claims that at fourteen years of age Chou could laugh or cry on command when he played girls' parts in the school plays, roles he was fond of taking. Chou En-lai is unquestionably a master of gesture and, for all his uncompromising Communist attitude of mind, an outstanding and patient tactician who is fully versed in the various styles of deportment and behavior appropriate to any occasion. He is the *grand seigneur* among the Communist elite in Peking.

In 1952 he handed over his job as Foreign Minister to Marshal Chen Yi. Many people thought at this time that Chou had fallen into disfavor, but it soon emerged that the intelligent mandarin's son had been called on to relinquish the Foreign Ministry to take up more important work in the ruling inner circle. He became the third pillar of the triumvirate with Mao Tse-tung and Liu Shao-chi. Foreign policy problems were still within his jurisdiction. In 1961 he was given the difficult task of being the chief delegate of the CPC at the 22nd Party Congress of the CPSU in Moscow; after the fall of Khrushchev he was given the delicate job of sounding out the Soviet leaders in Moscow; he manages the relationships between China and countries abroad and is almost permanently on the move, traveling to Asia and Africa.

Close behind Chou is the massive figure of his successor as Foreign Minister, the Politbureau member Chen Yi. Chen has none of Chou's elegance. Most of the time his small, cunning eyes are concealed behind large sunglasses. He is seldom without a cigarette in his mouth. His walk is military, his bearing upright: his military background is unmistakable. In conversation he tries to be jovial; his remarks are characterized by robust self-assurance. Behind the pose of the clowning military man there is intelligence and a gift for tactical argument, qualities not to be underestimated. Chen Yi has undoubtedly gained in stature within the Chinese Party hierarchy, but Chou En-lai is still the authority in all matters to do with Chinese foreign policy.

One man who is particularly warmly applauded by the assembled cadres whenever he appears at public functions is the aging Marshal Chu Teh. What the Chinese revolution owes to Mao Tse-tung's political and organizational genius in the decisive years of the civil war, it owes to Chu Teh in the military sphere. He was the guiding mind behind the battles and the skirmishes —a man, moreover, who was animated by high idealism, which is more than can be said for the majority of the military on the opposing side in the civil war.

Chu was the son of a wealthy landowner and was born in Szechwan Province in 1886. As a young man he led a riotous life as a warlord in the extreme South, but after a while this pointless way of life began to pall. He got rid of his harem of beautiful women and signed on aboard a British coaster as a drastic method of curing himself of his opium habit, opium smoking being strictly forbidden on British ships. Thereafter he went to Paris and Germany, studied military science and sociology and finally, in 1924, joined a Communist cell in Berlin. After a stop in Moscow, where he studied Marxism and economics for a time, and a short period as a Kuomintang military commander, he joined Mao Tse-tung and his band in the soviet enclave in the mountains. Here was forged the bond which has lasted until today.

Chu developed into an ingenious strategist. Innumerable legends, have been woven around him. His ability, his courage and his selflessness were as essential to the victory of Communism in China as those of his Party leader, Mao Tse-tung. Today Chu is old and weak. Two attendants have to help him on and off the stage of the Great People's Hall. The features in the peasant's square head are flabby and the joviality senile. But the eyes under the bushy eyebrows proudly light up when he receives the homage of the cadres. Chu's influence in the ruling group may nowadays be minimal, but the respect he enjoys is universal.

One Party celebrity who did not mount the stage was Teng Hsiao-ping, the General Secretary and the Party's chief ideologist, the man who led the Chinese delegation in the momentous negotiations with the Soviets in 1963. He was walking with a stick. (Some people thought this was the result of an old war wound, others that he once had polio, but nobody knew for certain.) Among his guests he seems modest and reserved. He is not a man for grandiloquence, nor a demagogue. The large clear eyes in the young-looking face and the high forehead radiate intelligence. He has all the marks of the spiritual self-possession which is so often to be seen in highly intelligent people who have some physical disability. Teng Hsiao-ping is the key figure on the Chinese side in the ideological debate with the Kremlin.

Much of his previous career is a mystery. There is no firm information on his social background or even on his date of birth. He comes from Szechwan, like Chu Teh, is certainly over sixty but looks much younger. Teng also studied in France; he, too, fled to Kiangsi to join Mao Tse-tung's small band of followers in the years when the CPC's fortunes were at their lowest ebb; and he, too, is one of the ten thousand survivors who came through the heroic Long March to Shensi in the North.

But he did not finally come into the Party limelight until 1955, when he became a member of the Politbureau. A year later he was already a member of the Standing Committee. Mao Tse-tung obviously values his penetrating intelligence very highly, for when he went to Moscow in November 1957 for his important discussions with Khrushchev, Teng Hsiao-ping was the only assistant he took with him. Teng is the main speaker at Party conferences to decide on future policy and it is still his hand that wields the dialectical sword in the ideological controversy with the Soviet Communists. His thought is sharp and aggressive. He is one of the most important men in China today.

Of the omnipotent seven, I had an opportunity to see and observe only five. The other two, Lin Piao and Chen Yun, were always missing from the Chinese state functions. It is known that Defense Minister Lin Piao has been ill for a long time and must take care of his health; nonetheless the comparatively young marshal—he was born in 1907 in Hupeh Province—may still be playing an important part in the deliberations of the Party's top men. Lin Piao was one of the most loyal and reliable Party stalwarts. At the age of thirty this manufacturer's son was already one of the most important Communist military leaders. In the Communist headquarters in the Yenan caves during the civil war he took over the training and political indoctrination of the officers of the Red Army. He was the most successful field commander in the final phase of the war against the Kuomintang. Today, as far as his health allows, he sees to it that the colossal army strictly toes the ideological line.

The absence of Chen Yun from official functions is due to quite a different reason. Chen fell into disfavor in 1959. Until then this son of a laborer, born in Kiangsu Province in 1904 (and incidentally the only man in the very top ranks who can boast a really proletarian origin), was in charge of China's economic affairs. However, he could not bring himself to go along with the Great Leap and the People's Communes concept and disappeared from the scene. Now, following the failure of the drastic economic measures, his star is once more in the ascendant. In the summer of 1962 the Peking daily newspaper carried a photograph of Mao Tse-tung shaking hands with Chen Yun. In the fall of 1964 Chen was re-elected to the National People's Congress and in the following December, at a meeting of the Congress, he was confirmed in the position of Deputy Premier. Economic experiences since the difficult years have proven that Chen Yun was right. It is therefore possible that he will be restored to high office in the near future. Meantime he is remaining in the background.

The Chen Yun affair is characteristic of the way in which the top men of China's Communist Party stick together. However much the individual members may differ in character and temperament, the Party's all-powerful ones give the impression of forming a solid group, linked together by their destiny. They have been bound to one another now for decades, sticking together throughout the difficult years of the civil war and the revolutionary struggle. It has very seldom happened that one has attacked another. Only one of the mighty men of the Party has had to be dethroned on serious charges. This was Kao Kang, the former Party leader in Manchuria, who was said to have been trying to make himself independent and working too closely with Stalin. Other cases of demotion are wrapped in silence, cases like those of Chen Yun or the Defense Minister Peng Teh-huai, Lin Piao's predecessor.

But since the Communists took over in China there have never been any of the weird-sounding, absurd, personal vilification and slander such as occurred in other Communist countries when one or other ventured to hold an opinion at variance with the views of the majority of the ideas of the *primus inter pares*. Of course there are discussions, arguments, differences of opinion and tendencies to pull in different directions; but they have never been carried on with such primitive brutality as in the other capitals of the Communist world. This perhaps may change, just as many other things could change once the present governing team of the sixty-five-to-eighty-year-olds quits the political stage. But until then the world has a solidly united governmental group to deal with, who are just as unlikely to bow to the pressure of foreign wills and foreign power, even that of ideologically like-minded governments, as they have always been.

But what of their position within their own country? What standing do they enjoy outside of the Party faithful? What do the seven hundred million people think of the Communist ideas and methods imposed on them by this small group of omnipotents?

Chapter 15

THE PERMANENT CLASS STRUGGLE
CONTINUES

It is difficult to get an accurate picture of the domestic political situation, the real balance of power and the mood of the people in China. The country is vast and many-layered. Conditions and circumstances differ from place to place, just as much as the temperament and mentality of the people. Then, too, it is not made easy for the stranger to get to the heart of things. Certain areas, perhaps indeed the most interesting ones, are barred to him. He is not allowed to see what goes on inside important sections of the machinery of government. His view is in danger of being obscured or his attention drawn in the wrong direction by a powerful, intelligent and cleverly manipulated propaganda machine.

It is thus not to be wondered at that in the West the gamut of opinions about the position of the Communist regime in China ranges from one extreme to the other. Some believe that the Giant of the Far East is coming to life and putting a people seven hundred million strong into a state of fanatical delirium, which will lead to accesses of power and success hitherto thought impossible; others are convinced of the exact opposite. As these others see it, the mass demonstrations, the big words about solidarity, the voluntary labor and the popular campaigns are only a screen for the weakness, bewilderment and vacillation of the governmental machine.

What is the truth of the matter? There is little point in expecting to find the answers to such questions in conversations and chance meetings during a trip through China. Most of the time one only hears the official line, anyhow. It is true that occasionally, in the course of an unchaperoned conversation, one's partners will give vent to some pretty strong anti-Communist comment, and this may lead one to think that the range of political opinions is as wide in China as it is everywhere else in the world. But one cannot, merely on the basis of such private, amateur canvassing of opinions, form a generally valid picture which will even faintly correspond to reality.

So one is forced to continue to rely on indirect analysis. Using the regime's political methods, so evident to every visitor to China, as a starting point, the aim is to try to establish, by personal observation, why just these methods are employed and what effect they have. In many respects the methods used in a totalitarian system demonstrate the country's political situation. They provide an indication of the difficulties the regime is faced with. But it is not until one has seen for oneself the actual conditions and circumstances, heard hints in personal conversations and observed people's visible reactions to certain governmental measures that one can achieve a better understanding, a clearer view of the purpose of party-political actions and thus a more lucid picture of the political situation.

There are three kinds of political methods that strike the traveler in China as especially conspicuous. First, the organizational ability of the cadres, which seems to extend with clockwork precision into every corner of the country and into every family. Secondly, the efforts being made to achieve complete indoctrination, efforts which shrink from no material sacrifice and are prepared to expend unlimited time and trouble. Thirdly and lastly, the idolization of Mao Tse-tung. Soviet and Eastern European observers in Peking were particularly fond of drawing my attention to this last feature. Here, they said, was a manifestation of a cult of personality such as used to be found all over Stalin's empire at one time. The results in those days were catastrophic. Similar results were beginning to make themselves evident in China.

And in fact the visitor does see frightening examples of glorification. It begins with the tiny children in the crèches and kindergartens. In Peking I heard some three to four years olds, enchanting little creatures, singing a little song: "The birds love to sing, the fish love the water, but we love Mao and the Party." In another Peking kindergarten the children performed a harvest dance from Sinkiang, ending with the refrain: "We owe it all to Mao, the liberator of Sinkiang, that we had such a good harvest."

The picture is not much different in the primary and intermediate schools. One class in a Peking primary school loudly and fervently recited for me, the guest from West Germany, the ode of Mao's portrait: "You are always present, looking down upon us with your gracious eyes. You watch us continually in all we do. We will not disappoint you: we will follow your wise counsel."

After experiences like these one has a fair idea what similar things must be done in the youth organizations and the lower levels of the Party organization. But in normal daily life, too, the visitor sees on every side the signs of Mao's idolization. In the moving-picture theaters the audience would break out into frenzied applause whenever Mao appeared on the screen. This can be a physically strenuous business, during the showing of a revolutionary film on the legendary Communist headquarters in Yenan during the long years of the civil war, for example. Since Mao was hardly ever out of the picture, the theater was permanently filled with deafening applause.

Films with more modern themes are also subject to the same sort of treatment. In Peking I saw a more recent Chinese production dealing with the story of a former Tibetan serf. Every detail of the cruel oppression and exploitation practiced by the perfidious feudal class was shown, and the hero's tribulations did not come to an end until the crushing of the Tibetan revolt by the Chinese in 1959. In the final scene, in which the Tibetan people are shown in the streets enthusiastically celebrating the victory over the rebels, the hero's girl friend says to him, "Well, say something at last!" The hero, who was charged with pilfering

as a boy and had his tongue torn out in a lamasery as a punishment, makes a supreme effort and manages to utter the guttural
reply "I have a lot to say! Thank you, Mao Tse-tung!" Upon
which the camera swings from the hero to a portrait of the
Chinese leader, on which there is a fade-in of the title "The End."

In every conversation in factory or commune the foreigner
will be told that all the progress they have made is due to the
wise Mao Tse-tung and his Party. In the Peking prison a woman
who was serving fifteen years for fraud told me, "I am so grate-
ful to Chairman Mao for making me into a new person." In the
bookshops and picture shops, old-style prints and watercolors are
increasingly giving way to representations of political scenes
based on poems by Mao Tse-tung.

The idolatry reaches a climax at the mass demonstrations on
political festival days and similar occasions. Then gigantic portraits of Mao are to be seen hanging on the walls of government
buildings, larger-than-life-size statues of him are paraded
through the streets and organized groups incessantly chant his
name. On the fifteenth anniversary of the revolution I was invited to the premiere of a play depicting in the classical Peking
Opera style the course of the revolution. In the final scene
hundreds of actors called on "the proletariat of the whole world
and all oppressed peoples" to show their unity and solidarity. On
the backcloth, on a red background, there appeared a picture
of Mao in gold, showing him as the sun sending palpitating rays
of light into the auditorium. The actors suddenly turned their
backs to the audience and made obeisance to the sun god, Mao
Tse-tung. A great choir struck up the final chorale: "Beloved
Chairman Mao, the sun in our hearts, your light shines forth
upon us whatever we do, you are with us wherever our steps
may lead."

Understandably the Western visitor tends to make comparisons
between this sort of thing and events that took place in Europe
not so very long ago. But although there are certain parallels,
there are also certain significant differences. In China they have
not yet gone so far as they once did in Nazi Germany, where

they had the inane custom of including the name of the leader in the greeting people gave each other. No towns, streets or squares have been renamed after Mao Tse-tung, as was commonly done with the name of Stalin in the Soviet Union and the satellite countries in the days when he was the unfettered ruler of the Soviet empire. From the very beginning the Chinese leaders resisted any attempt to introduce the custom, so common in other Communist countries, whereby the workers "spontaneously" report their production successes in messages and telegrams to their rulers. As early as in 1949 Peking issued a decree, still in force today, banning public celebrations of the Party leaders' birthdays. The world found it surprising that in December 1963, on Mao's seventieth birthday, there were no official celebrations anywhere in China to mark the memorable day, and that government publications gave it not even a passing mention.

The official political propaganda is not aimed primarily at the idolization of the person, at the wielder of supreme power, but at an amalgamation of the person and the gospel he proclaims. This was clearly illustrated by a visit I paid to Mao Tse-tung's birthplace in Shaoshan.

Pilgrimage to Shaoshan

Shortly after leaving the small town of Siangtan, our car is speeding along toward mountainous scenery, and soon we are surrounded by it. The road narrows, the curves multiply, woods extend from the tops of the hills into the valley below. The rice fields get smaller, hugging the sides of the mountains or cutting terraces into the woods. Some sixty miles after we started our journey in Changsha, the capital of Hunan, in the early morning, we reach the village of Shaoshan. This is where, in 1893, Mao was born.

Shaoshan lies in a valley, surrounded by wooded hills. It takes its name from Shao, the conical mountain that rears its head into the clouds. On its peak shines an ancient Buddhist temple amid dark green foliage. Shaoshan is neither a compact little settlement nor does it have a center. The two thousand or so inhabitants lived scattered across the valley. Paths running along the embankments between the rice fields lead from farm to farm. The people jog-trot along carrying their loads, baskets of rice, firewood and vegetables.

"So you are going on a pilgrimage to Shaoshan?" a Chinese had said to me with a twinkle in his eye in a conversation in Changsha the previous evening. And "pilgrimage to Shaoshan" was an apt description of what I experienced in the next few hours. First of all the landlord of the spacious inn took me to the most noteworthy spots in the village. A road lined with poplars runs along the side of a brook into another small valley. After a short ascent over carefully cemented flagstones a small farm comes into view. Shang Wu Shang, this spot is called. The house, broad and comfortable, lies on the side of a wooded hill, obviously restored, and with freshly plastered walls and new tiles. It is the birthplace of Mao Tse-tung.

Mao was not born and brought up in conditions of poverty. In my tour of the house I counted fourteen rooms, including six for living in and a large kitchen. For a family of not more than five, this cannot be called poor accommodation. The furnishings are simple but solid and practical. As a boy Mao had his own bedroom, which he also used as a study. The family owned twenty-two *mu* (about three and a half acres) of rice fields, a kitchen garden and some woods. At the back of the house are stables for cattle and hogs. The family was not short of the necessary farm implements or tools. At all events, the family's land holding was large enough to allow Mao's father to be able to hire hands, especially at the harvesttime.

Mao spent the first sixteen years of his life in Shang Wu Shang. To judge by the remarks of the guide, he must have been a paragon of a boy. And every inch of the property is being made into a historical spot. "This is where Chairman Mao used to swim as a boy," the guide says as we pass the pond in front of the farm.

"The Chairman was an assiduous vegetable gardener," he tells us in the garden. "He used to raise more than the family needed and gave away what they didn't need." Looking at the family's rice fields, I am told that he was a very hard-working boy. "Old peasants in the village still recall that whereas during the rice cultivation the village boys usually weeded twice before the rice harvest, the Chairman used to weed three times."

In the passage leading to the stables there is a glass case hanging on the wall. Inside it, reposing on red velvet, lies a bent and rusty currycomb. "That is what the Chairman used to use to groom the cattle, which he did very conscientiously." At the hog pens I am told: "He always used to help his mother feed them"; at the fishpond: "This is where the Chairman used to carefully restock the pond with young fish as a boy." Inside the house I am given similar pieces of information. In, at or on this or that piece of furniture the Chairman used to sleep, eat, read, work, write, reckon or study in his youth.

The same mode of presentation is applied to Mao's family life, which was governed by unity, love and harmony. "The Chairman particularly honored his mother, who was a kindly housewife. But his father was also an example to him because he was a hard-working farmer. Mao patiently instructed his two young brothers in revolutionary ways and methods."

It is noteworthy that Mao's Communist biographer Hsiao Chu-chang and Mao himself, in the biography he related to Edgar Snow in 1936, gave quite a different version. According to them, Mao's boyhood years were characterized by a continual state of fitful, angry revolt against his tyrannical father. It is impossible to fully understand Mao's career and ideas if this important conditioning factor is left out of account. But he who makes the pilgrimage to Shaoshan must be prepared for many a legend of this kind.

My road took me back into the village, to another attraction, the ancestral temple of the Mao clan, which belonged to everyone bearing the name of Mao—that is to say, practically the whole of Shaoshan, since nearly every inhabitant is called Mao,

or so I was told. Today the Mao ancestral temple is the headquarters of the district committee. The building is dilapidated;
yellowing placards and dust-covered pictures of Mao Tse-tung
and Liu Shao-chi hang on the walls. "As soon as the new accommodation for the district committee is ready," my guide
informs me, "we will make this temple into a worthy national
monument, too."

In the inside room of the temple the leaders of the cattle-
breeding brigades of the district's five communes are having a
discussion on how best to get the cattle and the hogs through
the winter. They have hard, open peasant faces and they listen
with great interest to my stories from another world. When I
ask how many of them are named Mao, two of the brigade
leaders rise. They belong to the Shaoshan commune. Their faces
reveal their pride, the pride that all Chinese feel when one of
their clan has risen to high office in the state.

Next door to the temple a new group of buildings has been
put up. This, opened only a few weeks before my visit to
Shaoshan, contains a museum of items to do with Mao's revolutionary struggle in his boyhood days. Here is assembled everything that could be found in the way of documentation. Photographs of the Mao family, Mao with his grim-faced father and
his helpless-looking mother, pictures of Mao's two brothers, both
of whom were later to die or be murdered in the cause of the
revolution. There are facsimiles of the books Mao read as a boy:
the classical Chinese novels and the works of the masters, Confucius, Lao-tse and Mencius; the writings of the man who is now
regarded as China's first materialist thinker, the sixteenth-century
Wang Shuang-shan; and the writings of Sun Yat-sen.

Mao also used to read Chinese translations of Western works
such as the historico-philosophical writings of the German Professor Pulsen, Rousseau's *Contrat Social*, J. S. Mill and Adam
Smith's classic *Wealth of Nations*. Karl Marx's works are not yet
included. Mao's comments on what he had read, contained in
letters to friends, are on display under glass. One sentence is
underlined in red: "The ideas which come to us from the West

are not all correct. They must be enriched with Eastern thought."

One section of the museum is devoted to the course of the Communist revolution. Here, too, Mao is presented as the central figure. Even historic decisions taken by the Communist leaders in which it is known that Mao took little or no part are presented in such a way that at least Mao's thoughts are represented. I ventured to suggest that this was not quite in accordance with historical fact, since up to the thirties the Party's course was being set by other people altogether. "Those other people took the wrong road," replied the museum director, a product of the Changsha Party School. "What is the point of putting mistakes on display?"

But what makes the visitor think is not the legends such as I was told in the course of my visit to Mao's birthplace, nor the tampering with history just described. Far more questionable is another tendency, manifested everywhere in the country but particularly here in the place where Mao spent his boyhood. It is known that Mao's career was influenced by impressions he acquired during his many travels through Hunan Province as a young man. He himself told Edgar Snow of the great impression made on him by the poverty and hardships endured by the peasants and how much he learned from seeing them. "In a sense," wrote Mao's biographer Hsiao Chu-chang, "he always vacillated between his admiration for the scholars and for science and his admiration for the peasants. He wanted to become a teacher and to devote his life to the peasants."

Thus it was primarily a thirst for knowledge and the desire to learn that sent Mao Tse-tung on his travels through Hunan. But in the museum in Shaoshan this emerges as something quite different. In a large number of enormous paintings Mao is represented not as a curious, wandering student, penniless, dressed only in a pair of trousers—all of which we know to be documented fact—but as the new Messiah preaching to the peasants in the garb of a prophet, his apostles around him, intent on spreading the new gospel of salvation throughout the world.

Mao Tse-tung to Replace Confucius

It may be argued that my experiences in Mao Tse-tung's birthplace are typical of a process which has invariably been set in motion everywhere in the world whenever attempts were being made to consolidate an authoritarian system. Of course no totalitarian system can escape its own inner dynamic. This is in fact what conditions the emergence of the person who holds the reins of power, in China more than anywhere else. After all, in China, the person who wields the power is identical with the one who led Communism to victory after decades of revolutionary struggles and has been responsible for all that has happened since the seizure of power. Moreover, in the Chinese view Mao is the only one left who is still pursuing the classic Marxist-Leninist ideal, now that the Soviets, according to Mao, have betrayed them.

Nevertheless, I do not feel that the cult of Mao is merely a manifestation of outward power or the lionization of a single person, but rather a means of helping the breakthrough of what is, for China, a completely revolutionary idea. How closely the person and his ideas are linked is clearly revealed in the symptoms that accompany the idolization. However much Mao Tse-tung's person is extolled and glorified, the same amount of breath is devoted to an equally insistent demand that his works be read—in other words, a demand for the same degree of devotion to his theories. I could hardly restrain a smile when, on entering the dining cars in the trains, I saw notices saying, "Read the works of Mao Tse-tung! Act according to his words!" Just as strange, it seemed to me, were the colorful placards I saw in the factory workers' clubs or in the administrative buildings in the communes, on which Mao was depicted as a sun, surrounded by dozens of workers intently reading the works of their idol, some with determined expressions and some looking radiant.

There is yet another reason why it seems to be wrong to brush off the glorification of Mao as exclusively a product of a totalitarian system of thought. Chinese tradition plays just as important a part. The written word has always counted for more than the spoken word in China, and it is not by chance that the Communist notables in Peking make great efforts to produce artistic Chinese calligraphy. People visiting Chinese diplomatic offices in foreign countries are occasionally suprised to find hanging on the walls of the reception rooms not portraits of Mao Tse-tung or Liu Shao-chi but the poems of the Foreign Minister, Chen Yi, whose written characters are said to be much finer than those of the other Chinese leaders. And it is not for nothing that Mao himself uses the style of a classical poet in his endeavors to spread revolutionary ideas and ingratiate himself with the people at the same time.

The decisive importance of the amalgamation of person and theory by means of a personality cult built around Mao seems to lie in the urgent necessity to overcome the traditional Chinese conception of society and its functions. For twenty-five centuries, with occasional breaks, Chinese thinking was governed by Confucius' teachings on society, the state and morals. For centuries Confucianism gave China the strength to survive in an overpopulated world. It was based on the search for accord and harmony and it had no room for a turbulent dynamic. Its main components were not basic questions of metaphysics or epistemology, but the shaping of one's daily life by the principles of harmonious order. Pedantic rules of ritual were more important than the nonconformist seeking after the unknowable for its own sake. The family and the clan were regarded as the basic unit of society, the yardstick of one's existence and the sole authority. They were the concern of every individual and only in them was individual and social security to be found. This attitude of mind was necessarily reflected in the social and state order. Custom and usage counted for more than law. The rulers were the closely-knit upper class, the gentry, trained in ethics, philosophy and history. The concept of the state and the nation in the real sense was unknown to the Chinese.

Confucius and his teachings are still firmly rooted in the Chinese—and particularly in the way they think of the family and the clan—even if they are only dimly conscious of it and even if it is much diluted. But no government today can hope to achieve a technically advanced society without simultaneously overcoming Confucianism. One of the principal reasons for Chiang Kai-shek's failure in the decisive years of the revolutionary civil war in China was that he was trying to work toward a modern democratic society while still remaining closely linked with the traditional pillars of Confucianistic society, the already declining gentry. The attempt could not possibly succeed.

On the other hand, in spite of their efforts to graft a new and revolutionary social system onto the Chinese people, the Communist leaders have been made aware of the enduring power of ancient beliefs, which were the cause of many of the failures of the Hundred Flowers period in 1957 and the harsh Great Leap in 1958. Was it mere coincidence that shortly afterward Mao Tse-tung resigned all his offices of state and has since been only the Party Chairman and theoretician? Was it coincidence that it was at this time that the idolization of his person and his theories first began? One cannot help feeling that the Peking leaders, having learned by experience, realized that the first thing they had to do was to try to replace Confucius with Mao Tse-tung and begin a massive campaign to substitute revolutionary Marxist ideas for the teachings of the ancient master. Only then would the revolutionary heritage of the fighting old guard, bought at the cost of so much sacrifice and so much bloodshed, be safe. The way the regime is trying to indoctrinate the people certainly suggests this conclusion.

There is no denying that many of the things I saw and experienced during my travels through China reminded me of a previous personality cult. When I once told a functionary in Peking that the idolization of Mao Tse-tung as a kind of sun god in China today probably outdid even the Stalin cult in the

Soviet Union some years ago, he replied: "There is no question of idolization. We love Chairman Mao sincerely and ardently because he is the greatest leader China has ever had. This is why it is permissible to depict him as the sun, because he *is* our sun."

Nevertheless, the indoctrination process is being mainly concentrated on another area. Everywhere in China, in the schools, the factories and the communes, there are political and reading circles. Political instruction periods are held during working hours (usually once a week), in meal breaks, in other breaks caused by mechanical breakdowns and, of course, after working hours. The central feature of all these meetings, apart from the reading of newspapers, is the works of Mao Tse-tung and the anti-Soviet pamphlets—particularly the Nine Commentaries on the Open Letter of the CPSU Central Committee—containing Mao's thoughts on the most important political questions of the day.

Wherever he goes the visitor sees how potent the effect of this indoctrination is. If he happens to be in the company of an official escort, many of the conversations touching on political instruction verge on the grotesque. "What do you do in your spare time?" I asked a nineteen-year-old girl in a rubber-boot factory in Changsha in South China. Immediately and with every appearance of sincerity she replied, "I like reading, especially the works of Mao Tse-tung."

Of all Mao's works, propaganda attention centers on the theory of the so-called "Contradictions among the People." This includes the thesis that even in a socialist society, class conflict still exists —in other words, that there are still oppositional forces. The purpose of this theory is clear and it possibly testifies to the leaders' realistic assessment of the situation in the country. What it is intended to do is equally clear, but what sometimes comes out of it can be astonishing to the foreign visitor.

In a commune near Shanghai I asked a middle-grade functionary to explain the Maoist theory of contradictions to me. Probably under the stimulus of excessive fearfulness, he made up an explanation. It was really very simple. "Look," he said, "last year we had a poor harvest. This year we have a good one. Isn't that proof of the correctness of the thesis that there are still contradictions?"

Even more bizarre was another incident. A popular volleyball team was having a spell of poor form. All their training, all their best efforts and all the pep talks were having no effect. "Then we passed a unanimous decision to intensify our study of the works of Mao Tse-tung." And lo, the miracle occurred. "After a few months we were back in our old form. We won one game after another."

That such absurd arguments are not solely confined to isolated utterances by particularly fanatical functionaries was demonstrated during the training of the Chinese team for the world table-tennis championships in Ljubljana in the spring of 1965. The so-called "spiritual preparation" occupied a prominent place in the training schedule for the elite players. Su Yin-sheng, one of China's foremost table-tennis players, gave the top women players a talk on the techniques of table-tennis play. No player could reach peak form, he said, if he only set out to achieve athletic skill and did not devote some attention to politics—if, in fact, he did not give politics pride of place. He must study the works of Mao Tse-tung and then think how he could make use of Chairman Mao's words when he came to play. The official Party newspaper, the Peking *People's Daily*, reproduced Su's talk verbatim on its front page and the state publishing house brought it out as a pamphlet, printing a huge number of copies.

The examples I have given may perhaps be regarded as amusing sidelights. But at the same time they illustrate the intensity of the impression made on people and the way it sometimes leads to the distortion of a theory whose sense and logic, seen against the background of the whole of Communist teaching, is clear and convincing; and the way it is applied to all sorts of situations in daily life. The words and teachings of Mao Tse-tung become a sort of miracle drug, which will supply a remedy and bring success in every difficulty.

The foreign guest is made particularly aware of this when

he is given an insight into the way the propaganda and agitation machinery deals with people who have distinguished themselves as stubborn opponents of Communism. I was given permission to visit Peking's only prison, in which 40 per cent of the inmates are said to be political prisoners or, as the Chinese put it, reactionaries. This is where indoctrination is practiced in its purest and most concentrated form. A great deal of time is spent on political education. Voluntary self-confession, examination of one's crimes in group discussion, unceasing instruction in "what is going on in the world" and "what has already been accomplished in this country in the way of socialist achievements," communal criticism and self-criticism of individual political beliefs—in short, all the procedures which have come to be known in the West as "brainwashing"—still have their fixed place in the methodology of "political education."

And here once again the teachings and the works of Mao Tse-tung play a decisive role. In the prison corridors leading to the cells hang dozens of wall newspapers written by the prisoners themselves. Sometimes one can hardly believe one's eyes. Letters from relatives are reproduced, reporting in detail on the "achievements" or saying that "Mao Tse-tung's teachings are the only way." Prisoners write long essays giving their thoughts on some work of Mao Tse-tung's they have just read. Or there is a letter from a prisoner's twelve-year-old son who writes his father promising to send some of Mao Tse-tung's works to him in prison. The prisoners write regular reports on what they have been reading or what they have learned. "At the moment they are engaged on preparing an account of their attitude to modern revisionism," the prison governor told me.

I had a conversation with two of the political prisoners. One of them, a former Kuomintang agent, had been in prison for thirteen years. The country's leaders had convinced him of the correctness of the new ideas. "What finally brought about your change of heart?" I asked him. "Mao Tse-tung's thesis that there can never be peaceful coexistence between imperialism and socialism, between the oppressors and the oppressed," he replied.

The second one I spoke to had also been a Kuomintang member and had, I was told, murdered more than twenty members of the Red Army before the liberation. He was not denounced by "the people's masses" until 1958. He was condemned to death but the sentence was commuted to life imprisonment. Now he, too, had seen the light. I asked the same question, what had finally persuaded him. Without hesitation he replied: "The Fifth Commentary on the Open Letter of the CPSU Central Committee, 'Two Lines in the Question of War and Peace.' I now see that there are just and unjust wars, wars of liberation and wars of aggression. Before, I was on the wrong side, the criminal side. The just war will be victorious, socialism will bring a bright future and then there will be peace forever."

Prisons or labor camps are admittedly the ideal places for a determined indoctrination program. The conditions are perfect. First-class propagandists and intelligent psychologists have at their disposal a strictly disciplined society almost completely cut off from the outside world, and which can be worked on hour after hour, day after day. Conditions like these are to be found nowhere else, but in order to create at least a semblance of them, the regime is making every effort to create an organizational network which will be as complete as they can make it. The leaders believe that total organization is essential for the attainment of their goal, the elimination of all political opposition.

Every visitor from the West is as much impressed with the Chinese Communists' organizing ability as he is with their brainwashing techniques. Their gift for organization has its advantages, but it also has its drawbacks. Nothing seems to escape the notice of the Party. The stranger who takes a walk alone, without an interpreter or an official escort, is very soon aware of the watchful eye of the street or house deputy; and there is every reason to believe that the same goes for the Chinese themselves. In the towns, at any rate, it would be very difficult for a Chinese citizen to do anything not strictly in accordance with his normal daily routine.

Particularly impressive are the mammoth demonstrations on special occasions. Such occasions demonstrate the ability of the machine, as if guided by some invisible hand working to fractions of a second, to handle masses of people to a prearranged program with a degree of discipline and order that is nothing short of uncanny. When an African or Asiatic statesman arrives in Peking, millions of people line the streets, waving flags, artificial flowers or garlands, forming choirs to chant greetings, making an infernal din with drums and gongs and displaying a degree of enthusiastic hospitality that nobody can experience without being moved.

If protest demonstrations are required, the same masses of millions of people show up in the same perfect order. In place of the paraphernalia of ceremonial welcome there will be clenched fists, placards and banners bearing succinct formulas such as "Freedom for the Congo!" or "U. S. Imperialists out of Vietnam!" and so forth. The organizing machine reaches its peak performance on national festival days. Hundreds of thousands of people parade before the leaders in perfectly arranged formation. There are no pile-ups, no confusion and no misdirection. Nothing is left undone to demonstrate revolutionary ardor and the power of an idea, all mounted in a splendidly colorful and imposing show.

Nor is this confined to Peking. Similar demonstrations are to be seen in the provincial towns, too. In Kunming, the capital of Yunnan Province in the far Southwest, I witnessed the preparations for the fifteenth-anniversary celebrations of the seizure of power. In the square where the parade was to be held rehearsals went on from morning until night. People from one district after another were marched on according to a timetable worked out to the last second. Orders rasped out over loudspeakers and the incessant blowing of whistles made sure that the arrangements ran to the split second. The infantry battalions lining the streets even had to practice standing to attention, looking grimly straight ahead, hour after hour.

The organizational perfection displayed on these great occasions has its parallel at the lower level of political instruction, activist meetings, reading circles and discussion evenings, all of which are minutely planned to a fixed schedule. Nothing is too much trouble, no sacrifice is too great. One afternoon, in Sian, in Shensi Province, I wanted to inspect a plant making electrical measuring instruments. I was told this was unfortunately not possible, as political instruction was being given at this time. I said I did not think it likely that every single employee would be taking part in this instruction and that the visit could be confined to those parts of the plant which were working. They admitted that not all the workers would be taking part, but said at least half of them would. My spontaneous reaction was to suggest that such a way of doing things must surely mean a tremendous loss of production that they could ill afford. The reply was: "No, you are wrong, because after attending political instruction, the workers work all the harder."

Chapter 16

THE "FOUR PURGES" CAMPAIGN

Is the politicizing of the whole of Chinese public life intended to be nothing more than a spur? Is the method of total organization merely a rational means designed to bring relative prosperity and prestige to an overpopulated country, short of capital and technically backward? During my travels through China I saw many things which lead me to believe that there is another and more important reason for the gigantic indoctrination campaign, apparently the same as the one which gave rise to the idolization of Mao Tse-tung: namely, that the masses of the Chinese people are still far from being as convinced of the purpose and virtues of the new social order as the leaders think they will have to be if the goals are to be attained. The most important thing is not economic or organizational expediency, nor yet the desire to provide a national stimulus, but the urgent need to build up an ideological foundation in the people. Not so very long ago Mao Tse-tung stated that there was still a "spontaneous tendency toward capitalism" in China. Are words like these only intended to justify new governmental activities or do these "capitalist tendencies" perhaps represent a real danger to the existence of the regime?

In functionary circles in Peking there is told a story which, if it is true, gives the leaders grounds for anxiety and alarm. Even if the story is not true, it is doubly typical, for it not only conforms to the Chinese mentality, it also makes clear what is really going on behind the façade of a perfectly functioning propaganda machine or perhaps even what this machine has started and what it is still keeping going.

One day in the fall of 1963 the wife of President Liu Shao-chi decided to go on a tour of the country. She wanted to see what had been achieved and to find out what the people really thought of their leaders. She traveled incognito through Shantung Province, going from town to town and from village to village, and stayed in a large number of communes. What she saw and heard in the remote parts of the province horrified her. Wherever the full strength of the Party's arm had not been felt, there had been a relapse into the traditional evil customs of the old days. There were chairmen of communes who ruled over their domains like the notorious warlords of old. Party secretaries exercised a tyranny such as used to be the normal thing in China in the old days. Corruption, illicit deals, black-marketeering and illegal profits from undisclosed sidelines in the communes were the order of the day. It was even reported that the district bigwigs were keeping concubines again.

Madame Liu Shao-chi indignantly wrote a long report on what she had discovered and sent it off to the highest Party level. The reaction was swift. A campaign was ordered but officially kept secret. Unofficially the campaign was called *se ching*, "The Four Purges." During my stay in China I could not find out which four purges were meant. It was not until the spring of 1965 that some indication was given in Chinese official statements. According to these, the campaign was directed against four allegedly widespread manifestations: corruption in the communes, "bourgeois thought," "reactionary forces" and the "revival of capitalism."

By the late summer of 1964 the campaign was in full swing. Hundreds of thousands of cadres from the towns (in Peking they were even speaking of two million town functionaries) were moved out into the country districts to replace the old functionaries or to reinforce the Party machinery in the remote areas. Nobody knows which parts of the country were particularly affected and no one knows what the reaction was, but there were continual rumors to the effect that the campaign had not gone entirely without friction. It was reported that there had been violence and disorders. In some places deposed functionaries were reported to be in league with the peasants against the intruders from the towns.

There is no way of knowing the proportions of fact and fiction in these rumors and stories. But what is known is that toward the end of 1964 one of the prominent leaders in Peking, in the course of an attack on revisionist tendencies in the Soviet Union, let fall the remark that in China also there had been cases in which even the Party cadres had displayed "symptoms of bourgeois and feudalistic degeneration." Moreover, my journeys through the interior of the country confirmed that an organizational regrouping on a scale hitherto unknown in China was being carried out. Everywhere I went, on the railroad stations, in the trains, on the country highways I met columns of people from the towns, carrying bag and baggage and on the way to some People's Commune. The Party's strongest bulwark is in the towns. This is where there are reliable cadres and this is where the Party believes it has the young people on its side. Now they were leaving the towns in their thousands, functionaries, officials, state employees, students and school children.

There are a number of distinct points of difference between the *se ching* and the customary annual "out into the country" actions of previous years. They were mainly intended to provide extra hands in the fields for the harvest period, while the new campaign had new features. The cadres from the towns are supposed to stay in the communes for six months or more. Their main purpose is not productive work but the political education of the peasants. "We learn from the peasants, it is true," I was told by a convinced Communist student, "but the main thing is that the peasants learn from us."

Chapter 17

THE REACTIVATION OF THE
PEOPLE'S MILITIA

Another means of exerting political and ideological influence on the masses returned to the full glare of Party work at the same time as the Four Purges campaign. The People's Militia was reactivated. This para-military organization had been summarily created, almost overnight, at the time of the Great Leap and the founding of the People's Communes in 1958. "Let everyone be a soldier" was the motto at this time. Within a few months, according to official reports, 200 million men and women had volunteered for the militia. An entire people had been transformed into soldiers on the orders of the top leaders.

But like so much else that was created in the period of the Great Leap, that period of unbounded optimism when so much was done too quickly and without adequate planning and preparation, the projected vision of a trained people's militia, strictly in line with doctrinal objectives, also faded. In the years of the slump not much talk was heard about "a people under arms." It was not long before the militia existed only on paper, except for some well-trained cadre units in the border areas. Only in the fall of 1964 did anyone appear to remember it again. Then the top-ranking political bodies promulgated decrees and instructions defining the purpose and the value of the people's militia and ordering it to be reconstituted. In the towns, demonstrations and sports meetings were organized, at which military displays, arms drill and shooting competitions were laid on with the aim of popularizing the idea of para-military service. There were also conferences and discussions, at which high Party dignitaries pointed out the basic significance of the militia as China's "spiritual atom bomb."

To most people in the West, the idea of a people's militia appears to be the product of Mao Tse-tung's military and revolutionary attitude of mind. Furthermore, many foreign experts now tend to regard the founding of the people's militia in 1958 as one of the first effects of the Sino-Soviet conflict. In 1957 Peking had demanded that Moscow should supply China with atomic weapons, but the Soviet leaders had obviously thought that to allow the Chinese to have control of nuclear weapons would be too dangerous. In the summer of 1958, during a visit to Peking, Khrushchev flatly rejected the Chinese leaders' demand. Shortly after this, during the Quemoy crisis, the Chinese discovered how little they could rely on the Soviets in the matter of effective military assistance. In place of nuclear weapons and military assistance from China's main ally, a people's militia of millions and millions of people seemed to be asking to be formed. "If the imperialists ever attack China," Mao declared at this time, "they will find it very difficult to advance one single step."

Similar arguments could be advanced at the end of 1964. The war in Vietnam was intensifying. It seemed not impossible that the American government would accede to the demands being made by many of the military advisers for the extension of the fighting across the demarcation line between North and South Vietnam. This automatically brought military countermeasures from the Chinese side and a direct confrontation between China and the United States within the realm of possibility. Party and military leaders in the Chinese provinces bordering on Vietnam were openly stressing their "responsibility for direct support for the revolutionary struggle of the Indochinese people." In view of "the threats of war from the American imperialists," it was said, "the building up of the people's militia must be accelerated, in order to create a solid and determined people's armed force, capable of moving into action at the first sign of danger, and able to fight and win."

In fact, the task of the people's militia has always been something quite different. In the Great Leap years it formed the organizational skeleton during the attempts to implement political and economic aims. Its role in the newly established communes, for example, cannot be overestimated. "The people's militia," it was repeatedly said, "is the revolutionary school of the people." It served as a model, it was the Party's transmission belt in teaching the masses new ideas and new principles and it formed an inexhaustible reserve of activists, young people capable of immense enthusiasm and soldiers released from military service, who could be more easily thrown into unpopular "battles for production."

My observations during my travels across China lead me to regard this function of the people's militia as the more important, in fact the real purpose of its existence. During the whole time I was in China I never had the feeling, so widespread in the West, of a people of 700 million under arms. I hardly ever saw the people's militia, a fact which I did not really appreciate to the full until I spent some time in Communist North Vietnam following my journey through China.

In the North Vietnamese capital of Hanoi the movements of military or para-military units are an everyday sight. Many times, in my hotel room, barked military commands, the rhythmic blowing of whistles or the heavy tramp of marching columns would wake me from my sleep in the middle of the night or in the early morning. Particularly on Sundays and holidays I would meet in the center of Hanoi or in the suburbs military units, people's militia, armed students, and stern-faced uniformed women and girls marching smartly in step, their rifles on their backs. Sometimes the town had all the appearance of a real armed camp. On the way home, uniformed figures would swarm out on foot, on bicycles and in streetcars, like a swarm of locusts spreading out to take possession of the town.

The military element plays a much greater part in the propaganda intended for domestic consumption in North Vietnam than it does in China. In the domain of the Chinese Communists, "socialist construction" and "economic achievements" stay very much in the foreground. In Vietnam, however, the emphasis is on means of stimulating defense preparedness. In an industrial exhibition I visited in Hanoi there were displayed among the modern industrial products photographs and placards which gave the impression that the peasants and townsfolk of North Vietnam were in a permanent state of immediate alert, ready to sacrifice their lives for their fatherland. Serious-faced men plowed their fields with guns at the ready. Old men and women in a rice field, clubs, flails or pitchforks in hand, looked in the direction of the imaginary enemy with expressions of heroic determination. Other pictures showed the mass demonstrations regularly organized in the towns. One picture I found downright grotesque was that of a lovely girl smilingly holding to her breast a placard showing a caricature of an American general in the shape of a monster, out of whose jaws dwarfs, crippled to the point of unrecognizability and labeled "Saigon," were flying straight into a hail of bombs and rockets.

In their conversations with me, Chinese functionaries naturally tried to depict the character of the Chinese people's militia as being similar to the one I was later to find in North Vietnam, both in propaganda and in reality. But what I saw with my own eyes undeceived me. I very seldom saw the Chinese people's militia in the capacity of an auxiliary defense force. When I saw them they were generally doing normal work or, even more often, assembled for political instruction. The salient activities of the people's militia in China are quite different from those of the North Vietnamese militia, which suggests that each of the two parallel organizations has a different task to perform.

This supposition is corroborated by things other than purely personal observation. For example, it is significant that command powers over units of the people's militia in China are exercised not by the military but by the local Party committees. In the fall of 1964 there was an equally significant leading article in the Peking *People's Daily* which said that the exterior function of the people's militia was "to ward off imperialist aggression" and

20. The child and the rice bowl—symbols of China's greatest problem.

21. A Chinese family rests on the Great Wall near Peking.

22. Young industrial workers coming off shift in the Wuhan steelworks.

23. Chinese leaders take every possible opportunity to woo the very young.

24. A Chinese family out for a Sunday stroll on the grounds of the Temple of Heaven in Peking.

25. Propaganda posters decorate the interior of a peasant's apartment in a People's Commune.

26. Some farmers in the South can afford an ox. Most peasants in the North must rely on their own strength.

27. Scene in the Anshan steelworks.

28. Interior of a Peking textile plant.

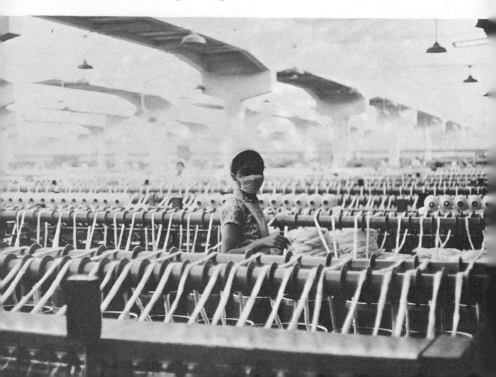

29. Making transformers in the "Horse Bridge" commune near Shanghai.

30. Stocking maker in Changsha. Output—one stocking per hour.

the interior function was "a means of ensuring that the dictator-ship of the people will prevail." How closely this thesis is con-nected with current events was made clear by a proclamation published at the beginning of October 1964 in Sinkiang Province, which borders the Central Asiatic republics of the Soviet Union, justifying the mobilization of the people's militia by "the need to thwart the subversive activities of the revisionists."

In China's border and coastal districts the people's militia does have a certain military value. Para-military units are stationed here, equipped with modern weapons. The militia is also charged with defense and internal security tasks. The Chinese newspapers regularly carry reports of heroic people's militiamen who have caught another Kuomintang agent or saboteur dropped by the Nationalist Chinese over the mainland. Perhaps, too, the leaders think there is something to be said for giving millions of people elementary instruction in the handling of simple weapons.

But in my view the deciding factor is the government's efforts, by the continual indoctrination of a gigantic organization, whose existence is justified not on party-political grounds but by a greatly increased national consciousness, to bind it more firmly to the regime and its policies.

Chapter 18

THE PARTY'S DIFFICULTIES IN
THE PROVINCES

The Four Purges campaign and the reactivation of the people's militia are good examples of the methods of total organization the regime in China has been using in recent years to try to indoctrinate the people. The question inevitably arises: why should such procedures be necessary, how successful have they been and what results have they achieved? The picture of China the foreigner gets is in the main put together from visits to a limited number of towns. Here the agitation and propaganda methods can be used to best advantage and it is not difficult to construct a perfect organizational network; so it may be that in the towns the agitation methods have produced some result. But out in the countryside, where more than 70 per cent of the Chinese people live, things look very different. There the Party has a very difficult task. It is doubtful whether it has been able to establish its control machinery to the same extent as it may have done in the towns and the areas surrounding them.

Not long ago the official Party organ of the Chinese Communists illustrated this by means of an example. Whereas in the towns, for understandable reasons, a great deal of trouble has been taken to train and influence young people, party-political work among the young people in the country districts still leaves much to be desired. According to the Peking *People's Daily,* only 13 per cent of the young people in the country areas were members of the Communist youth organization. Thirty per cent of the brigades in all the Communes had no youth organization at all, and a further 20 per cent had youth organizations consisting of only one or two members. In other words, half of all the People's Communes in China had not even attempted to get things going in a field of indoctrination that had been one of the main areas of political education for years. That being so, what did conditions look like in other sectors of party-political work in the country districts?

In these circumstances it is no wonder that old ideas and beliefs, traditional ways of life and ancient customs are more difficult to eradicate in the areas in which the majority of the population live than in the towns, whose population represents only a fraction of the total figure. The townspeople, moreover, are easier to organize and control and, because of the shifting sociological pattern in the industrial age that is dawning even in China, are much more open to progressive ideas.

During my travels in the interior I saw a number of indications of what the young Communists from the towns, who had been sent out into the provinces in connection with the Four Purges campaign, have to teach the peasant population in the backward country areas. I also saw more clearly why the people's militia organization was to be revived. One Party secretary, who had just been transferred to Hunan Province, frankly admitted that the greatest difficulties in his new post were caused by ideological matters. "Many peasants just don't want to do what we want them to. Some of them in fact simply will not work."

In the South I asked another new commune Party secretary whether it was true, as was being rumored in Peking, that in many places corruption had crept in. He hesitated for a while but then said: "Before my time there may have been some here, too. But there is definitely none here now—not since I arrived."

There were also a number of indications that relations between the simple country people and the Party functionaries were not of the best. "The *kang-pu* [Communist functionaries] are no better than the old bigwigs used to be," a confirmed anti-Party man told me during a chance meeting somewhere in the country.

"You can recognize them right away by their swelled heads and the good material their suits are made of."

In the South I thought I would put a well-known and widely propagated Party slogan to the test—the one that says that in order not to lose contact with the masses, the functionaries should not be afraid of physical labor. While inspecting work in the fields in a commune, I met an old peasant who was plowing a rice field. I asked the commune Party secretary who was escorting me to go ahead and prove that he could also do the work his peasants did. Full of energy and importance he took the plow over from the old man. It was a pitiful performance. The Party secretary could not keep the furrow straight, he stumbled over the clods and kept on overturning the plow. Very subdued, he tried to find excuses for his poor performance. The old peasant, however, was doubled up with laughter and gave me roguish looks, as if to say, "Well done! You really caught him there!"

The Revolutionary Theater as an Instrument of Indoctrination

If the visitor to China does not want to base his judgment merely on incomplete and more or less chance observations, he would be well advised to see as many modern Chinese plays and operas as he can. The themes and treatment of dozens of modern revolutionary plays throw a good deal of light on the problems facing the regime. Time and again the central theme of the events on the stage is the struggle between new ideas and old beliefs. And it was not by chance that the modern theater as an instrument of indoctrination began an all-out campaign at the same time that the leaders ordered the Four Purges and the reactivation of the people's militia.

In the summer of 1964 there took place in Peking an event that leading articles, commentaries and detailed reports in the Party propaganda media all proclaimed to be an occurrence of fundamental cultural and political significance. Twenty-eight companies of the Peking Opera from nineteen provinces assembled for a Festival of Modern Opera. Thirty-seven new plays were given their first performance. The entire Party old guard, including Mao Tse-tung, showed up. They praised the mammoth undertaking as a revolutionary turning point in traditional Chinese art, which would completely change the course of Chinese cultural life.

To the Western observer claims like this may appear to be the standard kind of exaggeration one gets with all the political campaigns the regime engineers from time to time in one field or another. But the opera festival, opened with much pomp and ceremony, and the subsequent full-scale propaganda attempts to popularize modern themes on the stage, differed from the usual obvious routine propaganda. It was the first full-scale attempt to break into a field which had hitherto succeeded in maintaining its integrity within the traditional framework of Chinese art. It was an all-out attack on a bastion of Chinese culture that had been cherished and hallowed for centuries.

This was not the first time since the government came to power that the Chinese Communist Party had tried to change the character of the Peking Opera to bring it into line with Communist views. There had been condemnation of the idealization of the conventional social order contained in the traditional Chinese operas and calls for "the separation of the feudalist chaff from the democratic wheat." There had been occasional censoring of plays and deletions of "unsound" passages. But despite such measures the popularity of the opera remained undiminished. In contrast to the culture of the West, the opera has remained the most popular form of dramatic art in China right down to the present day. Even now, every Chinese child, for example, knows the heroes of the opera episodes taken from classical literature, the main characters in *Three Kingdoms*, *The Robbers of the Liang-Shan Bog*, *The Generals of the Yang Family* or the immortal mythological characters from *Trouble in Heaven* and *Sun Wu-kung Thrice Defeats the White Skeleton Ghost*. The interweaving of musical drama, ballet and acrobatics perfected to the slightest movement, the richness of invention and the unrestrained splendor combine to cast a spell on the audience that no Chinese seems to be able to escape, especially in these gray, monotonous, modern days.

From now on all this was to change. Heroes of socialist reality were to take the place of emperors, princes, generals, monks, concubines and good and evil spirits. "The themes of the modern Chinese opera," said a commentary on this festival, "are taken from the history of the revolutionary struggle or they describe the class struggle that is still going on today. They portray the conflict between the old and new ideologies in our modern society and the awakening of a new generation under the care of the Party. They sing the praises of progressive characters in our socialist construction or reflect the struggle of the national minorities, under the leadership of the Party, to attain their freedom."

These words clearly disclose the motives and intentions of the regime. The idols of the Chinese masses are to be replaced and the Peking Opera is henceforth to serve the purposes not of esthetic pleasure but of party-political indoctrination. Communist heroes of the revolution and the civil war are being exalted to the status of legendary heroes. In the opera *Azalea Mountain* the heroine is the Party secretary Ho Hsiang, who teaches the "iron battalions of the Red Army" revolutionary guerrilla tactics and leads the peasants to victory over the Kuomintang. In *The Fight to Cross the Dadu River* the heroes are an assault detachment in the vanguard of the Red Army during the legendary Long March, who fight their way across a river in Szechwan Province and by this means prevent the almost certain destruction of Mao Tse-tung's exhausted followers. In *The Red Women's Company* the heroine is Wu Chung-hua, who overcomes frightful obstacles to become a steel-hard, victorious revolutionary. In *The Red Cliff* the heroes are a troop of fearless Communists who withstand all the tortures practiced on them in a Kuomintang concentration camp near Chungking and are rewarded for their steadfastness.

A second group of modern operas deal with current themes. They are interesting to the Western observer for two reasons. They not only embody the heroization of the Communist elect, but they also unfold the whole range of internal political problems that the regime still has not by any means solved. *The Story of a Plow* deals with the tensions between simple peasants, still in the grip of old beliefs and ideas, and a group of politically ambitious intellectuals from the towns, who have been sent out into the country "to get into closer contact with the masses." Variations on this same theme turn up in other operas. In *The Saga of the Young Girl Farmer* the heroines are high school graduates who almost collapse under the weight of their fight against old country traditions. In *The Daughter of a Commune Chairman* even the son of an old and trusted Party functionary, educated in a town high school, looks as if he will fall a victim to the influence of "feudal ideas."

The difficulties caused by old family traditions are illustrated in *Never Forgotten* or *In a People's Commune*. One pokes fun at the wicked mother-in-law who tries to maintain the influence which is hers by the ancient laws of the family order against the power of the Party. The other condemns the attitude of a young girl engineer who, after finishing her studies, under the influence of a patriarchal family structure, thinks herself superior and very nearly succumbs to "bourgeois tendencies." *Forward with the Stream* deals with the "modern class struggle in the factories of Shanghai." *A Bucket of Dung* shows how selfish motives and socialist consciousness clash in a marriage in the country. In an endless series of arias the conflict between the young couple is shown, culminating in the question of who is right, the husband, who wants to use their own feces to manure their private land, or the wife, who thinks the commune's fields should have precedence.

But how do the opera-loving Chinese people react to this flood of modern productions full of party-political propaganda? "The modern opera is a necessity for the great mass of the people," the directress of the Peking Opera School told me. As proof of this she cited the fact that "if we show a classical play today, we can fill the house for about ten performances. But we can put on a modern play a hundred times or more and you will still not find an empty seat in the house."

This piece of information must be taken with a grain of salt for more than one reason. It is an open secret that the "popularity" of modern operas is considerably helped along by official action. For example, factories, schools and offices are ordered to arrange collective visits to the theater, free of charge. The difference in reaction between the voluntary audience at the classical opera and the involuntary audience at a modern opera is evident to any impartial observer from the West. Seldom if ever does the audience applaud in the middle of a scene during a modern opera, as they regularly do at the classical opera. Another irrefutable piece of evidence is the difference in the number of curtain calls at the end of the performances.

There is also a significant difference in the expressions in the faces of the audience during the shows. Of course one does occasionally see emotional reactions during modern operas. During the play *Dock Gate No. 6*, all about the class struggle, the audience sitting in front of me had tears running down their cheeks as the hero, distressed and despairing, finds himself obliged after a long fight to sell his child to a "capitalist." As a rule, however, the audience sits in passive curiosity without any personal participation.

It is very different at the classical opera. The audience unrestrainedly goes along with the action, is ecstatic when one of their favorite performers pulls off a particularly difficult piece of business, and every face is alight. "I tell you, the modern opera can't hold a candle to it," a Chinese student told me excitedly when I asked him for his impression after seeing *The White Snake*, one of the finest of all the traditional Peking operas. "Every piece of action is full of wisdom. It makes you think, whereas the modern opera is simple and banal."

The functionaries in charge of cultural affairs are well aware of the state of affairs. The deputy editor of the official theater magazine, Liu Ho-cheng, admitted, "Many people don't like modern opera. They think it is neither attractive nor exciting." For the present, the classical opera is coming off best. And it is true that the esthetically sensitive Chinese, well versed in the harmonious sweep of the Peking Opera, can well appreciate the difference between the simple movements of a Red Army soldier in a revolutionary play and the stylized, majestic tread of a legendary general in a classical opera; or between the gestures of the heroine of *In a People's Commune* as she picks a flower in her plain blue cotton clothes and the elegant grace of an emperor's cocubine doing the same thing. "We must see beauty not in the form but in the content," the cultural functionaries conclude.

It is doubtful whether this will ever succeed. "There is probably nothing quite so difficult to stage as everyday problems," Mr. Liu frankly admitted. This is particularly true in China, where the standards of taste in the elegant and formal things are still very high and where the people already have their fill of the country's problems. The Party never stops recommending measures for solving these problems in school, political instruction or the continual collective meetings; so how can the people be expected to feel any enthusiasm when the same things are presented to them on the stage in their free time?

The Party knows all this. According to an instruction issued not long ago by the Chinese Ministry of Culture, only 30 per cent of the repertoire of the municipal Peking Opera theaters is to consist of modern plays. It is evidently thought that overcoming the opposition and the antipathy toward the modern revolutionary theater will be a long and gradual process. At the moment it is still an experiment and even the responsible authorities do not seem to be at all certain that it will succeed.

The Masses Are Like a Padded Wall

However, the fact that the survival of tradition or apparent antipathy to change has caused signs of domestic political difficulties should not be taken to mean that there is a widespread spirit of resistance or indeed some kind of strong opposition to the Communist regime in China. Certainly there may have been spontaneous unrest in various places during the years of the emergency, between 1959 and 1961; and even today there may be occasional isolated incidents in which groups of people air their discontent. But these things are not, in my view, characteristic of the present political situation in the country. China has to a great extent recovered from the setbacks of past years. It is true that the enthusiasm and confidence felt by many sections of the people in the early years of Communist rule may have diminished, but as against that, the people in both town and country still have vivid memories of the chaotic and unpleasant conditions during the Kuomintang period. What really worries the Communist cadres and sometimes drives them to despair or resignation, or even to relapses into the practices of the old feudalistic order of the kind that has been mentioned, is a certain fundamental attitude in the people, an attitude which makes itself obvious even to the visitor from the West after only a few weeks of his stay in China.

Some important conclusions can be drawn from the experiences I have described in previous sections of this book. On the one hand, the Chinese has shown himself to be prepared to give uncritical and unhesitating obedience to the commands of his leaders; and it does not seem to bother him in the least if this excessive zeal leads to grotesque distortions. On the other hand, there are a great number of indications, both official and unofficial, that the much-vaunted solidarity is not worth very much in reality. For most people the official version seems to serve as a kind of armor that they put on in order to ward off outside influences while they quietly follow their own pursuits as far as possible undisturbed. This attitude may be peculiar to the Chinese mentality, which is said to lean to conformism. It may correspond to the attitude of mind, so clearly revealed in classical literature, which only makes use of violence and open resistance in times of real emergency, preferring otherwise to try to overcome the opponent by cunning and trickery. Or it may be the result of the traditional refusal to accept any jurisdiction outside of the family, the traditional source of social authority.

Whatever the reason may be, for the cadres it means that they cannot get a grip on the masses. The people may look as if they are faithfully obeying the regime's commands, but the effect the leaders really want to achieve just is not there. Hundreds of millions of Chinese are like a padded wall. They offer no resistance; they do as the Party tells them, but not in that spirit of genuine, fanatical enthusiasm the Party would like to see.

It cannot be denied that the number of convinced believers is on the increase. This is also a question of the difference between the generations. But the overwhelming majority still think and act as they have done for centuries. As a shrewd Eastern European observer, who has lived in Peking for years, said to me: "Slogans, mottoes, campaigns, American imperialism, Vietnam and all the rest have little interest for the ordinary Chinese. The only thing that bothers him is whether he will have enough rice in his bowl this winter and whether he will be able to buy himself a new pair of pants next year."

In conversations with me, senior Party officials confirmed this fundamental attitude of the Chinese people, even if in other, less candid words. The leaders, it seems to me, are under no illusion. They admit that the ideological struggle—and consequently their efforts to consolidate political power—will go on for decades yet; or, as it was put on one occasion, "for five to ten generations." They realize the situation and are arming themselves for the future.

Chapter 19

TAMING THE REFRACTORY
INTELLECTUALS

Disinterest, ignorance, lethargy or pretended conformity on the part of the majority of the Chinese people are not the only things bedeviling the efforts of the Communist leaders to abolish political and ideological opposition. There is also a good deal of opposition in the ranks of the people on whom the regime will particularly have to rely in the future development of the country—the Chinese intellectuals. These are always a thorny problem for any totalitarian system, but they are especially so in China, where there has traditionally been a highly educated elite. A Chinese cultural functionary once described the problem in the following drastic words: "The transformation from the old to the new is a painful process for the intellectuals. They have to be dipped three times in clean water, bathed three times in bloodstained water and boiled three times in salt water."

Since the Communists came to power there have been innumerable purges of the intellectuals, dozens of more or less extensive "rectification campaigns" and a constant hail of Party slogans at cultural congresses and public discussions of the arts. How little effect all these early measures produced was revealed in 1957, in the Communist leaders' attempt at liberalization, which went under the name "Let a Hundred Flowers Bloom, Let a Hundred Schools Contend." The Chinese intellectuals exploded into revolt against the guardianship of the Party and the lack of intellectual freedom. Many of their spokesmen had to pay heavily for this when the regime struck back. Since then the leaders have been more cautious. They insist on rigid adherence to the Party's guiding principles and step in immediately and forcefully whenever thought or theory seems in danger of running counter to the current official line. For their part the intellectuals have also learned caution. Everyone is careful not to say anything in public that might be used against him. There is talk of a "conspiracy of silence" among the Chinese intellectuals. This was all the more regrettable from my point of view in that just at the time I was in China, a massive campaign had been started against a group of Chinese intellectuals who must be regarded as representative of certain currents in intellectual circles in China. Premier Chou En-lai had described this campaign as "the Great Debate," which affected a whole list of leading Chinese philosophers, university professors, scientists, authors and artists. Eastern European observers in Peking told me that the effects of the Great Debate were already more far-reaching than the "rectification campaigns" of the period following the Hundred Flowers episode in 1957. Never a day passed during my stay in China without some heated polemic on the debated questions in the leading Chinese newspapers, yet in all the conversations I had with intellectuals, I never came across anyone who even hinted at daring to diverge from the official Party propaganda line on this particular issue.

It is not difficult to establish what the issue is. It is not, as one might think, concerned with the refutation of anti-Communist views; on the contrary, the polemics center on the views of certain Marxist theoreticians, some of whom occupy senior positions in the Party machine. It is precisely for this reason that the leaders regard the campaign as particularly urgent, and it is precisely for this reason, too, that the intellectuals consider it a particularly delicate matter.

Everyone had been fully alive to the dangerous consequences that might follow a slip of the tongue ever since Chou En-lai, speaking to the National People's Congress at the end of 1964, referred to dangerous attacks made by people at home, who "have expressed bourgeois and revisionist views which distort the general line of our socialist development." What is particularly causing the Chinese leaders such a headache today, therefore, is the group of ideas known collectively as "revisionism."

It started with the condemnation of the prominent Party theoretician Yang Hsien-chen, a member of the CPC Central Committee and formerly Director of the Party Higher School in Peking. In the early summer of 1964 there began to appear isolated articles in Party journals criticizing theories Yang had put forward in lectures at the Party Higher School. The initial, relatively mild criticism soon developed into a flood of abuse. The actual wording of Yang's theories was never quoted, but extracts ascribed to him in the critical articles gave the general gist of his ideas.

Yang was alleged to have taken up a position in opposition to the basic philosophical ideas of Mao Tse-tung. His views on the theory of dialectical contradictions were summed up in the thesis: "Two Become One"; that is to say, the antitheses in the development of a society tend to lead to the formation of a new and more advanced synthesis. This, his critics claimed, was contrary to the logic of a truly revolutionary philosophy. Mao himself had said that the unity produced by the synthesis of antitheses was limited, temporary and relative, whereas the conflict between them was absolute. Therefore the phrase should be put the other way around: "One Becomes Two."

The significance for the political field of this apparently abstract and scholarly philosophical dispute is clear. If Yang's thesis —that it would be in harmony with the nature of antitheses to try to attain unity—were correct, the result would be that the Party's task would be to look for the common bases and to allow variations to continue. That, according to Yang's critics, would be equivalent to substituting social adjustment for the class struggle. It would mean negating the historical task of the proletariat in the struggle with the bourgeoisie and striving to reach a compromise with the class enemy. Peaceful coexistence would be possible, even with the "imperialists," and the necessity for just "revolutionary wars" would be a thing of the past.

Another leading Party philosopher was drawn into the attacks

on Yang Hsien-chen, Feng Ting, professor of dialectical material-
ism at Peking University and doyen of philosophic society in
Peking. Like Yang, Feng had acquired his basic theoretical
knowledge through years of study in the Soviet Union. Feng's
ideological works are to be found all over China, and their total
sales are estimated at nearly two million copies. The attacks on
Feng, which began in the fall of 1964, are mainly directed against
views contained in the more important of the works he wrote in
the fifties.

Feng is charged with a whole row of ideological crimes. Like
Yang, he is said to have denied the necessity for the class struggle. He once wrote that this was a waste of human spirit and
human energy. "As long as control over the revolution is in the
hands of the working class, the victory of the revolution will be
attained by peaceful means." Feng sees the relations between
the nations in much the same way. "Our main task must be to
enter into peaceful competition with the peoples of the world
who have different social systems. We must make it possible
for people to compare the good and the bad, so that they can
finally make their own choice." This statement brought down
devastating criticism on Feng's head. "Feng is simply mouthing
Khrushchev's lesson" was the unanimous view of the Chinese
press.

Feng also burdened himself with the mortal sin of "bourgeois
individualism." In his book *The Communist View of Life* he had
declared: "If happiness is to become the daily portion of the
people, we can achieve it only if we are at peace, not if we are
at war: if we can eat well, wear nice clothes and have large,
clean houses; and if love and harmony prevail between man and
wife and between children and parents. There can be no doubt
that this is right and this is what we must strive for." These
words, written in 1956 (and approved by the Party at the time),
were to be Feng's undoing. At the end of 1964 the Peking press
were printing almost daily articles sharply condemning him.

Chu Ku-cheng is the third victim of the Great Debate among
the Chinese intellectual elite. Chu is a professor at Futang Uni-

versity in Shanghai, a member of the National People's Congress and the author of a number of books on Chinese history and esthetic theory. Chu's critics deduced from his works that he was an execrable "subjective idealist and bourgeois humanist" and, what was more, that he had been a traitor during the Sino-Japanese war. The criticism was mainly based on an essay Chu wrote in 1962, "The Historical Position of Artistic Creation."

In this work Chu denied the absolute class character of artistic creation. "Emotion is the driving force behind all art and all spontaneous emotion is stronger than all class consciousness." Great art could never be a stereotype of the current historical epoch but only the purely original expression of the artist's feeling of "the spirit of the age." There were various forms of thought in various epochs, but all these forms flowed together to produce "the spirit of the age," which had always been and always would be a unified whole in every age, even though it was differently viewed by many classes and individuals.

What Chu was opposing was not only the prevailing thesis of the indisputable class character of all art. With remarkable courage he has also evolved historical interpretations which, in the present phase of Communist development, are being used against him. In his chief work, *A General History of China*, which was reprinted in 1955, he makes the claim, *inter alia*, that many of the peasants' revolts in the history of China were not attributable to feudalistic exploitation, as the Communists claim, but were simply the result of overpopulation.

Particularly unfortunate for him was his attempt to present the actions of Chin Kwei, a famous chancellor of the Sung Empire at the turn of the thirteenth century, in a new light. At that time Chin Kwei was pursuing a policy of appeasement toward the Mongols who had invaded the Sung Empire. (From my description of Hangchow earlier in this book, the reader will remember that a statue of the treacherous Chin Kwei in that town is still the object of public contempt.) Chu's cautious attempts at rehabilitating Chin Kwei are now being interpreted as attempts to seek peace at any price. This, it is claimed, is particularly reprehensible in that Chu wrote this work during the Japanese occupation. (The first edition of *A General History of China* appeared in 1939 in Shanghai, which was occupied by the Japanese at the time.) This, in the view of his critics, gives rise to the suspicion that Chu was openly pleading the cause of the enemy and the collaborators.

The effects of the Great Debate were not confined to these celebrated scholars. Creative writers also felt the weight of the widespread "rectification campaign." These also were charged with having ignored the role of the class struggle in social development. The attacks were concentrated on three men whose works have suggested that Chinese official cultural policy is too one-sided. Yang Han-sheng, a well-known film producer, U Yang-shang, a novelist from the South, and above all, Shao Chuan-lin, the deputy chairman of the Chinese authors' association, favor depicting people as they really are, with all their human faults and virtues. But under existing circumstances this would mean that the author or artist would have to devote particular attention to those who, as Shao Chuan-lin openly said at a meeting of the Chinese authors' association in August 1964, were "still undecided between the socialist and capitalist roads." In Shao's opinion, this means the great majority of the Chinese population. The artist must concern himself with them. They could only be brought to gradual, "painful" ideological awakening if the artists and authors created characters with whom they could identify themselves. "Everything we have been doing up to now is nothing but eyewash. All the heroes we create in our writings have red faces [the traditional makeup of the "good" personages in the Peking Opera]; and this is why nobody wants to read our books."

In the eyes of loyal Party functionaries, views such as these were shocking not only because they are in opposition to the official line, but also because they endanger the existence of socialist society. The official Chinese literary journal said in the fall of 1964: "If such views spread, our art and our literature will be robbed of their revolutionary spirit. Socialist literature will gradually be transformed into a bourgeois, reactionary form of art which would ruin the economic foundation of socialism and would pave the way for the peaceful transition from socialism to capitalism."

These arguments do not exactly reveal penetrating logic. What they rather show is the fact that the regime is afraid of even the smallest indications of "revisionist" thinking and takes immediate steps to stamp it out root and branch, although to judge by the experience of the last fifteen years of Communist rule in China, they are having only limited success. The intellectuals will certainly become more cautious than they already are; but what they are really thinking will be all the more difficult to discover for that.

Failing Socialist Consciousness Among the Young People

The Great Debate became the platform for a declaration of war on Party theoreticians, scholars and men of letters who have diverged from the current Party teachings and guiding principles, even if they remain within the framework of Marxist thought. The attacks were not only directed against the wrongdoers themselves; they also served as a warning to those who, as eager disciples of the wrongdoers, might themselves one day follow the same path: namely, the young intellectuals.

As early as the summer of 1964 there were increasing indications that all was not well with the "correct" attitude of mind of the Chinese young people. In June of that year the 9th All-Chinese Congress of the Communist Youth Association was held in Peking. The atmosphere of the proceedings was strange. The whole of the Party leadership attended, including Mao Tse-tung. One leading personality after another went to the rostrum to encourage the young functionaries—indeed, almost to implore them—not to lose the traditional Party fighting spirit and attitude, whatever happened. The old guard was clearly worried about the lack of revolutionary enthusiasm and the influence of modern revisionist ideas among the young people.

This was made particularly evident in the main speech of the meeting, given by the First Secretary of the Communist Youth Association, Hu Yao-pang, who frankly named the three main things about the young people that were bothering the Party. First: there was still a remarkable amount of social class difference left among young people. "Young people from differing classes and social backgrounds are marked by differing class ideas." Second: there was a noticeable drop in revolutionary ardor among the young people. "Young people who are brought up in peaceful and secure surroundings," said Hu, "tend to think that everything in the garden is lovely, and as a result they lose their alertness. This leads to a demand for a more comfortable life." Finally: it was becoming more and more obvious that young people were not being toughened up in revolutionary battle. They no longer appreciated the harshness and many-sided demands of the revolutionary cause that the fighters of Mao Tsetung's generation went through. For this reason the young people were being "corroded by bourgeois ideology. New bourgeois symptoms are appearing among them."

Were these words and the imploring manner of the old guard intended only as an admonition and a warning? Were these frank disclosures only meant to be a shot across the bow, not to be taken too seriously? To find out the real position among the rising generation of intellectuals I paid a visit to Peking University.

This university is particularly rich in political tradition. It has always been a cradle of libertarian thought and a breeding ground of revolutionary ideas and activities. The "May Fourth Movement," which is so highly extolled in China today, was started by students of Peking University. On May 4, 1919, the students organized violent demonstrations against the humiliating provisions of the Versailles Treaty, which made over to Japan all the rights and interests previously possessed by the German empire, without paying the slightest attention to China's interests in the matter. The demonstrations became the scene of bloodshed and were a political event of the first importance. But the Communists were also to be made sharply aware of the libertarian attitude of the students of Peking University in the summer of 1957, when the leaders in their confident optimism thought it would be safe to proclaim the liberal Hundred Flowers campaign and the university was the scene of an access of anti-Communism that was to become a signal for the whole country.

In view of these facts, I was surprised to find that the Vice Chancellor of the University, Tsui Yun-kung, responded to my questions with a frankness that was little short of astonishing. "It is precisely in the intellectuals that bourgeois and feudalistic leanings are still most deeply rooted," he bluntly told me, "and these ideas get automatically transferred to the younger generation, who consciously or unconsciously absorb them. So we are quite aware that as far as the ideological front is concerned, the class struggle will go on at the university, not just for a few years but for many decades."

The range of "bourgeois and feudalistic leanings" among the students at Peking University seems to be fairly extensive. "To give you a few examples," said Vice Chancellor Tsui, "many students just do not grasp the purpose of their studies. We believe that study must be completely devoted to the service of the people, but there are many students who are only studying to gain personal advantage or personal reputation. Again, there are some who show little interest in political studies, which occupy an important place in all our faculties. Many try to avoid collective work, and there are also those who dislike physical labor, are afraid of dirtying their hands, or who despise soldiers and peasants—in short, who display the kind of intellectual arrogance that used to be so common in the old days."

"Revisionism in the Communist movement" also played a considerable role, the Vice Chancellor assured me, a role that should not be underestimated, "since revisionism and bourgeois leanings are closely connected." Naturally, the conflict with the Soviet comrades had caused great confusion among the students, even if only a minority shared the Soviet views on specific issues. "We still have not found anyone in the university who completely accepts the whole of the Soviet viewpoint."

As proof of his assertion that only a minority leans toward "deviationist ideas," the Vice Chancellor gave me some figures on the social backgrounds of the students at Peking University. At the same time, these figures also show why ideological difficulties were bound to arise. In contrast to the standard practice in the Eastern European Communist countries, admission to a university in China is not restricted to the so-called worker and peasant class; the intellectuals are needed, no matter what class they spring from. "No less than 53 per cent of the students come from workers and peasants' families. Only 5 per cent can be considered as springing from the genuine exploiter class," Tsui proudly told me. As to the other 40 per cent or so, he maintained a discreet silence, which probably means that they come from the real former bourgeoisie. "Yes, we still have our difficulties. But our struggle to overcome them will be a purely intellectual one. We have discussions and we try to convince and help all those who have taken the wrong road." And with that Vice Chancellor Tsui concluded his report on the situation.

Are the functionaries justified in feeling optimistic? I thought I observed in the students an attitude comparable to the one I had seen among a large section of the people in another connection—namely, the faculty of being able to wrap themselves in ideological armor that conceals their true inner motives. In a conversation with students taking German studies, I asked them why they had chosen to study German. They replied: "Learning a foreign language is a weapon in the class struggle, a weapon in the fight against imperialism and revisionism." I asked them to elucidate. They promptly answered: "We are learning German as an important political task." It was only later in the conversation, when the atmosphere was more relaxed, that the individual motives came out. Being a teacher, said one, was a fine and pleasant profession. Another said that working as an interpreter gave one the opportunity to meet interesting people from abroad. Moreover, as I later found out from another student in Central China, there are better prospects of advancement because only a few people take German, in comparison with the number taking English or Russian.

These and similar experiences show that the orthodox Communist teachings are far from being firmly anchored, even in the minds of the younger generation.

Chapter 20

REVISIONISM IS THE GREATEST
THREAT TO THE REGIME

The refusal of the leaders to budge from the orthodox revolutionary line and the tenacity with which they defend the so-called "purity" of the gospel is not merely a question of ideological faith and uprightness; it is of fundamental practical importance. This emerged from another interview I had, in which I had a long discussion with the Chinese economist Yung Lung-kwei. Some years ago he was the Vice President of the State Planning Commission. Now he is the deputy chairman of the Council for the Furtherance of International Trade and professor of economic science at Peking University. The subject of the discussion was China's future domestic, economic and social policies.

Professor Yung opened his remarks by saying: "You know the Marxist theory of socialist development. First of all the bases of socialist productive conditions must be created; then the productive forces must be developed. We think we have not even dealt with the first point yet. It is true that there is no longer any private ownership of the means of production; and the administration of the economic sector and the system of distribution have both been socialized. But all this has not yet been sufficiently consolidated. There are still a great number of social evils that must be wiped out, and this cannot be done overnight. We shall need decades. Why? Because China is a very large and backward country with a population of some hundreds of millions. To achieve success we shall need a long time to develop the creative impulses of the people. Only hard work and the right motivation can help us, and even then only if we build on sure and strong foundations."

Yung Lung-kwei illustrated what he meant by "sure and strong foundations" by means of a comparison with modern developments in the Soviet Union. "The Soviet leaders maintain that the basic socialist productive conditions have already been created. Therefore, according to the classic theory, the productive forces must now be developed, by which they mean that the important thing now is to increase production and attain a higher standard of living. That is also our aim, naturally. But the consequences can be very unfortunate if one starts from wrong premises, claiming that the foundations for socialist development have been not only created but also consolidated, and then it turns out that in reality they are weak and fragile.

To drive home his point, Yung quoted some glaring examples. "Look at what is happening in the Soviet Union, where profit has been made the main yardstick of their economic policies. I do not deny that our firms have to produce profits, too. But in socialist production this must not be allowed to become the deciding factor. If it does, it cannot help but have harmful results. The Soviet comrades continually put forward the argument that since there is no private ownership of the means of production, there can be no exploitation or great personal wealth. But what is the point, when many a factory director in the Soviet Union can cheerfully put large sums of money into his own pocket through bonuses or surreptitious profits? What is the use of planning or state control in the public interest if, as is happening in the Soviet Union today, plants are allowed to buy raw materials and other production requirements just as they see fit, to suit their egotistical profiteering plans?

"Or again, look at the privileged caste in the Soviet Union. When they introduced the idea of so-called 'material incentives,' they did away with the sound socialist principle of payment by results. Today the motto in the Soviet Union is: everyone will work hard if it will bring him more money. So every Soviet citizen is eager to get his hands on as much money as possible. The only thing the privileged class of big money earners think of is buying a house, a car, a villa and so on—even a private swimming pool or a private plane, for all I know."

The conclusions drawn from these observations by my distinguished host were simple: "A spontaneous movement toward capitalism is under way in the Soviet Union. It is being stimulated by the thesis that what has to be done now is to adopt the so-called positive aspects of a free economy. As far as we are concerned, this thesis is completely unacceptable. If it were correct, it would mean that in the advanced stage of a socialist economy, principles of capitalist production would automatically come into play, even in a socialist country. That is a completely false and absurd theory. In reality the situation is merely this: no socialist development can be carried out—or it must automatically lead back to capitalism—if socialist consciousness is weak and if the foundations, the necessary conditions and the bases of socialist development are rotten. The mistakes being made by our Soviet comrades only reinforce the view we have taken for years and years, that it is still going to take a great deal of time and hard work before we can get rid of the contradictions in our social structure and the remnants of the old ideological and political ideas." With these words, one of China's leading economists was saying with astonishing frankness that the reason why the mailed-fist policy had to be maintained at home was not sheer pleasure in theoretical argument or an urge to apply the genuine classical teaching, but cogent and realistic political considerations. Unless the requisite political and ideological conditions for "socialist development" have been created, unless the "existing contradictions in society" and the "remnants" of traditional beliefs have been abolished, there will be an automatic reversion to "capitalistic" conditions. In other words, because these essential preconditions do not yet exist in China, the fight to achieve the regime's goals and aspirations must still be carried on stubbornly and uncompromisingly.

This accounts for the ordaining of a series of widespread

220 REVOLUTIONARY ROAD TO NATIONAL REBIRTH

campaigns and actions such as the Four Purges, the reactivation
of the People's Militia and the Great Debate. If *per contra* Peking were to follow the same "revisionist" path as the Soviet
Union, to slacken the reins once more or to be too generous with
subjective "material incentives," then—or so the Chinese Communist leaders fear—given the existing political situation, Communism might be swept away. These fears seem to dominate
the thinking of the old guard of the omnipotents, accustomed to
thinking in terms of guerrilla fighting and the civil war—all the
more so in that they will have to quit the political stage in the
not-too-distant future and want at all costs to avoid the possibility that their revolutionary inheritance will fall into decay.

In China, more than in any other country in the world, domestic policies are paramount. This was made clear to me by a
circumstance connected with the interview with Yung Lung-kwei
just described. I had not asked for the interview. It was offered
to me unexpectedly, a few days after Khrushchev's fall from
power—that is to say, at a moment when speculation in the
Western world on the possibility of a *rapprochement* between
Peking and Moscow had assumed some highly curious forms. As
far as I knew, Yung's comments in his conversation with me
were the first direct statement made to a Western visitor on the
Chinese attitude toward the change of leadership in the Kremlin.
For this reason, they seemed sensational to me, and I asked
Yung if I might cable my paper a report on the main points
of our conversation. With a charming smile he pointed out that
for obvious political reasons the interview had been regarded as
confidential from the beginning, and that an immediate report
on it would not be fitting. Once I had returned home I would,
of course, be at liberty to make use of it in the appropriate con-
text.

The Chinese leaders seem therefore to have thought it important even at this stage that my general reports from Peking
should give some indication of their skeptical attitude toward
the new turn of events in Moscow. They were above all concerned to make very clear one important point in the Sino-Soviet

dispute, perhaps the most important of all. This point was undisguisedly revealed in what Yung Lung-kwei said, and is plainly purely domestic in nature. The ideas and methods of the Soviet type of reformed Communism cannot be expected of China at this time. To adopt them might be to shake the foundations of the Communists' power in the country.

Both analyses of the Sino-Soviet conflict and assessments of Chinese foreign policy will therefore have to take much more account of this basic domestic political aspect than has generally been done up to now.

Chapter 21

WHITE DEVILS AND
COLORED BROTHERS

Chinese foreign policy is motivated by a number of different forces. Irredentism; emotionally and historically conditioned anti-imperialism; the desire, natural to the most populous nation in Asia, to become the political leaders of the continent; the resolve to increase the prestige and standing of a country that has led a humiliating shadow existence for over a century; the effects of the belief that ideologically, as a result of the break with Moscow, China has become the only representative center of world Communism; all these are unrelated factors, whose influence and intensity are continually changing and can never be exactly determined.

Other elements of Chinese foreign policy must be regarded as resulting from the internal political situation and methods. First: the efforts to achieve economic self-sufficiency and the desire to accomplish everything without help from outside compel the Chinese to follow a policy of the greatest possible independence of other powers. But conversely the Chinese are trying to prevent the threat of isolation in the foreign policy sphere by making special, and usually immoderate, efforts. Second: if the principles of revolution and the class struggle are valid in the internal political field, they are necessary much more so in the foreign policy sphere.

Finally, there is a factor which should not be underestimated and which can perhaps be described as a defensive element in Chinese foreign policy. In all nations and in all ages the practice of overcoming domestic resistance and internal difficulties by undertaking some activity in the fields of foreign policy has been a tried and tested procedure, even if not always free from danger and not always successful. A resolute foreign policy is especially likely to have favorable results for the government's internal policies if it runs parallel to a strong emotional current in the people. This is precisely the case in China.

There can be no mistaking the signs of a strengthening as of national feeling in China. The Middle Kingdom is in a phase of national rebirth. The successful overcoming of a period of intense difficulty unaided; the absence of any catastrophic famine in three successive years of natural disasters; the entry of China upon the world political stage as a power to be reckoned with; the increasing number of countries according China diplomatic recognition; the atom bomb, and Peking's revolt against Moscow's claim to leadership in world Communism —all have produced in the people a feeling of pride and confidence which the regime is now trying to exploit for its own purpose. The fact that the totalitarian propaganda methods employed to do this produce frightening excesses is another story. By energetically fostering a spirit of national consciousness, the Communist leaders are gradually and systematically endeavoring to bring about a state in which the entire people will wholeheartedly identify themselves not only with the national but also with the ideological and internal political aims of the regime.

The foreign visitor to China perceives signs of open nationalism wherever he goes. On the journey from Peking to Inner Mongolia, our train made a short stop in Ching Lung-chao, "the Bridge of the Blue Dragon," the place where the railroad pierces the Great Wall. All the passengers tumbled out of the train. In an endless procession, soldiers, peasants and officials made a pilgrimage to a small memorial at the end of the station. Here there is a portrait in bronze of Chang Tien-yu, the first Chinese engineer to build a railroad in China. It is not this fact alone which appeals to the imaginations of the passengers, but rather a chain of circumstances which preceded it. Japanese and British engineers had previously been given the job of building a stretch of railroad in this mountainous region, but after making exhaustive studies of the area they believed it could not be done. Thereupon Chang made some investigations of his own and came to the conclusion that if special precautions were taken the project was not impossible. He was given the contract and successfully carried out the work.

The unsensational little everyday event I have just described demonstrates the elements which are helping to accelerate the growth of Chinese national consciousness. Chinese imagination, Chinese inventiveness and Chinese initiative are believed to be capable of outdoing the knowledge and technique of other nations, be they ever so powerful and advanced.

This underlying feeling is demonstrated in sublimated form in the Peking revolutionary museum. The unprejudiced visitor may perhaps expect to find presented here a heroic epic of the Communist movement in China; and this is to some extent so. But what will surprise him in the portrayal of the Chinese revolution is the way the accent has been shifted to correspond to deeply felt popular sentiment.

The exhibits do not begin with Sun Yat-sen's republican movement in 1905, as the visitor might expect, or the fall of the Chinese empire in 1911; nor with the founding of the Communist Party in 1921 or even with the rise of Mao Tse-tung, beginning in 1927. They begin with the Opium War against the British in 1840. Basically, therefore, the Communist revolution has been transformed into nothing less than a century-old war of liberation against Western imperialism. A large number of pictures and documents depict the heroic struggle of the Chinese against the foreign invaders during the Opium War, the Taiping Rebellion and the Boxer uprising. The rooms are decorated with a captured cannon, equipment, flags and other war trophies.

The thousands of visitors are particularly interested in the "unequal treaties" imposed on the helpless and humiliated Chinese empire in the nineteenth century, forcing China to cede territory or sovereign rights to foreign powers. The collection does not yet include the "unequal treaties" with czarist Russia. When I asked why these documents were not also on display, the director of the museum replied that this was "a complicated matter"; but his expression revealed that the eventual publication of these degrading documents was only a matter of time and not of principle.

It cannot be disputed that China is entitled to present this epoch of Chinese history even in this form. What foreign imperial powers perpetrated on Chinese territory at this time, even allowing for a good deal of stupid and arrogant behavior on the part of the Chinese, constitutes one of the blackest chapters in the annals of world history. The carving up of the country into spheres of interest, the establishment of extraterritorial concessions in the most important commercial centers, the annexing of border territories by foreign powers, "gunboat diplomacy" in relations with the Chinese government—all these things were hardly calculated to make the Chinese people trust the foreigners and their modern ideas. It would go beyond the scope of this book to describe these historically fatal events in detail, but their effects are still felt in China even today. For the Chinese, the word "imperialism" has associations far beyond anything the concept evokes in other countries, where it has almost become an empty slogan.

Mistrust of the West

As a result of his historical experiences with them, the Chinese, even without the ideological gloss, views the Western nations with skepticism and mistrust. This is understandable in a people accustomed more than any other to thinking in terms of historical epochs. There are some slight variations, admittedly. The states that have lost their imperial power, mainly France and Germany but also including Great Britain and Japan are less severely judged. Chinese attention is consequently concentrated on the only genuine world power left in the West—the United States of America.

Official propaganda consistently exploits the people's emotionally conditioned nervousness to help to put across the regime's political ambitions. In the distorting mirror of Chinese propaganda, the truly fearsome devils are the American imperialists. America governs the Pacific; American guns, rockets or divisions threaten the Chinese mainland from Formosa, Japan, the Philippines or South Vietnam; the Seventh Fleet, with its colossal fire power, cruises in Pacific waters off the coast of China. The United States is doing its best to limit China's influence by means of political and military alliances and open intervention in the Far East. China feels herself hemmed in. The world power called the United States of America is constantly harassing the Red Dragon. It is no wonder the U.S.A. is still proclaimed to be China's archenemy. If anything, recent developments in South Asia and the Caribbean area have only increased the Chinese leaders' anti-American feelings. The President of the United States has become a "bandit chief" and his government the initiator of "unbridled aggression" and "brutal oppression."

On the twentieth anniversary of the end of World War II in May 1965, the Chief of the Chinese General Staff, Lo Jui-ching, writing in the Party journal *Red Flag*, took the trouble to make a comparison between the American government and Hitler. But the United States of America was much worse than Nazi Germany, he said, much more perfidious, much more dangerous and much more insidious. "American imperialism is even more murderous than Hitler. The United States makes use of even its closest allies and partners, such as Great Britain and France, or its most devoted lackeys, like Synghman Rhee and Ngo Dinh Diem, just as long as they are of use, and then, when their services are no longer required, it kicks them out—sometimes, in fact, once the ass has done its work at the wheel, it is simply killed off."

It is pointless to try to get Chinese into a sober discussion of

American policies. Any attempt to explain or justify the bases and principles of American actions seems quite useless. The picture the Chinese has of America is full of resentment and prejudice. Hatred of America is unbounded and deep-seated, and there is not the slightest indication that there will be any change in this feeling in the foreseeable future.

The anti-American campaign still dominates everyday propaganda. At the Great Wall in the Northwest I came across a young girl functionary in her Sunday best. On her blouse she had embroidered a heavy boot stamping on a map of the United States. In the May Day festivities in the Summer Palace in Peking the same characters appeared again and again—the caricature of the "American imperialist," complete with sunglasses, and the bearded liberation hero in the uniform of the Fidelists. In the modern opera the presentation is always the same—boorish GIs with red hair and fat noses are easily defeated by Chinese, Korean or Vietnamese champions of the revolution. The imperialists, wearing ties and European suits, are shown as the quintessence of baseness and cunning.

There is one experience that I remember particularly well because it was so blatant an illustration of the anti-American campaign. During my visit to the Anshan steelworks in Northeast China I was taken to see the kindergarten belonging to the workers' estate. Here the children performed the little games usual on these occasions. But in addition to the nursery rhymes and dances, I was clearly intended to see the patriotic attitude of the three-to-four-year-olds.

One tiny fellow had a machine gun slung around his neck. He climbed onto a chair and lifted his voice in a song about the soldiers on guard in Fukien Province, across from Formosa, in which the singer swears to thwart any attack on the fatherland by the American imperialists. The song was hardly through when American imperialism entered in the shape of a four-year-old girl on hands and knees and with a wolf's-head mask over her face. With a loud cry the hero of the piece saw the wolfish intruder, swung the machine gun and fired at the invader.

Meanwhile three little girls jumped into the fray and pretended to bayonet the American pseudo-wolf until he quivered and gave up the ghost.

Friendship with the Developing Countries

But if there are unmistakable signs of implacable hatred of America, there seems to be a natural counterbalance in China's decided friendliness toward the uncommitted developing countries. Not only does this fit in with the anti-imperialist theme, but the political, social and economic conditions in the countries concerned are very similar to those obtaining in China; and this approach offers the Peking government a promising field which suits China's aims, both ideological and foreign.

The *People's Daily*, the CPC's main organ, once gave a very clear exposition of what the Chinese leaders are primarily out to achieve. Speaking of all developing countries, the paper said: "We are all in the same boat, all striving, now that imperialism and colonialism have been driven out, to develop our economies and overcome our poverty and our backwardness. For this reason we must wholeheartedly trust the strength of our own peoples, make full use of our own resources and, relying solely on ourselves to help each other, afford each other as much material aid as possible and exchange ideas on economic development." To rise to the leading position in an association of young, striving but backward states, and by this means to become an important element in world politics, seems to Peking to be an important political target for the immediate future.

The various good-will trips Premier Chou En-lai has been making in Africa and Asia in recent years underline this aim. People in the West have often thought there were more superficial reasons, such as the hope of recruiting support for China's standpoint in her dispute with India, a plea for China's admittance to the United Nations or peddling the Chinese point of view in her quarrel with Moscow. Certainly such topical

questions are discussed, but Chou En-lai's extraordinary flexibility and his willingness to adapt himself to the specific interest
of the country he happens to be in reveal his anxiety to avoid
even the suggestion that Peking is concerned with defending
or furthering China's own interests. What Peking is after is
solidarity, a suitable vehicle for China in her attempts to attain
international standing and influence. A good example of this attitude was contained in the communiqué issued at the conclusion of Chou En-lai's discussions in Ghana at the beginning of
1964. This said that Afro-Asiatic representation in the United
Nations must be strengthened, although this question "must
not be regarded as having any connection with the demand for
the restoration of China's rights in the United Nations." The
shrewd efforts to establish a kind of United Nations of the "have
nots" and the deprived are an illustration of the Chinese leaders'
tactical moves.

The emphatic friendliness toward the African, Asiatic and
Latin American developing countries—except for such countries
as India, which could dispute China's claim to leadership—also
turns out to be a useful device in the domestic political field.
There was good reason for launching the slogan "The circle of
our friends is continually growing." The energetic building up of
connections with the neutral countries is intended to be a justification for and a confirmation of the correctness of the regime's
political actions and to take the wind out of the sails of possible
critics at home, particularly following the break with Moscow.

So when the Chinese leaders issue a flood of invitations to
citizens of the underdeveloped countries, they are pursuing not
only a foreign policy aim but a domestic one as well. There can
be no mistaking the success internally. African and Asiatic
friendship delegations, Latin-American emissaries and cultural
groups, statesmen and university students from underdeveloped
countries all over the world are now a familiar sight in the towns
and cities of China. As far as I could see, the reception given
them by the people was altogether friendlier than that given to
members of other nations. The leaders seem to have succeeded

—at least as far as the more enlightened among the Chinese people are concerned—in creating a feeling of solidarity and sympathy and to have strengthened the belief that the Chinese and these peoples share a common fate and have common problems to master.

At the foreign policy level, the results seem to vary. My own observations and conversations I had with visitors from developing countries during my journey left me with an over-all impression that on the whole these visitors would take with them a fairly favorable picture of what the Chinese were doing. Here are some examples. On my first flight to China, about a dozen young Africans from Rhodesia boarded the plane in Karachi.

In the course of conversation I learned that they were members of the Rhodesian People's Party, and had been invited to go to Peking to study for six months. The most intelligent of the group gave a perfectly understandable reason for accepting the invitation. "I am no Communist," he assured me, "but we are being bombarded with so many political programs from all sides that it seemed to us that it would pay to see what the situation really looked like, so that we can judge for ourselves."

Less than a week after this meeting I ran across the likable young African again, this time at the Great Wall near Peking. He was surrounded by a group of intelligent-looking Chinese students and functionaries who were respectfully and courteously explaining to their guest the history and architecture of the Great Wall. The African visitor was taking a cheerful and relaxed part in the conversation, but as soon as he saw me his expression changed to a helpless smile. He was clearly embarrassed by our meeting and the reason was only too clear. What met my eyes was a transformation that verged on the grotesque, for the Rhodesian had put off his sloppy clothes, the red checked shirt and faded blue jeans, and had exchanged them for the standard uniform of the Chinese functionary. The change made him look more dignified, without a doubt; but the feeling of having, for transparent reasons, been forced into much less comfortable apparel—and one, moreover, which indicated a particular form of political belief—embarrassed both him and me because of its symbolic significance.

On the return flight from Shanghai I traveled in the company of a group of Africans from Tanzania. They were of all different types, both as regards age and as regards their educational level. Next door to the plump, elderly African woman, who had to sign her customs declaration form with a cross, sat a young student thinking deeply about all the things that he had seen in the three weeks of his stay in China. "There was a lot I didn't like," he said soberly. But this critical comment was followed in the next sentence by a comment that demonstrated both the political ambitions of the Chinese and the success of their efforts to woo intelligent Afro-Asians. "One thing I became firmly convinced of in Peking is that it is useless to rely on help from the West or from the Russians. Both of them only want to make us dependent on them and to create new forms of colonialism. We must build up our future state exclusively by our own efforts and with our own resources."

In theory, the Chinese Communists' pretensions look very good, and visitors to China from the underdeveloped countries may be impressed. But in political practice Peking is meeting with some difficulties. These are simply and solely caused by the weakness of China's economic position. China may be able to deliver fine-sounding phrases and persuasive arguments but she is hardly in a position to offer any worthwhile material assistance to the "weak ones." For this reason the developing countries will continue for a long time to give a skeptical reception to China's efforts to woo them. On the other hand, China's claims to leadership might develop into a force to be reckoned with if the present steadily widening gap between the poor nations and the rich ones reached a stage which would promote revolutionary activities on the Chinese pattern. This is all the more so because hand in hand with this process goes a growing dislike of the advanced white industrialized nations.

Events in various parts of the world in recent years have provided support for this hypothesis. Peking has suffered setbacks in Africa, it is true. For example, I was reliably informed in Peking that invitations to attend the splendidly ceremonial fifteenth-anniversary celebrations of the Communist seizure of power were sent to the heads of state of all the countries Chou En-lai visited during his extensive African tour at the beginning of 1964. Peking was particularly anxious to have Ben Bella, the Algerian leader, and was banking on a momentous political demonstration that would not fail to have its effect in both Washington and Moscow. But instead of the great demonstration of fraternal solidarity there was only exasperation. The presidents of Mali and Congo-Brazzaville were the only prominent representatives from Africa who showed up.

But Peking is by no means giving up, as is clearly shown by the activities of Chinese functionaries—particularly in East Africa—and Chou En-lai's journey in the spring of 1965. Particular attention is being paid to the Arab countries. No miscalculations or setbacks can shake the center in Peking. Patiently and tenaciously the Chinese are sticking to the course they have charted.

In contrast to Africa, the situation in China's own Asiatic neighborhood in 1963 and 1964 looked much more hopeful. The position in South Vietnam was encouraging. The pro-Chinese swing in Cambodia was regarded as proof of increasing Chinese influence.

In the meantime the situation in the continent of Asia has changed considerably. The increase in American military effort in Vietnam has created a new situation in Indochina and despite Chinese support the outlook for the Vietcong and North Vietnamese is much less favorable than it was in 1964. The Chinese intervention in the Indo-Pakistan conflict in the late summer and fall of 1965 led to a fall in Chinese prestige. Finally, the failure of the attempted Communist coup in Indonesia at the end of September 1965 made it plain that for the Chinese the road to absolute leadership in Southeast Asia will be a hard and painful one.

However, all these things have failed to induce the Chinese to modify their general line. The Chinese leaders are accepting these setbacks and regarding them as a purely temporary impediment. The authorities in Peking still believe there is reason to work out tactical maneuvers against the day the Americans will relinquish South Vietnam and the power grouping in the whole Southeast Asian area will be transformed overnight. In Indonesia the "progressive forces" will come into their own and Burma and Thailand would hardly be able to withstand Chinese requests for "friendship." In highly industrialized Japan there would be a reinforcing of the view that this of all times was not the moment to run risks in seeking to play a more important role in the Pacific area. Finally, looking far ahead, the possibilities of making a political thrust against the two bastions of India and Pakistan would have to be considered. Already, in spite of anti-Communism and the revulsion against Chinese methods felt in the ruling circles of these two countries, there is a growing if grudging admiration for the Chinese. They wonder how China has managed to achieve this steady increase in prestige and political influence and to become the dominating power in Asia. These gains are in direct inverse ratio to the growth of the political standing of these two countries in the eyes of a large part of the world.

Even if such considerations appear premature, it is certain that the countries of South and East Asia—and in many other parts of the world, too—are fascinated by the colossus and the way it has succeeded in acquiring so much respect for its political importance and its potential might, so suddenly and with such brutal force. The developing countries will continue to feel skepticism and fear toward China; in some cases these may even increase. But along with this skepticism and this fear there will also be admiration, respect and a desire to follow the same road as China.

Chapter 22

OPPOSITION TO MOSCOW

China's negative attitude toward the leading Western power, the United States of America, on the one hand, and her positive attitude to the uncommitted developing countries, on the other, are two of the basic elements of Chinese foreign policy. These two opposite poles seem logical and comprehensible, but a third feature of present Chinese foreign policy—the state of open hostility to the Soviet Union—needs some explanation. For many years Moscow was hailed in Chinese propaganda as a loyal and helpful ally. Suddenly that stopped. Just like the U.S.A., the Soviet Union is now the object of violent polemics, is accused of fraud and disloyalty, abused as a traitor and stigmatized as an enemy of China.

In the course of a journey through China undertaken at the height of the Sino-Soviet conflict, it was inevitable that the dispute between Moscow and Peking should come up time and again in conversations with functionaries, officials and the ordinary man in the street. The arguments put forward by the people I talked to were a mixture of ideological justification and realistic political motivation. The current Western belief there can be only either one cause or the other, either the ideological issue or a palpable clash of national interests, may make this compound seem unlikely. In fact, however, it emerged from the various comments made to me that both of those elements can exist at the same time without difficulty; indeed that they are actually compatible with Marxist thought.

Before I go into detail on this point, I should like to deal with a piece of wishful thinking common in the West. This arises from the belief that the Chinese are a people without room to expand in. This leads to the thesis that if the existence of China is to be assured, China needs more territory. The most promising possibility lies in a northerly direction, it is thought, where the vast, unpopulated areas of Siberia lie, expanses which the hard-working Chinese could transform into fruitful farms and gardens. According to this thinking, Chinese pressure northward is natural, urgent and logical. This theory has been hawked around for years, its very simplicity assuring it eager acceptance. It was inevitable that a number of political commentators should regard the thesis of the Chinese urge for expansion at the expense of the Soviets as the final and decisive reason for the controversy between the two world Communist centers.

Now it is a fact that there have been tense situations on the long Soviet-Chinese border in recent years; they have been openly reported in the Chinese press. But all the information that has emerged from various sources makes two facts quite definite. In the first place the border disputes were never the cause but, at most, incidental results of the quarrel between Moscow and Peking, which had already begun and which had quite a different origin. In the second place the difficulties in the border issue, which have arisen mainly in the Central Asian sector of the border, are primarily ethnological in character and are governed by questions to do with membership of the largely nomadic Muslim Uighur and Kazakh minorities living on both sides of the border.

There is another reason why the theory of the pressure for expansion northward is a weak one: the premises are questionable. As I have already shown in the second part of this book, the Chinese leaders do not regard their people as having inadequate living space. In Peking they are well aware of the country's problems, particularly those having to do with the food supply and the population question; and they have drawn the necessary conclusions in word and deed. To suppose that the leaders would pursue a naïve policy of expansion that would do nothing to solve the nation's basic problems would be to misjudge the hardheaded sense of the responsible leaders in Peking.

Equally, the northward expansion theory would presuppose that the Communist leaders in Peking are liable to run amuck. Everyone in China knows the level of the Soviet Union's military might and the dangers involved in a military clash in which China would be completely on her own. Any drastic forward move in the territorial question would be tantamount to suicide. It is therefore not surprising that both in the violent polemics between Moscow and Peking, in which no argument of any kind has been omitted, and in all the conversations I had in China, the border issue played a very minor role, if indeed it played any part at all. Peking may occasionally bring it up for tactical reasons and it may, years from now, play a more important part if the Chinese ever feel themselves strong enough to clear up the matter of the "unequal treaties"; but in the present state of affairs and as a reason for the break with Moscow it is completely unimportant. In any event, to overdramatize the territorial question is to divert attention from the real cause of the Sino-Soviet conflict.

If you ask anyone in China what the aims of Communism are, you will receive the same answer as you would get in Moscow, Prague, Bucharest or in any other Communist city. The creed is the same everywhere. Everyone believes in the inevitable downfall of capitalism and the certain victory of socialism. Everyone is convinced that an organized and determinedly led class struggle will bring about this economic transformation on a global scale. They all insist on the social transformation that has taken place in the countries in which Communism has come to power, and all are working hard to attain rapid socialization, collectivization and industrialization. There is universal agreement that the influence of these can extend outside the boundaries of the countries concerned and can contribute to a slow but sure change in the balance of forces between capitalism and socialism in favor of the development of Communism. In addition, all the Communist command staffs equally firmly believe that this process can be accomplished only in the face of internal opposition or threats from without provided that the Communist parties keep a tight hold on the reins of power and provided the unity of all Communist parties is assured. This common faith, which I call the heart of the doctrine, embodies a clear aim supported by all Communist parties.

However, in addition to the common doctrine just described, the Communist ideological concept contains another component. This is the claim to be entitled to issue basic instructions to all members of the Communist community on the methods to be employed in attaining the doctrinal aims. This element of the ideology is referred to as the direction or guiding line of Communist tactics. It is discussed at regular intervals by representatives of the parties and subsequently declared to be binding on all.

While the doctrine remains unchanged, therefore, the program of action can change, depending on the current internal or external outlook for the chances of increasing Communist power at the given moment. Without the doctrine, the ideology would sink to the level of pure pragmatism; if there were no program of action and if it rested only on the doctrine, the ideology would be nothing more than a rigid, stereotyped dogma. It is this amalgamation of doctrine and action program into an ideology that gives Communism the impact that manifests itself in a mixture of unbending will and flexible maneuverability.

From this abstract delineation of the situation it can be seen that the ideological concept can be changed only if, as a result of a change in political conditions, an alteration in tactics is called for. A modification in methods can be justified by a shift in the basic political situation or a reappraisal of it. There is thus a constant possibility that differences of view will arise among the alliance of the Communist parties in the evaluation of the political situation and that as a result a dispute will break out on the need to alter the common program of action. Differences in evaluation can come about for a number of reasons, but what is important is that they all have their origin in differences in assessment of purely political factors. In that case, there is of course a likelihood that in view of the close links between doctrine and action program, a clash of ideological principles will be inevitable. What appears at first sight to be a conflict of concrete political interests is necessarily reflected, in the next phase, in the ideological sphere, becomes a separate, independent issue, and then, in the guise of the "correct" ideological postulate, reacts on the political action to be taken.

This process is demonstrated in the long development of the Sino-Soviet conflict. The Chinese with whom I talked left no doubt about the clash of interests in the political sphere, which have now been amply publicized in the undisguised polemics between Moscow and Peking. The Chinese Communists regard the Soviet concept of "peaceful coexistence" as prejudicial to their interests, the Moscow action program calling as it does for a measure of agreement with the leading power in the West to adopt measures to prevent an atomic holocaust. Moscow's constant willingness to talk to Washington arouses in the Chinese leaders a fear that their Soviet allies would be quite willing to ignore Chinese interests—for example, her claim to Formosa—in favor of their own. This leads Peking to conclude that Moscow is conspiring with "the gendarmes of world imperialism."

Similarly, the Moscow thesis of peaceful economic and political competition in the developing countries conflicts with Chinese interests. This has been made particularly manifest in the diametrically opposed attitudes of the two Communist centers toward India. Moscow has been courting the favor and friendship of New Delhi for years. In the border dispute between India and China the Kremlin maintained an attitude of semineutrality, which Peking could not help but regard as an unfriendly act.

India is perhaps a special case, since specific national Chinese interests are at stake. But the basic principles underlying Moscow's policies toward the developing countries clash with China's interests for other, more general reasons. It is just in this field that China's material resources are limited, which is why the Chinese leaders are aiming at grasping the leadership of the "deprived" group in the world-wide altercation between the "haves" and the "have nots." This is in line not only with the elementary principles of basic Marxism, which demand that Communists should support the cause of the weak and oppressed in all countries, but also with the Chinese aim of creating between the two previous centers in the East and the West a third force that will cluster around Peking and receive its impulse from there. This conflict of interests is what leads to the ideological claim that Moscow is "betraying the Marxist-Leninist concept of the class struggle."

Another important difference of interests arose in the internal sphere of "socialist development." Earlier in this book I gave a number of examples to explain why China cannot accept the reformed type of Communism that has become necessary in the Soviet Union. China, with its enormous economic and population problems, is still in a transitional phase in which any undue relaxation might endanger the existence of the regime. The organizational and indoctrination measures seem to show how seriously this danger is taken by the Peking leaders. In the ideological debate it gave rise to the charge that Moscow had succumbed to "symptoms of bourgeois and capitalist degeneration." I increasingly incline to the view that this aspect of the conflict, conditioned by China's domestic situation, is the most important of all.

I agree that this seems to be contradicted by the fact that the strictly orthodox considerations and measures taken by the Peking leaders, aimed at iron austerity and rigid discipline, have obviously not provoked a wave of detestation in the country. The foreign policy aspects of the conflict with Moscow, the controversy over the principles of peaceful coexistence or the rigmarole about the divergent views on how the class struggle is to be continued at the international level have little interest for China's millions. They have other, more trivial problems to think about and even for the great majority of the lower-level functionaries, who daily have to worry themselves about more modest but equally difficult matters, these important issues are mainly of theoretical significance.

After the painful experiences of the brutal methods of the Great Leap and the welcome liberalization period that followed, it might be thought that a program of modified Communism such as the Soviets are promulgating must meet with the approval of wide sections of the people and the lower functionaries in China. That this appears not to be the case and that the Chinese leaders have obviously succeeded in suppressing any leanings in this direction is, in my view, very largely due to Soviet actions in one particular phase of the Sino-Soviet quarrel. The sudden withdrawal of the Soviet experts in the summer of 1960 had not only material but also far-reaching psychological results, whose influence on the political consolidation of Communist China is generally underestimated in the West.

"Upright Communists" Are Transformed into "Vindictive Imperialists"

One of the most astonishing things about my journey through China was the fact that official quarters attached great importance to my being shown in detail, everywhere I went, the serious consequences of the breaking off of Sino-Soviet economic relations and the withdrawal of the Soviet specialists from China that Khrushchev decreed.

Shortly before I left Peking for the interior, the internal information service for middle- and higher-grade Party officials—which has a circulation of half a million and gives considerably more detailed coverage of world events than, say, the official mouthpiece and Party organ, the *People's Daily*—printed extracts from a report of mine on the Soviet-Roumanian dispute that appeared in the *Frankfurter Allgemeine Zeitung* in the fall of 1964. I was assured in Peking that this had been done with a purpose. "You will get to hear a lot of things," said a connoisseur of the subtle informational methods of the Chinese Communists in the capital. "The local functionaries in the provinces are prepared for your arrival and now they know what particularly interests you and what they are to tell you about."

And that was the way it happened. During my tours of plants and factories, my Chinese escorts would frankly tell me all about the course of events and the consequences of the Soviet Party leader's sensational move in the summer of 1960, which was intended, by means of an abrupt and complete cutting-off of all economic assistance to China, to bring the Chinese leaders to their knees. The departure of just under fourteen hundred specialists and technicians and the cancellation of some 250 joint scientific and technical projects may appear to the observer from a highly industrial Western country to be unimportant, considering the size and requirements of China. But a country that is still in many respects in the elementary stages of industrialization sees it from quite a different angle.

Some examples from the mass of material I collected particularly illustrate the importance of Soviet economic aid and the catastrophic results that followed when it was cut off.

An agreement was concluded with the Soviet Union covering technical assistance in a heavy industrial plant in Shenyang, in Northeast China. Soviet specialists were to introduce a rationalized, modern electro-welding technique, enabling "large machines to be assembled with small welding outfits." This new method necessitated a complete reorganization of the manufacturing process. When the Soviet engineers were withdrawn overnight, taking all the plans with them, there were still, according to the agreement, one and a half years of technical assistance to go before the reorganization would be completed and the Chinese technicians fully trained. "The departure of the Soviet colleagues caused a very long period of lost production," the director of the plant told me. "Our engineers set about experimenting and trying to figure out how to carry on by logic and experience. It cost us months of very hard work and desperate fumbling, months in which practically nothing could be produced."

In the Anshan steelworks, also in the former Japanese northeastern industrial center, I was told about similar happenings. "The Soviets had contracted to deliver and properly install a modern rolling plant in the rolling mill belonging to the combine. By the summer of 1960 a part of the rollers had been delivered, but after the breaking off of economic relations Moscow stopped the delivery of the rest. So for a long time our plant was just standing idle. We still can't produce modern rollers like those we got from the Soviet Union. In the end there was nothing for it but to try to use the old rollers longer."

The contract to install new cutting machines for the rolling mill at Anshan was also broken. "By the summer of 1960 the Soviets had only delivered the subsidiary components; the main parts have never arrived to this day. So there we were, stuck with our old plant." Other projects were also broken off. "All over the plant area there are a number of installations for the expansion and modernization of the whole complex, still standing in the same half-completed state they were in when our Soviet colleagues left them in 1960."

Moscow's action in the summer of 1960 had particularly serious results in the ancient imperial city of Sian. The capital of Shansi Province, with its one and a half million inhabitants, was to be expanded into an industrial center for the Northwest. More than two hundred Soviet specialists and dozens of experts from the other countries of Eastern Europe supervised the construction of factories, particularly for the manufacture of machinery, electronic products and chemicals. "They were given three days to pack up and leave," a senior provincial administrative official told me. "It was simply frightful. Many factories have not been finished. Others were completed only with tremendous difficulty and long delays. Production at our switch-gear plant, for instance, was three years late in starting."

In the tractor plant in Loyang they had different troubles. The plant had been completed in 1959. Thereafter Soviet experts pro-

31. Enormous statues of Mao Tse-tung are carried through the streets on public and national holidays.

32. Mao's portrait is woven in silk in a mill in Hangchow.

33. A reading room in the workers' club, property of the rubber-boot factory in Changsha, Hunan Province.

34. High school children digging drainage ditches in Shenyang.

35. & 36. Scenes from the modern revolutionary opera. Above, a scene from *The East Is Red*. Below, a scene from *The Red Sister-in-law*.

37. A young hero in an Anshan kindergarten sings the song of the patriotic sentry on guard against "American imperialism."

38. Communist functionary in a state holiday center in Hangchow.

39. The modern young Chinese Party functionary.

40. People's Militia during a parade in Peking.

41. Miniature shooting gallery in Nanning, near the Vietnamese frontier.

vided technical advice and assistance in the installing of new and improved processes. For example, in 1960 it was decided to build a new oil pressure device into the standard tractor to simplify the feeding of the fuel oil from the tank to the motor. In the middle of the turnover the Soviet technicians were taken away, and took the blueprints with them. "It took us a year to work out how the new system worked. All that time production was at a standstill."

It was also in Loyang that I heard about another cause of friction, one that is practically unknown to the West. After the stoppage of technical aid, the Soviets suddenly demanded to be paid for their technical and other work in the construction of the Loyang tractor works. "They wanted an additional five million rubles," the director of the plant indignantly declared, "even though we had not only paid off all our debts, but could have demanded the return of seventeen million rubles from the Soviets for installations they had failed to deliver. This Soviet demand was disgraceful not only for that reason but also because some of the things they did deliver were old and out-of-date and the price demanded was much too high anyway."

The most calamitous results of the Soviet reprisals, however, were caused to the modern steel-making complex in Wuhan on the Yangtze Kiang. This plant, constructed with Soviet help, went into full production in 1960. "Just at the very moment when we needed them most, the Soviet specialists left us in the lurch," the director of the complex complained. Almost every branch of production was affected, the ore preparation, the steel manufacture and particularly the rolling mill. Only the trained Soviet experts could have kept this modern plant running. "Our people were too inexperienced. They lacked the necessary technical skill and knowledge: they couldn't cope with the problems that came up. The damage caused by the loss or fall-off in production was incalculable. To this very day we still can't cope with the continuous process from the mine to the most modern production of sheet steel."

It was planned that sheet metal was to be produced in Wuhan

by the end of 1960, and this was the basis of the agreement. But even today only the naked concrete housing for the metal-rolling plant stands in the vast factory grounds. "We are considering whether we should make a start on building up this branch of the complex. In the meantime we have been able to produce the necessary components ourselves."

All the people I spoke to assured me that the damage caused by the Soviet actions in 1960 had been made good. "The Soviets' treachery has taught us to stand on our own feet, to take the initiative ourselves and to rely upon our own resources in building up our industry. We have succeeded completely," I was told again and again. This claim became a national slogan. Nevertheless, it cannot disguise the fact that the setbacks caused to the country's industrialization program were enormous and that the effects are still felt today.

More important, however, in my view, than the material losses caused by the Soviet reprisal measures in 1960 were the psychological effects on the Party officials and the great mass of the people. For over ten years there had been a massive propaganda effort to sell the Soviet Union as the Chinese people's great and helpful brother, friend and ally. Efforts were made to wipe out any lingering feelings of resentment among the people by pointing out that Communist Russia was a completely different thing to czarist Russia. Where socialism prevailed, it was said, there was only brotherliness.

But in 1960 the illusion was shattered. Hundreds of millions felt their long-standing bias confirmed—Communist or not, once these long-nosed foreigners think they have the upper hand of the Chinese, they all turn into "imperialists," try to blackmail China, to humiliate her and make her the object of their rapacity and intrigues, just as, in the view of the ordinary Chinese, they have now been doing for over a century.

In the years that followed, the official propaganda line, arguing that China could only rise again by her own efforts and using her own strength, did much to nurture this deep-rooted feeling in the people. It was accepted, understood and respected, and to a certain extent it created a kind of solidarity between the leaders and the people; and this undoubtedly played an important part in the process of internal consolidation that followed the three catastrophic years of 1959 to 1961.

Bitterness and Dislike Still Continue

The effects of the Soviet move in 1960 are important in another respect, too. They impede any *rapprochement* between Moscow and Peking. The prospects of a rapid reconciliation are in any event slight, on account of the growing number of causes of friction through the years. Even the fall of Khrushchev in October 1964 did not make much difference.

I was in Peking when this happened. The sensational events in the Kremlin did not evoke anything like the same astonishment or the same torrent of speculation in Peking as in other world capitals. The faces of the functionaries revealed their satisfaction at the downfall of the chief exponent of "modern revisionism," but this satisfaction never grew into transports of victory. Official press media recorded the event in unemotional, laconic statements. Questions I put to official agencies or to Communist functionaries during my travels in the next few days were answered with a skeptical shrug, as if to say they were harboring no illusions and were still suspicious. The chief matador of modern revisionism had disappeared from the political arena, no doubt, but his clique was still in power. The Chinese were waiting to see if there had been any significant change in Moscow's political and ideological views—that was the invariable tenor of the reaction.

And in the closing months of 1964 and early 1965 it did occasionally look as though Moscow was intent on trying to patch up the quarrel. There was no lack of attempts from the Soviet side to bring about a kind of armistice or truce in the conflict with Peking. It began immediately after the fall of Khrushchev with the postponement of the preliminary conference of the Communist parties, at which it had originally been intended to "excommunicate" the Chinese Communists. Later this conference was turned into a harmless consultative assembly.

The polemics suddenly vanished from the controversy, to be replaced by assertions on the absolute necessity for "the unity of the socialist camp." The new premier, Kosygin, undertook a good-will journey to the Far East. In the North Vietnamese capital, Hanoi, under the influence of the first American air attacks, he even went so far as to declare that these air attacks brought the Soviet Union and China closer together, just as the removal of Khrushchev had opened the way for "increasing unity."

But nothing came of it at this stage. The Chinese wanted not merely fine words but deeds. The halfhearted Soviet plotting during the conference of the Communist parties seemed to the Chinese to prove that the Soviets still maintained their claim to exclusive leadership in world Communism, even if they were going about it more cautiously. But above all it was in the realm of foreign affairs that the attitude of Khrushchev's successors did not suit the Chinese book. The Chinese could not accept the way the Soviets went on strictly following the peaceful coexistence policy Khrushchev had developed. On this basic issue the Soviets did not budge an inch from their previous position, simply because it would obviously not be in their interests to do so. Moscow's equivocal attitude to the war in Vietnam and continued willingness to talk to the West had shown this.

In the developing countries, the targets of so much wooing, the Kremlin is still pursuing a moderate course, the policy of political and economic competition and not of revolutionary fervor. The visit of the Indian Premier Shastri to Moscow in the spring of 1965 was a clear demonstration of this.

Nor has there been any narrowing of the differences of view on the important matter of "socialist development." The new duumvirate of Brezhnev and Kosygin remain firmly attached to the economic and cultural policies already set out by Khrushchev; in certain questions they are even venturing beyond the previous "revisionist" limits. The new party program of CPSU is still claimed to be the authoritative guide along the road to Communism. The Chinese have repeatedly described this program as revisionist to the highest degree and have demanded that it be scrapped if there is to be the slightest chance of rebuilding a common foundation. The plenary sessions of the Soviet Central Committee that have taken place since Khrushchev was deposed have consistently followed a course that is regarded by the Chinese Communists as the continuation of a pseudo-capitalist economic program aimed at increasing consumption.

Naturally, the Kremlin is trying to pacify the Chinese or at least to mark time in the conflict with Peking. The violent Chinese agitation that Khrushchev allowed himself to be drawn into led to defeats for the Soviets in world Communism and undermined their standing and prestige. All the same, the Kremlin's tactics in the months following the fall of Khrushchev brought no change in the conflict of interests between Moscow and Peking. Occasional apparent flickers of change cannot disguise the fact that for the Soviets charity begins at home. At the end of 1965 the Chinese leaders made unmistakably clear what they thought of the apparent Soviet attempts at appeasement. They proclaimed the thesis of "the three illusions and the three realities." What Moscow was doing was nothing but "pretended anti-imperialism, in reality capitulation; pretended revolution, in reality betrayal; pretended unity, in reality division."

In November 1965 the polemics between Moscow and Peking flared up anew. The Chinese Communists unleashed a flood of bitter invective against the Soviets, whose behavior, the Chinese said, had created a final gulf that could no longer be bridged: in Marxist jargon, "the contradictions" had become "antagonistic." The Soviets had no option but to make some reply. Their response, while still restrained, unequivocally rejected the Chinese criticism as slanderous and provocative. The statements by both sides gave no hint of the slightest readiness to yield or compromise.

The greatest difficulty is still the fact that the quarrel has been raised to the ideological level. A Communist party's claim to political power rests on the "correct" interpretation of the ideology. Ideology means power, just as Communist power is unthinkable without ideological justification. Any party which bows to the ideological criticism of another Communist party not only loses standing and prestige within the world Communist movement but in addition inevitably raises doubts about its right to rule inside its own country. For this reason, as soon as ideology comes into play in political differences, there is not much room for maneuver in the settlement of the actual or original issues through reciprocal give and take.

All these political and ideological factors standing in the way of an adjustment of the differences between Moscow and Peking were only added to by the psychological effects of the Soviet actions in 1960. The reason why these are so important is that their traditional and emotional character evoked an unusually vigorous response among the people, much more strongly felt than all the political and ideological arguments. The result was that in addition to the hatred of the leading Western power, the United States, there was now disappointment, bitterness and disgust at the former friend and ally, the Soviet Union, and her loyal satellites.

Chapter 23

THE THEORY OF THE
"INTERMEDIATE ZONES"

Today China stands in opposition to the other two atomic powers. She has swum free politically, so to speak, but in doing so she has put herself in danger of ending up isolated. The leaders must fear that left to herself, China will never be able to fulfill her planned ideological and political mission. The Chinese diplomats have therefore been trying for a long time to make contacts outside the two atomic giants. They are everywhere trying to create understanding, trying to find friends, to establish connections on all sides—or at least to spin threads— that will lead to the power-political status in the world for which China is striving. From whichever point of view she argues, whether political, ideological or economic, in the end it all amounts to one thing—China is determined to create for herself an independent position as a factor in the association of great powers.

As we have seen, Peking's political and diplomatic efforts are being concentrated on wooing the African, Asiatic and Latin American countries. But the Chinese leaders are levelheaded enough to be able to make an objective assessment of the advantages of these connections for their country's power-political standing and the real benefit for her own development. It is not surprising, therefore, that Peking is now paying special attention to other, avowedly pro-Western countries in the area between the United States and the Soviet Union's loyal Eastern European satellites.

It was not difficult to find ideological justification for this foreign policy tactic. For years Peking has been proclaiming that the United States of America is the real enemy of socialism and the center of imperialism. The CPC's famous 25-Point Program, issued in the summer of 1963, said: "The strategic aim of American imperialism has always been to invade and take control of the intermediate zone between the U.S.A. and the socialist camp, to wipe out the revolution of the oppressed peoples and nations and then to destroy the socialist countries and enslave all the peoples and countries of the world, including America's own allies, and put them under the control of monopoly capitalism." Accordingly, the guiding principles of Communist foreign policy must be "to unite all the forces that can be united, to exploit the differences between the enemy countries and to create the broadest possible united front against the American imperialists and their accomplices." This united front is intended to include not only the neutral countries of the intermediate zone—called the "first intermediate zone"—but expressly those also that are allied with the United States. These are referred to as the "second intermediate zone."

This new foreign policy theory of Peking's is not, as might appear on the surface, directed exclusively against the United States but is also aimed at Moscow's power-political claims. This was made clear by the Soviet leaders' hysterical reaction to the Chinese theses with regard to the so-called intermediate zones. The Kremlin has repeatedly and violently attacked Peking's intermediate zone theory. The CPSU Central Committee's ideological journal, *Kommunist,* opened the assault on the Chinese theses in October 1963, and Suslov, the Party theoretician, continued it in his speech to the CPSU Central Committee in February 1964. Chinese propaganda, he claimed, was currently being restricted to the fight against the United States and skirting around its allies. Seen objectively, this meant that Peking was "trying to whitewash the imperialists in England, France, West Germany and Japan. We are justifiably worried about the fact that the Chinese leaders are *de facto* making common cause with the reactionary, warmongering elements of imperialism."

At first sight the Soviet arguments may seem surprising, considering that for years now the Soviet Union has been doing its best to play one Western ally off against another in order to torpedo their alliance with the United States. Depending on the situation or the opportunity, one or another of America's allies has been courted for obvious reasons. It may therefore appear that the Soviets are annoyed that the Chinese are now trying— and perhaps with more success—to wrest from Moscow the initiative in the attempts to subvert the Western alliance. Moscow's anxiety may not be entirely unfounded. Mao Tse-tung made known his views on the balance of forces in a very unorthodox way at the beginning of 1964. Answering a question from a French parliamentarian as to what he thought of a "third force" in the world political arena, he said: "For me, the third force is France, Germany, Italy, England and—provided it stops being an agent for America—Japan."

Peking's Interest in West Germany

One element in Moscow's attempts to subvert the Western alliance is particularly important. Since, in spite of all the Soviets could do, it proved impossible to separate the Federal Republic from the Western alliance by dangling dreams of a new Rapallo before her, the indicated line seemed to be to make Bonn the whipping boy. For some time now, the main aim of Soviet policy on Germany has been to denigrate West Germany in the eyes of her allies, to represent West German political aims and ambitions as disruptive, troublesome or even dangerous to all attempts to achieve peaceful cooperation between the nations; and by this means to split the Western alliance.

These subversive efforts are not an end in themselves, of course. Back of them lies the intention to maintain and secure the integrity of the possessions that fell to the Soviet Union after

World War II. Divided Germany is still the most sensitive point in the area bounding the Soviet empire. For this reason alone West Germany is bound to occupy a special position in Communist foreign policy. Bonn is inevitably the chief target of Soviet diplomacy and propaganda, the purpose being to achieve a revaluation, consolidation and finally general recognition, *de facto* and *de jure*, of the East German government.

As long as there did not appear to be any essential conflict of interests between Moscow and Peking, the Chinese solidly supported Moscow's point of view. For Peking also, Bonn was the great troublemaker, whose "revanchist machinations" threatened the socialist camp. Parallel with this, Peking fostered good relations with East Germany. In fact, relations between the Chinese and East German Communists were most cordial for many years, both sides quoting their common functions and common tasks. Both of them said they had "unsolved national problems," both of them claimed to be "outposts of the socialist camp, one in the West and the other in the East." Close economic relations followed, and in 1959 East Germany was China's second most important trading partner after the Soviet Union.

All this changed when the Sino-Soviet conflict became public and East Germany came out unconditionally in support of the Soviets. At first the Chinese tried to win the East Germans over to their side. The pro-Chinese leader of the Albanian party, Enver Hoxha, was brought into action, when in the fall of 1961 he accused the Soviets of timidity and retreat in the Berlin question. When the Moscow atomic test ban treaty was concluded in the summer of 1963, the Chinese themselves entered the arena, declaring that the form of the declaration of accession accepted by Moscow was "a betrayal of the interests of the East German Democratic Republic." The Soviet leaders had "sold out the interests of the German people." The agreement had increased the status of Bonn and at the same time lowered the standing of East Germany.

When the East German Communists showed no sign of changing their attitude, Peking tried another tack. The thesis of the intermediate zones provided an opportunity. The theoretical Party organ *Red Flag* had already expressly included West Germany in the new Chinese foreign policy concept in March 1963, and at the beginning of 1964 Mao Tse-tung repeated this in the conversation with French parliamentarians already mentioned.

Moscow reacted strongly, as already indicated in the extract from Suslov's speech to the CPSU Central committee in February 1964. But the reaction of the East German Communists was nothing short of hysterical. Their chief ideologist, Kurt Hager, speaking at a plenary session of the East German Central Committee in July 1964, described the inclusion of West Germany in the Chinese intermediate zone theory as a "thoughtless underestimation of West German imperialism."

Particularly instructive, however, was an attack made by Hermann Matern, a member of the East German Politbureau, in April 1964 in his speech on the occasion of the Lenin commemoration ceremonies in East Berlin. According to the incomplete extracts quoted in the East Berlin newspapers, Matern is reported to have said: "The final result of the Chinese leaders' plan would be the complete selling out of East Germany as the Western outpost of the world socialist system in Europe and a revival of the Beria clique's policy on Germany."

This reference to Beria, whom the Soviets had repeatedly accused of intending to betray the East German regime by a too-daring reunification policy (although they never produced any evidence to prove it), not only suggests that the arguments used against the Chinese Communists may have been conditioned by considerations of propaganda, but provides striking evidence of the nervousness in the Eastern European Communist camp about the catastrophic effects that might result from even the most harmless-seeming Chinese attempts at a *rapprochement* with Bonn. And this in spite of the fact that the Chinese have never given the slightest indication of wanting to drop Ulbricht and in spite of the fact that at no time during the Sino-Soviet controversy has there been any indication that the Chinese were about to make any radical change of course in the most important issues in Communist policy toward Germany.

There were, it is true, a number of indications at this time, in the spring of 1964, that Peking was making serious efforts to get West Germany into the intermediate zone concept. The Chinese press campaign against West German "militarism" and "revanchism" was stopped. The English-language *Peking Review* simultaneously printed a sober and not at all polemic analysis of the position of West Germany in the balance of world political power. The essential point of the article was that West Germany would increasingly let herself be guided by her national interests, and that Bonn was no longer an "American protectorate." In conclusion the *Peking Review* stated that "for the near future Bonn's chief policy line, for practical reasons, will be to try to gain the friendship of a number of countries."

Several equivocal statements made by the Chinese Foreign Minister, Chen Yi, to a small group of international journalists at the beginning of May 1964 startled Moscow and East Berlin. I was one of these journalists and handed in several written questions on German-Chinese relations, including a particularly ticklish one on the reaction of the Chinese government to the statement by Hermann Matern that the aim of Chinese policy, like that of Beria, was to sell out East Germany to the West. Chen Yi did not answer it.

He did, however, deal in detail with another one. This asked how the Chinese government envisaged measures to improve German-Chinese relations and whether the setting up of a West German trade mission would be a suitable first step. Chen Yi replied: "Our trade relations are quite good, and are improving year by year. We have not yet considered the establishment of trade missions, but when the requisite conditions are ripe, then we shall of course consider it. It is our deeply felt wish that both parts of Germany shall be reunited in genuine peace. It is definitely not our intention to exploit connections with West Germany to put pressure on East Germany or our relations with East Germany to put pressure on West Germany. Despite the fact that the East Germans belong to the group within the international Communist movement who condemn China, we are still not willing to abandon our correct attitude toward both parts of Germany. We shall continue our trade relations with West Germany. We are and shall continue to be especially interested in importing precision instruments from West Germany. But we are resolutely opposed to the policy, which started with Adenauer and is being carried on by Erhard, of relying on the United States for the realization of revanchist aims."

These few sentences embodied the whole of Chinese policy vis-à-vis West Germany: China was interested in good trade relations with West Germany. At that time, on the other hand, she was also interested in irritating the Soviet and East German governments with vague and ambiguous statements. This was shown in the use of the wording "both parts of Germany" and not, as is customary in the Eastern camp, "the two states." The expression "German Democratic Republic" was not even mentioned in Chen Yi's statement: he spoke only of "East Germany" and "West Germany." But on the other hand he left no doubt as to the Chinese government's intention to maintain its basic stand on the German question and to try to prize West Germany loose from her close alliance with the United States.

The West German government did not respond to Peking's first cautious feelers, even though there was a possibility of undermining the Soviet Union's basic German policy. First contacts between Bonn diplomats and Chinese representatives seemed to bring assurance that the Chinese would be willing to agree to include a special clause on Berlin in the final text of an official trade agreement. But when Chancellor Erhard declared in June 1964, after a visit to President Johnson, that West Germany, in deference to her American allies, was opposed to the establishment of any official relations with the Chinese, the picture changed in a flash.

All at once the Chinese press revived the old propaganda attacks on West Germany, and shortly afterward China concluded two economic agreements with East Germany. In the spring of

1965, at the time of Ulbricht's visit to Cairo and the West German diplomatic crisis in the Middle East, the Chinese leaders vehemently supported the viewpoint of the Soviet Union and East Germany and violently abused West Germany. On one occasion the Peking *People's Daily* said: "The Chinese people are resolutely opposed to the insidious plans of the West German imperialists to isolate and annex East Germany and unconditionally support the people of East Germany in their just struggle against the West German militarism and revanchism whipped up by the American imperialists, and against the notorious Hallstein Doctrine; and support the defense of East German sovereignty."

The heaviest attack was made by Peng Chen, a member of the Chinese Politbureau, in a speech he made at the end of May 1965 at the Aliachim Academy of Social Sciences in Djakarta. Referring to the Soviet Union's German policy, he said, "If they [i.e., Khrushchev's successors] are supposed to have altered Khrushchev's revisionist line, why are they carrying on with Khrushchev's policies, which are aimed at selling out East Germany? Why don't they have the courage to take measures to thwart the provocations by West German militarists, who had the impudence to hold a meeting of the Bundestag in West Berlin and thus challenge the German Democratic Republic and the whole socialist camp in the most shameless fashion? Why have they shelved the proposal for the quick conclusion of a German peace treaty and for a solution of the Berlin problem and don't dare even to mention it?"

The chronological course of events in the relations between China and West Germany illustrates Chinese tactical thinking. First of all the conflict with Moscow leads them to take measures to frustrate the plans of their former allies. Secondly they stick rigidly to their attempts to gain a foothold in the so-called "second intermediate zone," this all the more because General de Gaulle's actions have given Peking cause for optimism. Initial setbacks, such as the failure to get into contact with Bonn in 1964, will not shake the Chinese. When they think the time is ripe, they will make fresh moves. This thesis is supported by the ingrained conception the Chinese have of Germany, which is radically different from the one the Eastern European countries have.

How the Chinese See Germany

Although official Peking policy had been switched over to "anti-Bonn" in the summer of 1964, I made some astonishing discoveries in the fall of that same year. In my very first conversation with a young, intelligent functionary in Kunming, I was greeted with the words: "I am glad you have come to China. One can talk more sensibly with people from West Germany nowadays than with Khrushchev's vassals from East Germany." This was something I might have expected in the spring, on my first visit to China, but it seemed out of place now, in the fall.

On October First the speakers at the celebrations to mark the fifteenth anniversary of the founding of the Chinese People's Republic were entirely on the side of Moscow and East Germany as far as the German question was concerned. However, when the East German ambassador gave a speech on the Chinese national day a few days later, he did not feel called upon to return the Chinese leaders' compliment, even in the form of a passing reference. I asked East German representatives stationed in the Chinese capital the reason for this strange behavior. They answered that in view of all the chopping and changing in China's policy toward Germany in recent months, it would be unwise to put too much faith in the new course.

Both of these experiences induced me to do some research into what the Chinese think of Germany. At every suitable opportunity, in government offices, in factories, People's Communes, schools, or in conversations in trains or teahouses, I asked the same questions: "What do you know about West Germany? What do you think of the situation? What are the chances for a policy based on the commercial interests of Germany and China within the limits imposed by their differing political and ideological systems?"

The answers I got were variegated to a degree one would hardly expect in a country whose people are constantly being subjected to a flood of monotonous, uniform agitation and propaganda. These were simple workers, artisans and peasants, to whom the word "Germany" was like something out of the realm of fable. Many of them had never even heard of the division of Germany, much less of the German problem. Others replied promptly: "For me Germany means mainly industry and chemicals. That's all I know."

Junior functionaries and officials saw things differently, although they seemed troubled by uncertainty. And it must be admitted, it is not easy to align the old Communist picture of West Germany as a monopolistic, revanchist and militarist danger with the new version portraying the country as a potential partner in the intermediate zone. The more cautious among them played safe and confined themselves to ideological clichés. "I have seen a number of West German films and always recognize the real theme as being the social conflict in your society," a functionary told me in Kunming. "Social conflicts prevail in your country; the class struggle triumphs, even if the exploiters try to disguise the fact."

A woman functionary I talked with in a Peking textile plant thought the same: "The ruling circles in Bonn represent only a minority. Not everyone in your country lives well. A man who has a job today doesn't know if he will be on the street tomorrow." The editor-in-chief of a Chinese literary magazine was even more certain: "Freedom is only a disguise. In reality, what you have in your country is the dictatorship of the bourgeois."

But then, when West Germany's foreign policy problems came to be discussed, there emerged a characteristic that I found again and again in my conversations in China. In contrast to the picture of Germany painted by the Communists in the Soviet Union and the Eastern European countries, the Chinese Communists admit that there are extenuating circumstances. The leaders in Moscow,

Warsaw or Prague concentrate on "German revanchism" in their campaigns against Bonn, but in China I heard practically nothing of this distorted image. I had the feeling that this was something that one saw in the papers from time to time but nobody really paid any attention to. In conversation, at all events, the Chinese Communists seemed to regard West Germany mainly as a victim of "American imperialism," the object and not a participant in the European political tug of war. "The Americans have military bases in your country, don't they? Therefore the West German people are oppressed. You are not free to act as you choose," concluded the director of a Peking primary school.

The most interesting conversation I had on this subject was one I had with the Party secretary of a People's Commune in Hunan Province. This talk contained the elements I have already described, but it also showed how sober and unprejudiced Chinese thinking can be. For almost the whole day I had been pestering the intelligent and knowledgeable functionary with questions about Chinese economic, population and internal policies. Finally he asked if he might now put some questions to me.

"I have often wondered," he began, "why the German people's desire for reunification is so weak, in fact hardly noticeable." I tried to give some account of the position. When I had finished, the Party secretary replied with a smile, "Your explanation doesn't really convince me. What I rather suspect is that in this question, too, American imperialism is a serious obstacle. We at any rate have had experience of it in Taiwan."

My reply to this was that whatever the shape of Chinese experience in the Taiwan question might be, the German question was based on entirely different premises. I pointed out that Mao Tse-tung himself, in his conversation with Japanese socialists in August 1964, had denounced Soviet expansionist policies after World War II. In Mao's opinion the Soviets had annexed too much territory. In Europe, for example, Moscow had taken a piece of Poland and, in compensation, had given the Poles a piece of Germany. It was only natural, I went on, that a defeated and prostrate Germany should have looked out for a strong ally who could protect her against this kind of Soviet neo-imperialism. My companion grinned appreciatively at the words "Soviet neo-imperialism."

Even today, I continued, there had not been much change in this situation, which was why the West German people were happy to have American troops stationed on their territory. China herself had had a taste of "Soviet great power chauvinism." Another broad smile. The Party secretary, instead of simply quoting some propaganda cliché, as one might have expected, replied: "Your argument sounds very plausible. I can only conclude that conditions that apply in one part of the world can't be directly applied to another part of the world."

When national interests are under discussion, even the most dyed-in-the-wool functionary thinks realistically, even in regard to the German problem. I had this same impression when the conversation turned to East Germany. "Ulbricht is nothing but a lackey of the Kremlin," I was told in the South. Certain questions put to me revealed, moreover, how much the Communist functionaries know about the real conditions in divided Germany and the conclusions they no doubt draw in private. "I don't understand it. Why are you in West Germany so much better off than the people in East Germany?" Or, "I don't believe that the Berlin Wall is effective. Don't the people still go across to West Germany just the same?"

In conversations I had with functionaries and senior officials of the Foreign Ministry there were also a number of indications of a line of argument based more on power-political and national considerations than on ideological ones. It was openly admitted to me in the Peking Foreign Ministry that there had been great disappointment at the outcome of the first contacts between Bonn and Peking in 1964. "We don't understand the West German attitude," I was told. "At first it looked as though Bonn was also interested in taking some small steps toward trying to get nearer to each other, to our mutual benefit. Then your Chancellor went to Washington and suddenly the whole atmosphere changed. How can we possibly take you seriously as an independent partner?"

It was not easy to find some kind of acceptable explanation for Bonn's irritating methods in the preliminary negotiations in 1964, for it was undeniable that following the Chancellor's visit to Washington, official quarters in Bonn had made play with West Germany's unshakable and unconditional loyalty to the United States, although to judge by appearances they had ignored it before this. At all events Chancellor Erhard has never explained to the West German people the reasons for the difference between West Germany's China policy before his conversations with President Johnson and after them.

Nevertheless, the functionaries with whom I was speaking displayed a surprising amount of understanding. They understood the significance of the problems of Berlin and Germany for the Federal Republic and they were aware of the sensitivity of American public opinion, to which Bonn cannot be indifferent. One of them said: "We know it is not easy for you. There are too many people interfering, both at home and abroad. One just has to be patient."

This understanding of West Germany's difficult position and the evident willingness to be patient do not suggest that Chinese policy on Germany is governed by purely tactical intrigue. This thought did make itself evident in talks I had with Eastern European representatives in Peking, who seemed to fear nothing so much as a positive development in German-Chinese relations, which would deal a blow to the established Soviet policy on Germany and might weaken the status of East Germany. Similarly, many of the remarks and gestures made by my Chinese opposite numbers seemed to show how pleased the Chinese were that their brush with Bonn upset the hated rulers of both the Soviet Union and East Germany.

The question is, of course, whether these are the really essential features of Chinese policy toward Germany. My own view is that the Chinese are working toward much more concrete objectives for the distant future. The intermediate zone theory is not by any means just so much empty talk. I was repeatedly earnestly reminded of the similarity in the interests of China and West Germany. "The more centers of power come into being in the world political arena, the better for the cause of peace," I was told on one occasion. And on another, "You, like us, must be interested in seeing that the two super-powers, the Soviet Union and the United States, are not allowed to ride roughshod over us."

These and similar remarks might give the impression that Peking bases its policies purely on the requirements of the national interest at the moment; but this is not so. As in every Communist country—and in China more than anywhere else, now that the Chinese Communists claim to be the only prophets of the true gospel—ideological maxims vitiate the national political plan. However much Peking may wish to see Chinese power-political ambitions realized, the ideological criteria applied to the "capitalist" Western countries impose definite limits. Socialism is sacred, which means, taking the case of East Germany, that the East German Communist regime cannot be allowed to fall. This is the dilemma in Chinese policy toward Germany, a dilemma from which the Chinese would like to extricate themselves and one which offers a number of opportunities to an intelligent and imaginative West German diplomacy.

True, any West Germany government will be on the horns of a dilemma. The authorities in Bonn have long been aware of the possibilities that would be opened up by an advance toward China, made cautiously and step by step. They have not forgotten the violence of the reaction from Moscow and East Berlin to this first approach to Peking. After the failure of the West German China policy in the summer of 1964 there were occasionally soothing murmurs in Bonn that the solution of the most important question for all Germans—the reunification of Germany—could not be achieved through Peking anyway. The same could be said of Bucharest, Budapest, Sofia, Warsaw or Prague, and yet the usefulness of a limited degree of collaboration with these Communist capitals is now taken for granted by almost every politician in the Western world. It is illogical to say that just for that one reason a policy of *rapprochement* with Peking is pointless. West German policy toward China will therefore only appear plausible if Bonn's caution in dealing with Peking is admitted to be simply and solely due to consideration for West Germany's main ally, the United States of America.

This position is not only defensible, it is also of fundamental importance. West Germany cannot afford to pursue a go-it-alone policy toward China without regard to anyone else. More than any other member of the Western alliance, she must fit her policy in with the policy the free world ought to be trying to work out toward China. At present the Western states have no common line on China. The views held in some Western capitals are ingenuous or naïve, in others the picture of China is full of prejudice and ill feeling. In general there is a lack of farsightedness, which may prove fatal one day. The exciting events in the Far East should stimulate us to take a more realistic view of the possibilities that lie in a clear-cut policy vis-à-vis the future great power in this part of the world.

Chapter 24

PEKING AND THE
WESTERN POWERS

The distinguishing feature of the development of many Communist countries is nationalism. Nationalism played a great part in destroying the monolithic unity of the Eastern bloc that Stalin had created, gave the Eastern European countries the first impulse that set them on the road to independence and contributed to the breach between Moscow and Peking. This did not, of course, bring about any change in the revolutionary aims basic to every Eastern European Communist party, but it did cause a change in political methods according to the national interest of the country concerned.

China is no exception to this phenomenon of growing nationalism, as I have already tried to show. Peking is striving to attain a place in the sun: China wants to be able to stand as an independent power among the peoples of Asia and the world. However important and all-pervading a role ideological precepts may seem to the visitor to play in China, what is coming more and more into the foreground in current Chinese affairs is action conditioned by national interest. This is all the more so in that it reflects the feelings of the people. Nationalism still has deep roots in China.

The governments of the Western powers are unanimous in applying a special policy to the Eastern European states with the aim of gradually loosening the countries bordering the Soviet Union from the one-sided Eastern community of interests. They hope in this way to undermine Moscow's position and to weaken the foundations of the Soviets' anti-Western and anti-European policies. Toward China, on the other hand, the attitude of the West is in general one of reserve. Although Peking has been much more firm than the other countries in opposing Moscow's claim to be the absolute leaders in the Communist camp, she is excluded from the West's policy toward the Soviet satellites. Although China's military and economic potential is not even remotely comparable to that of the atomic giant, Soviet Russia, which still professes the revolutionary principles of Communism and the class struggle, there is a widespread tendency to regard China and not the Soviet Union as the real danger to the world. Moreover, many people seem to believe that the attempt to draw Peking into a scheme of global responsibility is inopportune or doomed to disappointment from the start. Many authoritative Western politicians think that a more promising plan would be to join hands with Moscow to isolate the awakening giant of the Far East and thus tame and perhaps even crush it. What lies at the bottom of this attitude? Will it prove to be correct in the long run?

Why China Is Politically Ostracized

There are three main reasons for the wish, so widespread in the west, to apply a complete political boycott to China. In the first place many believe it would cause the Communist regime to come to a standstill. The country's problems, they argue, are insuperable and can certainly not be solved by the methods so highly thought of by the Communists. Resistance to the absolute totalitarianism is too widespread and the example of Nationalist Chinese democracy in Formosa too seductive for the Peking regime to be able to survive if left to itself.

In the chapter "The Permanent Class Struggle Continues" I went into detail on the internal difficulties facing the Chinese Communists. The various methods and campaigns, at different levels and with varying aims, make it evident that the leaders and the Party functionaries are thoroughly aware of the real situation and are taking steps to deal with it. What the regime is trying to combat is established traditions, so-called "revisionist" tendencies, apathy and political disinterest. It is doubtless true that the continual efforts to indoctrinate the people indicate a state of uncertainty and instability, especially when one considers the gigantic tasks still to be tackled. But it is a long way from this situation to storms of protest and an even longer one to a revolt of the masses.

There are some effects of the Communist system that many Chinese dislike or even hate, but there are also a large number of positive developments, of which the following seems to me to be the most important. After years of humiliation and national disunity, a central power has for the first time given the country unity and thus created the basis for improvements in organization and supply. It cannot be denied that there is nowadays a degree of social and physical security in China that was unknown previously and that there have been great advances in education and hygiene. The political standing China has attained in the world, whatever the methods that may have been used to achieve it, fills every Chinese, Communist or not, with pride. Economically, China has recovered from the catastrophic setbacks of the years 1959 to 1961, and what is more, she has done it without outside help. Things are gradually moving forward, the leaders have learned from the mistakes they made at that time and there is less risk of mistaken decisions in the future.

Finally, the well-disciplined organization of loyal functionaries and the results of the rigid control they exercise must not be overlooked, just as the position and importance of the enormous army, trained in national discipline, and its part in holding the nation together, must not be underestimated. These most important elements of the power structure are deployed in conformity with the aims the leaders have set themselves. Within this area of power and control there is little sign of disloyalty or divergence of aims, much less indications of decay, opposition or indifference.

In short, if there was ever a possibility of eliminating Communism in China, it was in the years of general distress and economic difficulty, which even the Communist functionaries now admit existed—a time when it was a fair assumption that hardly anyone in China would have given a nickel for the regime's chances of survival. Today the position of the leaders has considerably changed for the better.

All this must lead to the conclusion that any Western policy and planning that is based on speculative and illusory premises, unable to stand up to sober and unemotional analysis, can only be described as foolish.

A second argument is that China is agressive and wants war. Therefore, before the West agrees to negotiations or *rapprochement* there must be firm Chinese guarantees clearly demonstrating Peking's desire for peace. Since this has never happened, everything is as it was.

It is doubtful whether this argument is logically sound. The Chinese leaders have never openly expressed a desire for war (unless it was in respect of what they called "just, revolutionary wars of liberation," which are also supported by the Soviet Communists); they have always based their public statements on the premise that "imperialism" is the only force in the world that actually wants war. Peking has many times rejected as absurd and slanderous the Soviet allegation that China wants war. The important difference in the attitudes of the Soviet and Chinese leaders lies in the fact that Peking has indicated at various times that it is less worried about the consequences of war than Moscow is.

The most important clue to the Chinese attitude on this was contained in a speech Mao Tse-tung made at the 1957 conference of Communist parties in Moscow. According to a Chinese source, Mao said at that time: "Is it possible to foresee the number of victims a future war might claim? The death toll will possibly amount to a third or even half of the 2.7 billion people on earth. . . . I discussed this question with a foreign statesman. He believed that if it ever came to an atomic war, the whole of mankind would be wiped out. I said that if the worst came to the worst and half the people in the world were to be killed, the other half would go on living. But imperialism would have been completely eradicated and socialism would triumph all over the world. After some years there would again be 2.7 billion people in the world—and more."

The Soviet theoretical Party journal *Kommunist* added some significant further details from Mao's speech. The "foreign statesman" was Nehru. When Mao said that a third of mankind would be destroyed in an atomic war, he also said *en passant*: ". . . that is to say, only nine hundred million people. I would regard this as a very low figure if atom bombs did in fact start to fall. It is a frightful thing, of course, but even if half of mankind were to be destroyed, it would not be so disastrous." Mao was also reported—according to Soviet sources—to have said on this occasion that the Chinese Communist leaders were ready to sacrifice 300 million Chinese for "the victory of the socialist world revolution."

There is little doubt that at this time (the conversation with Nehru took place in October 1956) the Chinese Communists were extraordinarily little worried about the risks attached to an atomic war. This may have been due to the fact that they were still influenced by the outcome of the Korean War, in which the Chinese had been relatively successful against a world power, the United States, and saw in the impending Soviet rocket lead over the United States an opportunity that world Communism should take advantage of before American science and technology closed the gap.

In subsequent years, however, Peking's official statements showed the Chinese were becoming less and less indifferent to the risks and sacrifices of a potential nuclear war. This may have been in no small measure due to their realization that Moscow was shying away from the risk of a nuclear war and was therefore by no means willing to afford the Chinese Communists military assistance whatever the circumstances. (The rapidity with which the crisis over Quemoy and Matsu died down in the summer of 1958 may be taken as evidence of this.) At all events, Peking changed its tone. The article in the April 1960 issue of *Red Flag* that first made public the controversy with Moscow, "Long Live Leninism," said: "We are completely opposed to allowing imperialism to unleash a criminal war, because an imperialist war would demand sacrifices from the peoples of many countries (including the United States and other imperialist countries). But should the imperialists impose such sacrifices on them, we believe they would not be made in vain. On the ruins of dead imperialism the victorious peoples would quickly build a civilization that would stand a thousand times higher than the capitalist system, and a truly wonderful future would be in sight."

From this time on Chinese propaganda increased its insistence on the thesis that China did not want war but only peace—ever. It was not China but the imperialists that wanted to impose on the peoples the sacrifices a war would entail. Everyone was realizing more and more clearly the heavy loss of human life that would ensue.

On the same level was the surprisingly moderate tone taken by the Peking Communists when the first Chinese nuclear bomb was exploded. An official statement declared: "China is developing nuclear weapons not because we believe them to be all-powerful; quite the contrary. China is developing nuclear weapons solely for defensive purposes and to protect the Chinese people from the consequences that might ensue if the United States were to start an atomic war."

I cannot help thinking that the view commonly held in the West, that the Chinese regard an atomic war as a good means of accelerating a world revolution, is wide of the mark, at least at the present time. Nowadays the Chinese seem to be taking a far more realistic view of the consequences of a modern nuclear war, even if they do not by any means rate them as highly as does the Soviet Union. This is made plain both in Chinese propaganda abroad and in internal indoctrination material.

In confirmation, I quote some remarks by the Chief of the

Chinese general staff, Lo Jui-ching, who said in May 1965 in an article in *Red Flag* on the occasion of the twentieth anniversary celebrations of the end of World War II, at the height of the Vietnam crisis: "In preparing to defend ourselves against an imperialist war of aggression we must assume the greatest difficulties and the worst situation that could happen. We must be prepared not only for a limited war but also for a medium-sized war and for the heaviest war the imperialists could wage. We must be prepared for the imperialists to use not only conventional but also nuclear weapons. If we work on this basis and take action accordingly, it is not only more realistic but we are in a better position to take the initiative." In October 1965, Lo spoke openly of the possibility of an American attack on China and made this the theme of an impassioned appeal to ten thousand assembled Party functionaries in Peking. "We must adjust our mental attitude to the possibility of every kind of emergency situation," he told them. "We must think back to the years of the revolutionary war." Lo put the rhetorical question whether a nation faced with an enemy armed with an arsenal of modern nuclear devices had any choice but to submit, and answered it with the flat statement that there should be no fear of death. "If we lack the necessary backbone, if we cannot endure hardships and triumph over trials and tribulations, then we shall never achieve the victory in our war against aggression." These words reveal more a fear of the sacrifices an atomic war would entail and of invasion by a militarily and technically superior enemy than the terrifying ignorance of the risks that seemed to prevail among the Chinese leaders even as recently as 1957.

One or two experiences in the country itself support this. Time and again in conversations during my travels my attention would be drawn to China's poverty and backwardness. "Do you think we want war? We have enormous tasks to fulfill and great problems to solve. A war would only put us right back."

Another experience made a particular impression on me. When the first Chinese atom bomb was exploded, I was in the train on the way from Peking to Inner Mongolia. The news of the explosion was given out at 7 A.M. over the loudspeakers, one of which is in every compartment. Neither among the passengers in the coaches of the packed train nor in the dining car nor on the various stations we stopped at en route were there any signs of spontaneous joy, excitement or great enthusiasm among the many soldiers, functionaries and peasants. Their faces certainly expressed satisfaction, but there were no transports of victory or patriotic emotion; it was as if an atomic explosion in China were the most natural thing in the world.

If the charge of warmongering is shown not to be substantiated, many observers still believe that at least a charge of extreme aggressiveness can be proved, aggressiveness, moreover, which goes beyond what would normally be consonant with Communist revolutionary aims. The public in the West quickly forgot dangerous Soviet moves, as in the Berlin ultimatum or the Cuba crisis, but they very clearly remember apparent Chinese expansionist moves such as those in Korea or Tibet or toward India and Southeast Asia.

If one carefully examines the Chinese Communists' alleged aggressive behavior from the point of view of its origins and the underlying motives, the picture that emerges is usually anything but that of a furious aggressor. Take, for example, Peking's intervention in the Korean War. There is little doubt now that the Korean War was planned and inspired not by the Chinese but by Stalin. The Chinese did not intervene militarily until the American forces, in spite of repeated Chinese warnings, crossed the 38th parallel and General MacArthur publicly declared that the Yalu River should not be allowed to limit American action either. This made the conflict in Korea into a matter of national security for the Chinese and no longer a question of active support for somebody else's steps on the road to world revolution.

The incorporation of Tibet in 1950 had a different origin again. Tibet was for centuries one of the outlying territories of the Chinese empire. The experts in international law have long been disagreed about how the relationship of the Tibetan theocracy to the Imperial Throne in Peking should be described, particularly as this relationship shifted and varied throughout the centuries. The reason it is especially difficult to categorize it is that concepts of international law as developed in Europe are very difficult to apply to Central Asian and Far Eastern territories because of the quite different mentality and ideas prevailing there. The nearest definition of the status of Tibet was given by the man who for many years headed the British trade mission in Lhasa, H. E. Richardson, who said: "Tibet was a kind of papal state under the protection of the Chinese emperor, whose supreme authority was recognized and with whom there were indefinable, mystical, political links."

Tibet did not declare itself independent until after the fall of the Manchu dynasty; none of the succeeding rulers of China ever acknowledged Tibet's independence and the Nationalist Chinese government in Formosa still ignores the claim to this day. Nor did the Western powers ever question China's claim to Tibet before Mao Tse-tung came to power. In 1943 the State Department in Washington issued a statement which included these words: "The United States government takes account of the fact that the Chinese government has long claimed sovereignty in Tibet and that the Chinese constitution lists Tibet among the areas forming the territory of the Chinese Republic. Our government has never at any time called either of these claims in question."

Misgivings at the manner in which Tibet was annexed to the People's Republic of China and the way the Chinese tried to "remodel" the Tibetan mentality and way of life may be justified, just as the reason given for the occupation of Tibet, as explained on one occasion by the Chinese Foreign Minister Chen Yi, is also difficult to swallow. While there were two million Tibetans living in undisputed Chinese territory, Chen declared, over a million Tibetans could not be allowed to exist in slavery in their native land, because to allow it would be a denial of the aims of the revolution. For all that, the fact remains that the occupation of

Tibet cannot be called an act of aggression in the real sense of the word.

The Sino-Indian border conflict and the advance by Chinese armed forces into Indian territory in the fall of 1962 are further links in the argument to prove the aggressive character of Chinese foreign policy. In my view there are two particularly important motives behind the actions of the Chinese in this affair. The first was the strategic necessity to secure Tibet and get it under strict control, measures which became particularly urgent following the Tibetan revolt in 1959. Even today the supply routes of the partisan groups of the Khambas, who are in revolt against the Chinese occupying forces, run from the South over the Himalayas. It is only from this point of view that the fixing of the previously undefined boundary in an uninhabited wilderness—in which the Chinese were anxious to secure strategically favorable mountain ranges and passes—is understandable. The clandestine building of the communicating road from South Tibet to Sinkiang through Aksai Chin (which the Indians claim as their territory) may serve to confirm this thesis.

A second feature developed only gradually, in the course of the boundary dispute. It has its roots in the rivalry between the two states on the continent of Asia, which was bound to end in a power-political demonstration. There is a tendency in the West to put all the blame for the failure to settle the Sino-Indian boundary dispute on the unyielding attitude of the Chinese. This seems doubtful to me, if only because India has given proof on more than one occasion that she is little disposed to negotiate and prefers the use of force to settle problems, or at least insists on getting her own way. The invasion of the Portuguese colony of Goa by Indian troops and the Indian arguments in the Kashmir dispute are evidence of this attitude (although this is not to say that Peking has shown itself any more reasonable or sensible).

At the beginning of October 1962 the Chinese launched an armed attack on Indian territory, describing it as a "counterattack" because, they said, the Indian high command in New

Delhi had ordered the setting up of Indian advanced posts on the flanks of the Chinese positions. Within a month the Chinese had occupied nearly thirty-five thousand square miles of Indian territory.

The unprejudiced observer finds it very difficult to sort out the truth from the untruth in the claims and explanations issued by both sides on the causes of the armed conflict. The one thing that is certain is that China's action cannot be interpreted as an "aggressive campaign of conquest." After an amazingly successful advance the Chinese suddenly and unilaterally declared a truce, withdrew their forces to a point twelve miles behind the 1959 boundary line and turned over all captured Indian soldiers and military equipment to the Indian authorities. This clearly marked the military action in the Himalayas not as a demonstration of the Chinese Communists' lust for conquest but as a demonstration of Chinese power in Asia, actual and potential.

The previously mentioned military actions by the Chinese Communists served to reinforce or to re-create the stability of the nation. There is a distinction to be made between this more or less legitimate aim and Peking's efforts to extend the Chinese sphere of influence on a global scale. If it were a case of purely political activity, as were, for example, the temporarily successful Chinese efforts in Cambodia or Indonesia, then their diplomatic maneuvers could be regarded as normal.

In the fall of 1965 the Chinese leaders unfolded a program of ambitious claims to predominance, claims that are to be realized in dangerous fashion. Several theses propounded by Lin Piao, the Chinese Defense Minister and a member of the inner government circle, had already been proclaimed by the Comintern as early as the 1920s and had been reissued verbatim by D. N. Aidit, the leader of the Indonesian Communists, in 1963. But when spoken by one of the Chinese Party leaders, these theses sound more menacing and are hardly likely to assuage Western bourgeois feelings. The world revolution led by the Chinese, Lin Piao declared, must take the form of the encirclement of the Western industrial nations by the Asiatic, African and Latin

American countries, growing in strength. Chinese Communism had come to power by way of a peasants' revolution, and the aims of the revolutionary idea could be similarly attained everywhere by "an encirclement of the world's towns" by the numerically superior "country areas of the earth."

The tactical and strategical instrument of this Chinese doctrine is the "people's war," the guerrilla warfare methods worked out by Mao Tse-tung during the years of the Chinese civil war. These methods are the same as those that have commended themselves in the Vietnam war, and the Chinese envisage similar methods bringing success in the world revolutionary struggle. The Chinese Communists charge the Soviets with having betrayed the concept of violent revolution by the "oppressed and exploited." They reject the Soviet argument that warlike means are too dangerous to use in the nuclear age and they regard as plain calumny the Soviet charge that the Chinese are bent on war. "Your insults only increase our standing," Lin Piao replied. "It is precisely our alleged willingness to make war that contributes to preventing the imperialists from unleashing a world war. We simply use revolutionary aggressiveness to combat counterrevolutionary aggressiveness."

The theory of the people's war and the encirclement of the strong nations by the weak ones seems to be in distinct conflict with the intermediate zone theory mentioned earlier, which is part of the Chinese Communists' official program. This apparent contradiction is only resolved when one considers the time and the circumstances of the proclamation of the "encirclement and people's war" theories. The rivalry between Moscow and Peking, which had reached a critical climax in the Vietnam question just at this point in time—in the fall of 1965—seems to have been the immediate reason for promulgating the new militant theories. If this is so, they were more the product of expediency than the outcome of mature deliberation.

In the Vietnam question, too, there is no attempt on the part of the Chinese at conquest or aggression in the real sense. They are trying to increase their influence and to drive the nation's declared Enemy Number One, the United States, out of this part of East Asia. The militant and subversive means required to do this are linked up with the world revolutionary Communist mission. "Just wars of liberation and civil wars" is the term used to justify support actions of all kinds. In theory this puts the Chinese Communists in accord with their comrades in Moscow, but in practice the two are acting quite differently. Peking is urging a continuation of the civil war, whereas Moscow is willing, on certain conditions, to consider negotiations for a peaceful solution. What is the reason for this crucial divergence of views?

To begin with, the Kremlin has a number of reasons of self-interest for proceeding cautiously. Moscow wants to avoid a direct confrontation with the strongest power in the world, the United States. Then there is the difficulty that the great distances involved limit the possibility of military intervention, an aspect in which the Soviets are at a disadvantage compared with the Americans, who have strong bases in Southeast Asia. Moreover, if the Soviets were forced to make common cause and undertake common action with the Chinese, they must fear that their ideological and political rivals' very much stronger position in this part of the world would increase their influence, a prospect highly displeasing to Moscow. But that is exactly what Peking is hoping to achieve by the determined continuation of the partisan war in Vietnam supported by all its Communist partners.

In this struggle for predominance in Indochina, the North Vietnamese Communists hold the balance. The fight to gain Hanoi's favor was demonstrated in the Sino-Soviet polemics of November 1965. The Chinese made the Soviets' attitude to Vietnam the basic issue of their charges against Moscow, reproaching the Soviets with trying to reach a compromise with the United States over Vietnam; and they produced evidence in the shape of revealing information on Soviet diplomatic practice.

Another Chinese charge concerned the extent of Soviet aid to North Vietnam. Peking claimed that while the Chinese were "helping the Vietnamese people to the best of their ability," the aid the Soviets were giving Hanoi "bore no relation whatever, either in quantity or in quality, to the strength of the Soviet Union." This particular assertion, unlike those in the political sphere, was not supported by any firm evidence, a fact that makes it seem less than credible, particularly as just at this time the West had become aware of vigorous Soviet military assistance to North Vietnam. American experts discovered that in the space of a few weeks the North Vietnamese air force had been reinforced by sixty to seventy new MIG jet fighters; the number of anti-aircraft guns near vital targets in North Vietnam had grown to between seven and eight thousand; and the number of surface-to-air missile units had risen to thirty, able to operate from at least a hundred sites.

Clearly, this reinforcing of the North Vietnamese defense potential by the Soviets did not suit the Chinese book. To this must be added a further fact. At this same time the London *Observer* published the text of two secret letters between Moscow and Peking, furnished by a source in Eastern Europe. The Chinese letter, the authenticity of which was not in doubt, showed that the Chinese had declined to provide the cooperation necessary for certain additional Soviet aid. First, the Soviets had wanted to station a force of four thousand regular troops, probably engineer and pioneer units, in North Vietnam: secondly, the Soviets had asked for the use and occupation of one or two airfields in Southwest China, with a Soviet armed force of five hundred men, for the defense of North Vietnamese airspace: thirdly, Moscow had asked the Chinese for an air corridor between the Soviet Union and North Vietnam in order to ensure the fastest possible transport of supplies. These Soviet plans for helping the North Vietnamese were rejected by the Chinese, who asserted that they were intended not to provide large-scale support for North Vietnam but to establish Soviet dominance in Southeast Asia.

This argument made it clear what was really at issue. Any increase in direct cooperation between Hanoi and Moscow is damaging both to the interests of the Chinese Communists in the immediate approaches to their own domain and to their ambitions in the global conflict with Moscow. Peking has learned from bitter experience. In 1964 and 1965, using promises of large-scale assistance, the Soviets succeeded in loosening North Korea's close political and ideological links with Peking. If the same thing were to happen in Hanoi's case, there would be no saying what catastrophic results it might have for the Chinese Communists.

Peking clearly feared that every instance of vigorous Soviet support for North Vietnam would increase the Hanoi regime's dependence on Moscow. This might initially be confined to the economic and military fields, but it could later have its effect on the political field. Since the Soviets still adhere to their policy of peaceful coexistence and the avoidance of a direct military confrontation with the United States, it is possible that increased North Vietnamese dependence on Moscow would enable the Soviets to apply pressure on the North Vietnamese to enter into peace negotiations that would lead to the situation the Chinese had plainly stated in their November 1965 polemics against Moscow, namely, the status quo in Vietnam, to be guaranteed in the North by Soviet troops and in the South by American forces.

This, if it came about, would mean an abrupt end to all the Chinese dreams of expanding their power in Southeast Asia. And what applies in the individual case of Vietnam and Southeast Asia is equally valid for the general political and strategic concepts of the Chinese Communists. This problem shows very clearly the nature of the Chinese position vis-à-vis Moscow, how completely differently the Chinese think and the ideological basis of their thinking.

For the Soviet Union peaceful coexistence has become the main plank of their foreign policy; the reasons have been given elsewhere. China rejects any too far-reaching interpretation of this concept, especially the possibility of peaceful coexistence with so-called "imperialism," that is to say with the United States, because she believes that in the end this is not in her own national interest. In the course of the years of controversy between the two centers of world Communism these basic positions have become more and more sharply defined and are now axiomatic and exhortative. They have become ends in themselves, the importance of which must be reflected in practical political action. The Chinese now believe they must remain inflexible, even in a situation in which some other way than the rigid and bloody "revolutionary" way might, seen objectively, appear to be more favorable. For example negotiations on Vietnam aimed at removing the Americans from the country—the aim of both Communist partners—would pave the way for a bloodless seizure of power on the model of the Prague *Putsch*. Nevertheless, the Chinese are unwilling to give up the idea of revolutionary victory because that is the unequivocal stand they have taken up within the world Communist movement. Any giving way in the Vietnam question would therefore automatically mean not only a diminution of Chinese power in Southeast Asia but also a loss of face and an admission of Chinese willingness to make concessions in respect of principles developed by Moscow.

The real motives lie deeper. They also explain how there ever came to be a conflict of opinion on the question of the historical mission of spreading world revolution. The Soviet Union is not only sated from the territorial point of view, but she has also reached a position of political power that has won her respect all over the world and assured her of ways of exerting her influence in many different spheres. China, on the other hand, has been able neither to satisfy her territorial demands completely nor to attain the international power-political position she thinks is automatically due to her as the most populous country in the world. One means of attaining respect, standing and influence is to carry out the traditional world revolutionary mission. This not only appears to serve Chinese national interests but also reinforces the ideological platform from which the Chinese may credibly claim the leading position within the confederation of Communist parties.

The Chinese are willing to accept the risks involved in this kind of action in the atomic age, risks which the Soviet Union, standing at the pinnacle of her power, is not willing to run because it just is not worth the trouble or because the damage might, in certain circumstances, prove to be too great. But above all because the Soviet leaders believe they can achieve the same goal using their existing position of power and different political strategy and tactics.

Not only in Vietnam but also everywhere else in the world, Western diplomatic action will have to adapt itself to this feature of Chinese foreign policy, which creates new defensive problems for the West. Although Chinese actions may be highly disagreeable and, in some cases, even menacing and dangerous, it must be distinguished from a policy of aggression or conquest. China is trusting to revolutionary "dirty" limited wars, which means at the same time that the Chinese Communists, too, want to avoid the possibility of unleashing a nuclear world war.

The fact, incidentally, that the Chinese leaders are perfectly capable—and perhaps even more capable than the Soviets, on occasion—of distinguishing between well-understood national interests and dangerous adventures undertaken for the sake of an idea, is clearly demonstrated by the continued existence of the British crown colony of Hong Kong and the Portuguese possession, Macao. The responsible authorities in Peking still regard the existence on Chinese territory of these "outposts of imperialism" as more profitable to them than any increase in prestige that would automatically follow a "cleaning up" of this situation.

However militant their propaganda may be, the Chinese leaders are well aware of the practical risks involved in too vigorous an advance in fact. Generally speaking it can be said that the basic principles underlying China's revolutionary foreign policy are exactly the same as those laid down by Mao Tse-tung decades ago for the civil war at home. No fighting except in self-defense, but then, strike hard; only attack when you are certain of winning; only ask for a truce when the enemy is in a position to start a new offensive. These were the principles that governed the action against India in the Himalayas in the fall of 1962, and it looks as though they still hold good in Vietnam.

But even if the reader cannot accept all these propositions and still believes China is an expansionist and aggressive power, the conclusion that China should therefore be politically exorcized is neither conclusive nor convincing. The Chinese Communists' revolutionary challenge in the foreign policy field is not only consonant with defensive internal considerations, the demands of a militant ideology or the plan to increase China's power-political status by this means, it is also definitely fostered by a profound mistrust of the rest of the world, both East and West. To fear the aggressiveness of a power while at the same time turning one's back on it politically—and thus increasing its distrust—seems to be an absurd proceeding, which would actually bring on the very dangers one claims to fear.

A third reason why it is argued that Communist China should be politically isolated from the West is one that deserves more serious attention. This arises from loyalty to Formosa. The United States, as the leading Western power, has guaranteed the existence of "Nationalist China," as was historically inevitable. But what still seemed a matter of course in 1945, or even in 1949, ceased to be so long ago. There is a growing feeling in the peoples of the West that we have got ourselves involved in a series of rear-guard delaying actions in East Asia. Not only in Europe but in America, too, the necessity to choose between moral duty to an ally and facing the historical facts is becoming more and more painfully felt.

What has been achieved on Formosa deserves credit, of that there can be no doubt. The Chiang Kai-shek government has given the inhabitants of the island a standard of living that is among the highest in Asia. Yet no one regards Nationalist China as the real China, certainly not in Asia and also not in Europe or anywhere else, notwithstanding the occasional statements to the contrary. Among the overseas Chinese and even on Formosa itself doubts are beginning to arise as to whether Taipeh's claim is justified and whether it can be maintained in the long run. However distasteful or hateful the Peking regime may be, the fact is that it stands for the Chinese nation *de facto* and in the eyes of the world.

This important point has a parallel in the German question. West Germany claims to represent the German people. She is also generally considered to be the real Germany, a fact that I seemed to hear hinted at particularly in conversations I had with Chinese. It was surely no slip of the tongue when Mao Tse-tung listed the countries which, belonging to the second intermediate zone, represented the third force in world politics and used the word "Germany," clearly meaning the West German Federal Republic.

Just as the Federal Republic cannot and must not waive its claim to represent the whole German people, so the Peking regime cannot waive its national claim, either. The consolidation of the *status quo* or the constituting of two separate states is unacceptable to Peking. There are a number of German politicians who argue for the easy solution, creating two states in East Asia; but what they do not appear to realize is the conclusion world opinion might draw in respect of the Central European area. The fact that Khrushchev himself, according to the Chinese, on one occasion, while he was in Peking, supported the creation of an independent state of Formosa was not only a warning to the Chinese: it ought also to have been a warning to the Federal Republic.

A Common Western Policy for the Future

The situation I have been describing shows the extent to which Western policies toward China have got themselves into a blind alley and how difficult it is to find a way out. This is particularly true of the United States, whose freedom of action is limited by treaties and alliances. The tedious and protracted negotiations between American and Chinese representatives in Warsaw, for example, have not been able to make any progress. They were bound from the beginning to founder on the national question, a fundamental one for the Chinese. The Soviet Union's willingness to establish a community of interest with the United States in measures to prevent war—for example, the setting up of the "hot line" between Washington and Moscow and the conclusion of the atomic test ban treaty—hardened Peking's attitude not only toward the Kremlin but also toward the United States. Finally, the way events in Vietnam have developed, the escalation and the undisguised engagement of American forces have for the time being made even the slightest attempt at reaching agreement between the two hostile states utterly impossible.

Any Western feelers toward a relaxation of tension in East Asia can therefore only be put out by countries that have indicated their support for Peking's case in international law or are as yet neither committed nor directly engaged in the Vietnam conflict. There has been no lack of such attempts, but so far without the slightest trace of the success that would be in the universal interest.

Britain has maintained diplomatic relations with Peking ever since the beginning of Communist rule, but this fact has obviously not been able to make much impression on the Chinese leaders, even though Britain is the only Western industrialized power to have decided on this step. To this day the authorities in Peking appear to give only passing attention to the existence of a British legation in their capital and even then purely of a formal nature. There has never been any possibility of making political contact and Britain's diplomatic mission is essentially left with nothing more to do than assist in arranging commercial transactions.

General de Gaulle's sensational decision to grant China diplomatic recognition at the end of 1963 has brought no noteworthy political results. Even the fact that France had to break off relations with Nationalist China did not succeed in increasing Peking's willingness to negotiate. This is all the more remarkable in that the French President has left no doubt that the real reason for the step he took was more the intention to affront France's

NATO ally, the United States, than a carefully considered new French policy toward China.

West Germany's short-lived attempt to establish contact in 1964 also did little to encourage the West to make new attempts at appeasement or to think up maneuvers to draw the West closer to China. Peking's reaction when the West Germans withdrew from the negotiations in their initial stage showed the considerations uppermost in the minds of the Chinese. For Peking mutual advantage is of limited importance: the really important thing for them is to try to exploit the position of their partner in the negotiations for their own political purposes. These purposes are and will remain for some time to come aimed at weakening the position of the Soviet Union and isolating the United States. It must not, incidentally, be overlooked that this political strategy is not an end in itself, but is in Peking's view necessary for the strengthening of China's power-political position and the increasing of her international stature.

If the policy of the West toward China is to make every effort to draw the future great power of the Far East into accepting her share of international responsibility, without on the other hand running the risk of splitting the West's own forces, then a common Western plan for China is essential. Today the thinking in some Western capitals may still be dominated by particularist and short-term tactical considerations, as in Paris, with De Gaulle's policy of anti-American pinpricks, or in Bonn, with the thought that if the Soviets were to apply a more stringent policy toward Germany this might be countered by West German contacts with Peking. But what the Western alliance ought to be doing is to make an urgent start on considering a plan for a common political strategy toward China. Western policy cannot go on indefinitely being conditioned by the present United States attitude, because relations between Washington and Peking have been made so difficult by the consequences of the historical and current factors I have described that any attempt at *rapprochement* would be certain to fail at the outset; nor can the members of the Western alliance go on trying out their diplomatic skill independently of each other, because any mistrust within the alliance would necessarily have dangerous consequences. Instead of gazing helplessly at the fire-breathing "Red Dragon" or letting oneself be cowed by talk of a "Yellow Peril," the essential thing to do is to reduce the feelings of resentment and prejudice toward China. However difficult it may seem to many people today, it is essential to create at least some understanding for the social and economic difficulties facing the most populous nation in the world, difficulties which lie at the root of many of China's reactions in foreign policy. Particular features of Chinese foreign policy must be carefully scrutinized with a view to seeing to what extent the West's own actions or too narrow a view of Western interests may have been a contributing factor. It goes without saying that the West will have to take a firm stand against Peking's subversive strategy outside China—in Vietnam, for example—but the question of the way this is to be done is a crucial one. Thus the continuing American air attacks on North Vietnam (where there are no Chinese troops), for example, have made some people fear that this is bringing about exactly the opposite of what it was hoped to achieve with regard to China. Instead of forcing the Chinese into a state of willingness to negotiate, the air attacks seem only to have increased their mistrust. The seven hundred million Chinese will not find it difficult to believe the Communist propaganda assertion that American activities in Vietnam are only a prelude to an attack on China.

An outstanding native expert on the Chinese political scene said to me in Peking: "There is no doubt at all that inside China a liberalization can be expected in the decades ahead. But as far as foreign policy is concerned, if the attitude of the West toward China remains as it is today, then that same period is more likely to see an increase than a decrease of tension."

One cannot dismiss out of hand the objection that any attempt at *rapprochement* is pointless because the Chinese have taken up an orthodox, revolutionary position that leaves them almost no room for maneuver in foreign policy. Why should the West be the ones to wear themselves out looking for points of possible contact and chances of decreasing tension? Any such attempt would be doomed to failure from the start. So runs the argument.

While this view may seem justified today, the premises on which it is based may change tomorrow, when the old guard of professional revolutionaries and civil war heroes quit the political scene. Not only that, but the nationalism that is already playing an important part in Chinese policies may in the not-too-distant future come increasingly into prominence and may lead to a change of attitude that will bring about a modification of the Chinese Communists' world revolutionary plans in our favor. These are possible developments that should be prepared for already, today. On the one hand, the West must make it clear beyond doubt that it is ready and able to beat off revolutionary subversion. On the other, it should show its willingness to accord China a position of authority within the community of nations, provided Peking abandons its alleged ambitions for world revolution. A persistent and intractable policy of isolating China risks the possibility that Peking will try to break out of its isolation by force. Therefore the West must not leave it at fine words. A strategy of advancing a little at a time, with each nation playing the role allotted to it, must be worked out and initiated, a strategy based on trying to make contact at the economic, cultural and finally political levels and accompanied by unceasing efforts to whittle away China's deep-seated mistrust and to induce Peking to relax its rigid foreign policy attitude. All this cannot, of course, be achieved overnight, but in my view it is the only way that offers any long-term prospect of success.

I feel myself reinforced in this opinion by my personal experience of conditions in modern China. The events and situations I have described in previous chapters have shown the extent to which the Chinese Communist leaders' thinking is dominated by the paramount importance to them of their domestic policies. Hardly a people in the world is so dependent on itself, so completely cut off from the thought and traditions of other countries as the Chinese, and this applies to their leaders, too. Sometimes the visitor to China, whether from the West or from the East, has the feeling of having been transported to some other planet, even though the visible propaganda and methods continually remind him of the pattern in other Communist countries. China is still a world of its own, in spite of Communism and modern industry and technology.

This view, engendered by a large number of personal observations, leads automatically to the question that has been so often asked, whether at bottom Maoism contains more Communist theory than reactivated Chinese native thought, or vice versa. In my opinion there is no such sharp dividing line: both of these motivating forces are interwoven one with the other. At the same time, however, I feel that the real determining factor in the policies of the Chinese Communists is the drive toward national regeneration. Communist theory and Communist methods are an instrument for the completion of the grand design of a unified, onward-striving and mighty Chinese nation.

Despite the tremendous efforts the Communists have made, their philosophy seems to have remained a foreign body, some theory that has been imposed on the people from outside. The comparatively short history of Bolshevism *à la chinoise* has already shown what strange and idiosyncratic teachings have developed and the extent to which it has been possible to adapt Communist methods to suit local requirements. Is it too much to expect that in the foreign policy field, too, there will one day be possibilities that will turn out to be more useful to the country's national interests?

To end this book I should like to describe an experience that was one of the most impressive of my whole journey through China and was the initial impetus for the thoughts I have been discussing. This was a visit to the temple caves of Lung-men. Not far from Loyang, in Honan Province, hundreds of caves and hollows have been cut into the steep cliff face. These contain statues, reliefs, sculptures or sacred inscriptions, testifying to an age of deep piety and spiritual refinement such as are to be found in very few places in the world today.

Here stand the imposing relics of a period in Chinese history when an alien philosophy from a completely different culture succeeded for the first and only time in conquering the Chinese mainland; the period when Buddhism became the dominant political and religious power in China. But not for long. Chinese individuality and Chinese spirit transformed Buddhism and so permeated it that although it continued to exist, it no longer had political or social influence. Chinese vitality and originality won through.

Neither destruction nor pillage has been able to rob the temples of Lung-men of their colossal power. From the end of the fifth century until the beginning of the eighth century men were building, creating and augmenting in Lung-men. The cave temple displays the development of an art form from primitive beginnings to a standard of sculptural art in the golden age of the Tang period such as has seldom been equaled in the whole history of sculpture.

A distinguished British art historian once said that if visible proof were needed of the proposition that faith can move mountains, the Chinese cave temples provided it. I share this opinion. But the strange thing is that the faith in question did not originate in China. Many experts on China believe that Buddhism had a most profound influence on the country, the only foreign culture to do so in China's four-thousand-year history.

Still, down the centuries the Chinese mentality and the Chinese world of ideas impressed the alien faith with their own stamp. This is also shown in the character of the artistry displayed in Lung-men. It has been established that the sculptors of the cave temples were inspired by the style of the Gupta period, the classical golden age of Indian art, and tried to imitate their instructors. But where the Indian sculptors were concerned to employ all their skill and cunning to use the clothing, for example, to emphasize the shape of the body beneath it, the

Chinese felt no urge to portray the sensual. They used the clothing solely to express life and movement.

This unique phenomenon of the adaptation of the features of an alien faith and its representation in artistic form is particularly illustratcd in the way the Chinese took over certain characteristically Indian ideas. They took over the Indian idea of communing with one's soul in the semidarkness of the grotto, where outside influences cannot divert men from their search for God. They accepted the Indian idea that death and darkness go together and that death is nothing more than a necessary transitional phase on the way to a new life. They accepted the Indian idea of the huge size and the multiplicity of the sculptured Buddhas, testifying to his omnipotence and the unlimited number of world ages, each with its own Buddha. How was all this possible, seeing that the world of Indian philosophical thought does not in any way fit in with the shape of life and thought in Chinese society?

Buddhism reached China in the early Han period, principally in the first century before Christ. Only a few educated people were willing to receive it, however, and even then it was not because of its philosophical or religious content but because of the modern scientific theories which reached China at the same time as Buddhism. The new faith did not gain a firm foothold until much later, now, in contrast to the first time, as a religious belief among the great mass of the people. This development was directly connected with the decline of the Chinese empire in the first five centuries A.D. After the collapse of the Han dynasty there was a period of disruption and breaking-up, first the period of the Three Kingdoms, then the split between North and South and finally the centuries-long struggle for power by various groups in the South and the invasions by non-Chinese nomadic tribes, who established their alien rule in the North.

These events resulted in want, exploitation and oppression among the Chinese peasant masses. It was therefore not surprising that the country people who had suffered so much through the centuries embraced the new faith with such fervor. This was due not to the philosophical and spiritual value of Buddhism but to the new and revolutionary teaching, the gospel of life after death. At their next rebirth, all those who were now enslaving and impoverishing the people would be punished by being born into a miserable existence, but those who lived in misery and were trodden down by their betters would rise to a higher station in their next life. Buddhism offered the people consolation, hope and conviction.

However, it was not alone the profound distress among the people that contributed to the spread of Buddhism. The Turkoman and Mongol alien rulers also fostered it for their own purposes. This explains why the outstanding testimonials to ardent faith—these cave temples—are only to be found in the North of China and not in the South. Of the many foreign dynasties it was the T'oba tribe, who took the Chinese name of Wei, that gave the strongest support to Buddhism. In the fifth century the power of their realm was growing, and with it the desire to have their own state religion. Buddhism suggested itself for a number of reasons, not least political. The tolerance enjoined by Buddhism suited the book of the alien rulers. The great mass of the people were devout in the faith, a factor which seemed to the Wei emperors particularly desirable, since they thought this would enable them to restrain the power of the strongest oppositional group, the Chinese gentry, the educated, landowning class, devoted to Confucianism and occupying all the key positions in the traditional structure of officialdom.

This period represented the heyday of Buddhist culture in China. It gave birth to monumental works like Lung-men, which for sheer creative skill are comparable with the artistic wonders of the world, such as the Egyptian pyramids or the ruined temples of Angkor. But this pinnacle of skill was the beginning of the end. The transferring of the Wei dynasty's capital to Loyang was to prove a fateful move, since it isolated the nobles of the nomadic T'oba. The enormous distances between Loyang and their own tribal areas led to their impoverishment. The influence of the Chinese gentry became stronger and stronger and with it the influence of Confucianism. When the Wei empire disintegrated, the political fate of Buddhism was sealed. Confucianism gradually displaced the state religion of the foreign rulers, as had happened once before, in the great Han period, and was to happen again later.

Although Buddhism remained alive in the people, exerting its influence on the other religious communities and philosophies, as they in turn influenced it, and continued to attract the masses of the people, it was never able to play any decisive role in political or social life again. The memorials in stone are all that remain of a great and distinguished past.

May it not be that one day we shall see a historical counterpart to today's new faith, also imported from abroad and equally revolutionary, which would correspond to the independent mentality, the native character and the deep-rooted obstinacy of the Chinese people, the obstinacy that has shown itself time and again over thousands of years? Historical comparisons are not always valid, admittedly, and it would be a mistake to use them as a guide to the conduct of our own affairs. Yet no less a person than Mao Tse-tung himself once gave reason to hope for a possible favorable change in Chinese Communism. In an interview with Edgar Snow in January 1965, replying to a question about the future of Communism in China, he said future events would be decided by future generations acting under the influence of conditions that no one could foresee. The youth of today and the generations to come would judge the achievements of the revolution by their own standards. "Conditions of human life on this earth are changing at an increasingly rapid rate. It may be that thousands of years from now Marx, Engels and Lenin will all seem rather ridiculous."

These words by Mao Tse-tung should not be too hastily dismissed as a sarcastic aside. They testify to a degree of historical perception that is part of the traditionally pragmatic Chinese way of thinking. They should not be lost sight of in considering and planning a common Western policy toward China. No matter how doctrinaire a basic attitude may seem today, this should not blind us to the possibility of a change in political methods tomorrow, if the conditions on which they are based were also to change. The history of Communism in the Soviet Union is as an instructive example. Communist China could develop in the same way. But this would entail the West's according the Chinese nation a place in the community of peoples worthy of their long history, their spiritual tradition and the greatness of their country.

SELECTED READING LIST

Barnett, A. Doak, *China on the Eve of the Communist Takeover*. New York: Frederick A. Praeger, 1964.

Barnett, A. Doak, *Communist China and Asia*. New York: Alfred A. Knopf, Inc. (Vintage Books).

Barnett, A. Doak, *Communist China in Perspective*. New York: Frederick A. Praeger.

Barnett, A. Doak, *Communist China: The Early Years, 1949–1955*. New York: Frederick A. Praeger, 1964.

Beauvoir, Simone de, *The Long March*. Cleveland: World Publishing Co., 1958.

Bodde, Derk, *China's Cultural Tradition*. New York: Holt, Rinehart & Winston, 1957.

Bowie, Robert, see Fairbank, John K.

Buss, Claude A., *The Arc of Crisis*. New York: Doubleday & Co., 1962.

Buss, Claude A., *People's Republic of China*. Princeton, New Jersey: D. Van Nostrand & Co., 1962.

Chao, Kuo-chün, *Economic Planning and Organization in Mainland China*. 2 vols., vol. 1, 1959; vol. 2, 1960; Cambridge: Harvard University Press.

Chassin, Lionel Max, *The Communist Conquest of China: A History of the Civil War, 1945–1949*, tr. by Timothy Osato and Louis Gelas. Cambridge: Harvard University Press, 1965.

Ch'en, Jerome, *Mao and the Chinese Revolution*. New York: Oxford University Press, 1965.

Clark, Gerald, *Impatient Giant: Red China Today*. New York: David McKay, 1959.

Clubb, O. Edmund, *Twentieth-Century China*. New York: Columbia University Press, 1963.

Crankshaw, Edward, *New Cold War: Moscow v. Peking*. Baltimore: Penguin Books, 1963.

Croft, Michael, *Red Carpet to China*. New York: St. Martin's Press, 1960.

Elegant, Robert S., *Center of the World*. New York: Doubleday & Co., 1964.

Fairbank, John K.; Reischauer, Edwin O., *A History of East Asian Civilization*. 2 vols., vol. 1, *East Asia: The Great Tradition;* vol. 2 (with Edwin O. Craig), *East Asia: The Modern Transformation*. Boston: Houghton Mifflin Co., 1965.

Fairbank, John K., *United States and China*. Cambridge: Harvard University Press, 1958.

Fairbank, John K., *Chinese Thought and Institutions*. Chicago: University of Chicago Press, 1957.

Fairbank, John K. with Robert Bowie, Communist China 1955 to 1959 (documents). Cambridge: Harvard University Press, 1962.

Faure, Edgar, *The Serpent and the Tortoise*. New York: St. Martin's Press, 1958.

Fitzgerald, C. P., *China, A Short Cultural History*. 4th rev. ed. New York: Frederick A. Praeger, 1961.

Fitzgerald, C. P., *Chinese View of Their Place in the World*. New York: Oxford University Press, 1964.

Fitzgerald, C. P., *Flood Tide in China*. Chester Springs, Pennsylvania: Dufour Editions, 1958.

Granet, Marcel, *Chinese Civilization*. New York: Meridian Books, 1958.

Greene, Felix, *Awakened China*. New York: Doubleday & Co., 1961.

Greene, Felix, *Curtain of Ignorance*. New York: Doubleday & Co., 1964.

Griffith, William E., *Sino-Soviet Rift*. Boston: Massachusetts Institute of Technology.

Hahn, Emily, *China Only Yesterday, 1850–1950*. New York: Doubleday & Co., 1964.

Halperin, Morton H., *China and the Bomb*. New York: Frederick A. Praeger, 1965.

Hobbs, Lisa, *I Saw Red China*. New York: McGraw-Hill, 1966.

Hughes, Trevor J., and Luard, D. E. T., *The Economic Development of Communist China, 1949–1958*. 2nd ed. New York: Oxford University Press, 1961.

Isaacs, Harold R., *Tragedy of the Chinese Revolution*. Rev. ed. Stanford, California: Stanford University Press, 1961.

Kuo, Ping-Chia, *China, New Age and New Outlook*. New York: Alfred A. Knopf, Inc., 1956.

Latourette, Kenneth Scott, *Chinese: Their History and Culture*. 3rd. ed., rev. New York: The Macmillan Co.

Levenson, Joseph R., *Confucian China and Its Modern Fate*. 3 vols.; vol. 1, *The Problem of Intellectual Continuity*, 1958; vol. 2, *The Problem of Monarchical Decay*, 1964; vol. 3, *The Problem of Historical Significance*, 1965. Berkeley and Los Angeles: University of California Press. [Vol. 1 also published under title *Modern China and Its Confucian Past*. New York: Doubleday & Co. (Anchor)].

Levenson, Joseph R., *Liang Ch'i-ch'ao and the Mind of Modern China*. Cambridge: Harvard University Press, 1959.

Mao, Tse-tung, *Selected Works*. 5 vols.; vol. 1, *Revolutionary Civil Wars, 1926–36;* vol. 2, *War Against Japan, 1937–38;* vol. 3, *War Against Japan, 1939–41;* vol. 4, *World War II, 1941–45;* vol. 5, *Third Civil War Period, 1945–49*. New York: International Publishers.

Myrdal, Jan and Kessle, Gun, *Chinese Journey*. New York: Pantheon Books, 1965.

Myrdal, Jan, and Kessle, Gun, *Report from a Chinese Village*. New York: Pantheon Books, 1964.

Newman, Robert P., *Recognition of Communist China*. New York: The Macmillan Co., 1961.

North, Robert C., *Moscow and Chinese Communists*. 2nd ed. Stanford, California: Stanford University Press, 1963.

Nossal, Frederick, *Dateline Peking*. New York: Harcourt, Brace & World, 1963.

Reischauer, E. O., see Fairbank, John K.

Riencourt, Amaury de, *The Soul of China*. Chester Springs, Pennsylvania: Dufour Edition, 1958.

Roper, Myra, *China: The Surprising Country*. New York: Doubleday & Co., 1966.

Rostow, Walt W., *Prospects for Communist China*. Boston: Massachusetts Institute of Technology, 1954.

Schwartz, Harry, *China*. New York: Atheneum, 1965.

Shabad, T., *China's Changing Map*. New York: Frederick A. Praeger.

Snow, Edgar, *Other Side of the River: Red China Today*. New York: Random House, 1962.

Snow, Edgar, *Red Star Over China*. New York: Grove Press, 1961; Gloucester, Massachusetts: Peter Smith.

Tsou, Tang, *America's Failure in China 1941 to 1950*. Chicago: University of Chicago Press, 1963.

Wint, Guy, *Communist China's Crusade*. New York: Frederick A. Praeger, 1965.

Wright, Arthur, *Studies in Chinese Thought*. Chicago: University of Chicago Press, 1953.

Zagoria, Donald S., *Sino-Soviet Conflict, 1956–61*. Princeton, New Jersey: Princeton University Press, 1962; New York: Atheneum (paper), 1964.

INDEX